Never Too Late To Be Great

Praise for *Never Too Late To Be Great*

'My most cheering read of the year so far is *Never Too Late To Be Great* by Tom Butler-Bowdon. If you haven't yet started up that dream company or written that book in your head, it's a hugely encouraging how-to manual ... Inspiring stuff.'

Red magazine

'According to a super inspirational new book *Never Too Late To Be Great* we are never too old to start something new no matter what our age. Author Tom Butler-Bowdon has provided the antidote to quick-fix life solutions as his studies revealed that the role of time in achievement is always woefully under-reported.'

Daily Express

'This classic motivational book sets out to explode the myth of overnight success and that age is against anyone who wants to break out in a creative or entrepreneurial new direction. Starting with Malcolm Gladwell's theory that significant achievements rarely happen without a decade of intense work, former political advisor Butler-Bowdon goes on to provide pages and pages of evidence to back it up.'

The Pulse, NHS Choices

'"At 40 you have 67% of your productive life ahead of you". Tom Butler-Bowdon's new book on this topic is great.'

Oliver Burkeman, author of *The Antidote: Happiness For People Who Can't Stand Positive Thinking*

'Loved the range of examples and stories – Anthony Robbins next to Antony Gormley, Napoleon Hill next to Jonathan Franzen. The breadth of the examples makes it very sympathetic to people who are not big readers of mainstream self-help. A great antidote to the "instant success" mentality of many self-help books.'

Jules Evans, author of *Philosophy For Life and Other Dangerous Situations*

'No, it's not another self-help book claiming to change your life in minutes. Tom Butler-Bowdon busts the promise of overnight success in his latest offering. By teaching the "power of thinking long", Butler-Bowdon relaxes expectations of success and believes it takes at least 10 years of hard slog and practice to achieve results. Willing to go the distance? Order now – we'd tell you how it works, but we've got nine years and 11 months to go!'

Healthy magazine

Never Too Late To Be Great

The Power of Thinking Long

TOM BUTLER-BOWDON

Virgin BOOKS

2 4 6 8 10 9 7 5 3 1

First published in 2012 by Virgin Books

This edition published in 2014 by Virgin Books,
an imprint of Ebury Publishing

A Random House Group Company

Copyright © Tom Butler-Bowdon 2012

Tom Butler-Bowdon has asserted his right under the Copyright, Designs and
Patents Act 1988 to be identified as the author of this work.

Every reasonable effort has been made to contact copyright holders of material
reproduced in this book. If any have inadvertently been overlooked, the publishers
would be glad to hear from them and make good in future editions any errors or
omissions brought to their attention.

Addresses for companies within The Random House Group Limited can be found at:
www.randomhouse.co.uk/offices.htm

The Random House Group Limited Reg. No. 954009

A CIP catalogue record for this book is
available from the British Library

The Random House Group Limited supports the Forest Stewardship Council® (FSC®),
the leading international forest-certification organisation. Our books carrying the FSC
label are printed on FSC®-certified paper. FSC is the only forest-certification scheme
supported by the leading environmental organisations, including Greenpeace.
Our paper procurement policy can be found at:
www.randomhouse.co.uk/environment

MIX
Paper from
responsible sources
FSC® C016897

Printed and bound by CPI Group (UK) Ltd, Croydon, CR0 4YY

ISBN: 9780753555309

To buy books by your favourite authors and register for offers, visit:
www.randomhouse.co.uk

For parents who patiently wait for their child's
promise to be fulfilled.

For partners who believe their loved one's
potential can be realised.

TABLE OF CONTENTS

NOTE TO READER   ix

PREFACE   xi

INTRODUCTION   xvii

1. WARMING UP
   Why what you've done so far may just
   have set the scene   1

2. LIFE ISN'T SHORT
   How increasing longevity is giving us
   multiple chances to succeed   9

3. THE LONG VIEW
   A simple way to join the elite   25

4. LEAD TIME
   It's the 'time in between' that matters   55

5. THE 40 FACTOR
   Why many people never do anything
   remarkable until their fifth decade   93

6. MID-CENTURY MAGIC
   'Now for my next half-century'   139

7. THE 30-YEAR GOLDMINE
   How many, usually without intention,
   save their best for last   165

8. THE BEAUTY OF PEOPLE
   How background shapes us, but only
   to a certain point   183

9. EVERYTHING BIG BEGINS SMALL
   And often starts slowly   223

EPILOGUE   243
ACKNOWLEDGEMENTS   249
ENDNOTES   251
INDEX   268

NOTE TO THE READER

You are invited to receive a free eBook, *Never Too Late Extra*, containing more examples and insights in relation to thinking long and slow-cooked success. To receive the bonus, just send me an email to tombutlerbowdon@gmail.com, with 'Power of Thinking Long' in the title bar. I look forward to hearing from you, and welcome any comments or suggestions.

Please visit my website, Butler-Bowdon.com, which has many free self-development book commentaries, interviews and other content. For news and updates follow me on Twitter @tombutlerbowdon, or befriend me on Facebook (my personal page, not the public profile).

PREFACE

At the beginning of his autobiography, the philosopher John Stuart Mill felt he needed to defend the indulgence of writing his own life story. Not having had a particularly adventurous life, he didn't feel that he was of great interest, but his famously intensive education – home schooled by his father, learning Greek at three, reading all the classics by ten, advanced in mathematics by his teen years – *was* remarkable, and he was happy to admit it.

My life certainly doesn't justify the logging of more trees, and my childhood education was in no way remarkable. However, the education I received as an adult, which fell to me by no great design, was lucky. This was the opportunity to systematically read, covering a ten-year period, hundreds of notable books in the fields of self-help, success, motivation, spirituality and psychology, to summarise their key points, and provide commentaries that put each title into the context of the whole genre, which can loosely be called 'self-development'.

As enjoyable and inspiring as it was, the more I got into

it, the more I felt the literature was lacking something, and this omission rendered it close to worthless for many people. With hindsight, I had been concerned with this missing element for most of my adult life, and only later did I see how my work and personal life had converged.

Since I was 20, I had felt like I was playing catch-up. On leaving school, like most of my friends I went on to further education, enrolling in an art college where I took courses in photography and film. My idea was to become an art photographer. However, after three years I decided that art school wasn't for me, and dropped out.

I left behind my hometown and comfortable life and started again with a new college degree in a bigger city. Now older than the other students, I felt pressure to do well to justify the decision I had made, and worked doubly hard. With no scholarships or loans, I had to pay my way with a variety of jobs that left little time for socialising.

One of these jobs was at a store selling newspapers and magazines. At the end of each week, my boss would give me the pick of the unsold stuff, and I would take them back to read in my room in a student house. One magazine really caught my attention, a title called *Success*. I was ambitious, but unsure about the future. I believed that successful people were a race apart, who got that way via fate or good luck. But *Success* told its readers that being an achiever was more a matter of *decision*. The hard part was allowing yourself the belief that you would be successful. Then, all that was needed was a certain amount of application and focus.

While this sounded fine, I couldn't ignore the fact that in terms of career progress, I was three years behind other people my age, and had already missed at least one important boat. But a positive outcome of this insecurity was that it led me to be interested in the age at which people made significant achievements. When reading a newspaper profile or watching a documentary, I found myself saying, 'Well, if he had done that by the time he was 27, how many years does that give me to do something great . . . ?' The media was full of stories of youthful success, and I didn't enjoy the contrast between these people and myself, still ploughing through university. I was delighted whenever I came across the biography of a person who had started out late, or who achieved something when a bit older. These examples let me relax a bit and focus on the tasks at hand.

I was 26 before, ensconced in my proper career job, I read my first motivational book. A couple of years later, I decided to leave this career behind and pursue what then seemed a very 'way out' option: writing about personal development. Though I loved the field, it struck me that it was at a similar stage that biology was before Darwin, and where economics stood before Adam Smith. That is, it was a realm of knowledge largely untested by evidence, and based on the assumptions and prejudices of its early practitioners. Much of it was about 'transforming your life', and hopefully in as short a time as possible, yet if these techniques worked as they promised, then everyone who read the books, listened to the audios or went to the seminars should have been a superstar in a year or two. I realised how little attention was given to the role of *time* in the progress of an individual. On the one hand, this was almost too obvious: of course significant achievement takes many years. And yet, none of the books

I read dared mention it; all were promoting a short route to success.

The vast majority of successful people I had profiled had taken years to achieve what they did. None had been overnight successes. What if, I wondered, 'slow-cooked' success was not only the norm, but the *only* path to genuine achievement? If individuals only had limited spans of years allotted to them, then success was surely about the rate, pattern, sequence or trajectory of achievement as it was anything else. How long did it take for her to complete that masterpiece? What was he doing leading up to his great discovery? How old was he when he first had the idea for the company, and when did it start to prosper? If 'personal success' was ever going to be a generic subject that could be studied, questions such as these – all of which involved time – should be basic.

A quote I had heard kept ringing in my ears:

> 'Most people overestimate what they can achieve
> in a year, but underestimate what they can
> achieve in a decade.'

This perfectly chimed with my experience and that of people I knew. I had been led to believe that time was the enemy, a force battled against to achieve our goals. Now, I began to wonder if this enemy, if we got to know it better, could become a friend. I was aware of the criticism of self-development that it got people to dream up audacious goals and plans which were divorced from reality. People are rightly sceptical that a rousing motivational seminar can lift a person from mediocrity onto the track of greatness. However, I had seen enough evidence that major goals can and are often realised by anyone, as long as they are cast within *appropriate timeframes*.

In writing my five books, I had been fed a daily diet of hardcore inspiration, and this material did improve me and increase my effectiveness in many ways. Yet inspiration itself had been no substitute for effort. It was not motivational talks that had got me to sit down and write the books, but the bare pressure of deadlines. I discovered that large projects, when broken up into smaller pieces, and spread over time, became quite doable.

I had also noticed that many of the great achievers I had read and written about had not even discovered their great project or passion until having done other things, lived other lives, had other careers. They nearly all took time to get into their stride. At many points they may have felt like they were getting nowhere, but when looked at from the vantage point of history, they were just getting ready to make their mark.

A revolution is needed in personal development. Instead of blinding people with visions of glory that can supposedly be realised in a year or two, surely it is ultimately more productive to accept the pivotal role of time in accomplishing our goals. This does *not* have to mean reducing the level of our ambition, but simply *adjusting the timescales* in which we should expect to achieve things. This alternative theory of success also takes account of the haphazard, circular, zigzagging and simply unclear paths that life so often takes us on. Life happens, as John Lennon famously put it, when you are making other plans.

Yet by taking a longer view of things, it is possible to shape life to a greater degree than you think. And crucially, with most of us living longer now, it is rarely too late to *begin* on a remarkable path.

It's not too late . . .

Maybe you have read plenty of motivational books that told you that you 'can do anything', but perhaps what you need now is not more fists in the air or walks across hot coals to 'pump yourself up', but examples of real people who only began to achieve at a similar age to you.

Included in this book are many potted biographies of conventionally 'great' people. Though these may seem like irrelevant figures who have faded into history, I ask you to bear with me in recounting their stories. Because they were once the age you are today, and they also had their own struggles – often long before they achieved any renown.

Just as you should never discount the effect that people's lives in the past have on our lives in the present, you too may do things in the next ten, 20 or 30 years that can reverberate in a positive way through successive generations. Here is your chance. It's not too late to seize it.

INTRODUCTION

Do you wish to do something remarkable, and feel you have a special niche just waiting to be discovered?

Do you feel there is still time to pursue something you have long desired?

Are you on the right path with your career, your company or your organisation, but still waiting for your potential to be fulfilled?

If so, this book is for you. If not, it may still be for you, or someone close to you. For in it I will show that it is rarely too late – and you are rarely too old – to achieve something that is truly important to you. Also, that the reasons most people give us – and that we give ourselves – for not doing something, lack foundation. Because the good news is that you have much more time than you think to achieve your goals.

Perhaps you feel that you have missed some great opportunity to progress, or are too 'past it' to take an exciting new direction. Maybe you have just missed a promotion at work, or some other big chance seems to be fading from view. Perhaps you wanted too much, you think to yourself. Family, friends or colleagues told you something is not possible, and perhaps you started to believe them. Who am I to think I can do something singular that will express my deepest interests and talents? If that is your thinking right now, here you will find another voice to listen to.

If you are like most people, you have no shortage of desires and dreams, and you do not need to be motivated by someone else to go after them. The motivational field does its best to make people more successful, but facts alone can be more inspiring than promises to 'change your life in seven days'. Ironically, I believe that your success is *more* likely to occur the moment you stop looking for 'great moments' of motivation and instead give yourself the time to bring real things into being. This way may seem less dramatic at first, but the end results may astonish you.

This book rests on two simple observations:

1. All great accomplishment may take longer than first imagined; and yet . . .
2. In the age we live in, it's rarely too late to begin something great.

With most of us living longer lives, we have an advantage over our ancestors in that we can expect to *complete* a great project. With this extra time, very little becomes impossible.

Anthony Robbins observed that *people overestimate what they can achieve in a year, but underestimate what they can achieve in a decade*. Does this ring true for you? We've all heard about the magic of thinking big, but perhaps it is the power of thinking *long* that can lift us above the pack. My experience is that it is rarely the size of a person's goals that is the issue, but the timeframes they give themselves to achieve them.

When people, companies or products become famous, their rise seems inevitable, yet nothing could be further from the truth. By exploring what the remarkable people were doing *before* they made their landmark contributions, this book aims to once and for all destroy the myth of overnight success, and show why the 'slow-cooked' way is the norm, not the exception.

The universe is filled with examples which suggest that all good things take time. No person is ever born successful, nor do great companies, products or movements rise overnight. Yet in our fast-moving age, we begrudge the role of time and are embarrassed by the time it takes to do worthwhile things. What is quick and takes less work is always more alluring, but the desire for instant results, while understandable, makes us less and less open to the paths that will lead to lasting, major achievement.

Pablo Picasso once said, 'I don't develop: I am.' He meant that everything he created already existed in some form; he just needed the time in which to pour them out. Appreciating life the Picasso way, we don't *become* something; we are it already and simply need a few years to properly allow it to be expressed.

Your life so far, and the success you have wanted, may have just been missing one vital ingredient, and that ingredient is what this book is about. I don't claim that it will 'change your life', but I'm confident it can reorient your thinking and give you another chance at being great – *in your own way, and in your own time.*

CHAPTER ONE:

WARMING UP

Why what you've done so far may just have set the scene

> 'No matter how great the talent or effort, some
> things just take time: you can't produce a baby
> in one month by getting nine women pregnant'.
> Warren Buffett

The modern world sees time as a commodity in short supply, or an enemy to be conquered, but Warren Buffett became history's greatest investor through seeing time as a *friend*. Having picked a company to invest in, he lets time reveal its true value, often holding on to a stake for decades. In a field where everyone wants good returns quickly, the Sage of Omaha's success comes from an opposite approach: make one good decision initially, then let time do the rest of the work.

With various wiles or technologies, we can manipulate the conditions to make something ripen quicker, but still the central aim is ripeness, which can't be hurried. A sage of another era, the former slave Epictetus, said:

'Nothing great is produced suddenly, not even the grape or the fig. If you say to me now that you want a fig, I will answer to you that it requires time: let it flower first, then put forth fruit, and then ripen.'

Epictetus completed his reflection:

'If then the fruit of a fig tree is not perfected suddenly and in one hour, would you possess the fruit of a person's mind in so short a time and so easily?'

In the logic of success, we are obsessed with questions of talent, ability and intelligence, but these make us overlook the power of our own natural unfolding. Many of us have a problem appreciating the role of time in our efforts because at first glance the 'march of time' seems to make us weaker, not more powerful. Perhaps, though, we just have the wrong pictures and stories in our heads, and simply need to replace them with ones that are about harnessing, not avoiding or fighting, time.

The Great Basin Bristlecone Pine (*Pinus longaeva*) is the oldest living tree on earth. Growing mainly on the high slopes of California's Inyo National Forest, some specimens are well over 4,000 years old. Bristlecones grow at 10,000 feet, on the edge of the tree line, and in cold to freezing temperatures for much of the year. Their 'soil' is actually a limestone substrate with little nutrient value, and rainfall on the slopes to which they cling is minimal. Largely protected from fire by the lack of surrounding vegetation and ground cover, their very dense and highly resinous wood offers them protection from attack by insects, bacteria and rot-causing fungi.

But the cost of these very effective adaptations is very slow growth. The period in which the Great Basin Bristlecone Pine can actually grow, flower and send forth new pine needles is limited to only six weeks a year. The way the Bristlecone grows is to send new shoots out of gnarled bits of ancient, dead wood. The result is not particularly attractive, but in their particular environment, slow, careful growth means they reign supreme.

The result is that what looks like a sapling may be over a century old, and a taller tree may have seen empires and civilisations come and go. The majestic Giant Sequoia is one of the Bristlecone's cousins in the pine family, and can grow to five times its height. But in the time that a Sequoia's life cycle has waxed and waned, many Bristlecones are only just branching out.

The Raramuri Indians of south-western Chihuahua in Mexico are well known for their long-distance running. Sometimes doing 200 miles at a time in bare feet from one community to another, their running heart rate and blood pressure can be no greater than if they were walking.

With their amazing stamina, the Mexican Olympic Committee thought they could blitz the field in the 26-mile marathon, and sent two Raramuri men to the 1928 Olympics in Amsterdam. But the Raramuri runners did not win the race – they did not even get close, coming in at only 32nd and 35th places.

What happened? At the finishing line, they kept on running, not realising that the race was over. When officials caught up with them, all that the men could say was: 'Too short, too short!'

The psychologist Milton Erickson liked to describe the incident to patients. 'They thought twenty-five miles was when you warmed up!' he would tell them. Erickson's biographer, Sidney Rosen, would think of the story when he could not seem to get started on a project, was frustrated by difficulties, or was on a run himself and out of breath. The phrase would come into his head, 'I am just warming up now'. By giving himself more time, he suddenly had more energy.

You may feel worn out by your efforts, but in these pages you will learn how you can get back your breath. You will discover that, in all probability, what you have been doing all these years is simply warming up. 'Life is short', you may have been told, or 'Life is a sprint with few winners'. But when faced with challenges, we would do well to remember the Raramuri runners, just getting into their stride after 50 miles, or be inspired by the image of the Bristlecone Pine, only just branching out when other trees have long expired, and all the more remarkable and beautiful because of its extremely slow growth.

It is in the nature of true success that at first, even for a long time, it seems like nothing is happening. In despair, we think that we have picked the wrong ingredients or got the recipe wrong. Peering into the oven, we see nothing. But come back later, and suddenly we discern a dark mass rising above the rim of the tin. Things of value often come into being too slowly for us to notice, working on timescales beyond normal apprehension. Just as the human eye and brain cannot 'see' plants growing in real time, but only notice growth in hindsight, so we often cannot appreciate the progress we have made.

You may be used to thinking of outcomes in terms of days, weeks or months, but real results usually take longer. An Italian proverb goes: *Che va piano, va longano, e va lontano*. 'Who goes slowly, goes long and far.' Note that it is not 'Who goes slowly, will do quite well', but who goes slowly will *exceed* expectations.

Tragically, people often give up because the indications of progress are too subtle, but as many of the stories in this book will show, the point at which we think we are 'finished' can actually mark the beginning of our rise. At 40, Bill Wilson was a destitute alcoholic without hope. Wilson was the scion of a long line of drunks, a heritage which may have crushed him. Instead, it made him increasingly desperate to find a way out of his apparent destiny. At 43 he launched a world-wide movement, Alcoholics Anonymous. At 38, Jean Nidetch was an office clerk losing her battle with obesity. Two years later she was a different person, the founder of Weight Watchers International. Both Wilson and Nidetch were at their nadir when they unexpectedly found success.

Each of us has foundations that we can build on to create something remarkable. At the time, our experiences may seem exactly what we *don't* want, and only later do we come to appreciate them as building blocks. The key is to take the longer view, and continually ask ourselves how we can use our background and experiences to good ends. Modern life is set up to reward the ego, but in only ever thinking what is always best for us, our lives will be severely limited. In raising our minds to what can benefit many people beyond ourselves, it is much more likely that our potential will be realised.

When Arthur Schopenhauer was 77, he felt compelled to explain why he was putting out another edition of his great work *The World as Will and Representation*. In his preface to the new edition he included a Latin quotation: *Si quis tota die currens, pervenit ad vesperam, satis est.* 'If anyone who wanders all day arrives towards evening, it is enough.' The quote reminded Schopenhauer of an old rule, which he felt also justified his late-in-life work: 'Influence lasts longer in proportion to the lateness of its beginning.'

The laws of probability suggest we are all entitled to some lucky breaks, but the universe rarely offers shortcuts to anything. By once and for all admitting the truth of this, you are on the way to genuine achievement. For it is not as if slow-cooked success is an alternative route to succeeding, it is really the *only* way if you are talking about real accomplishments that come from insight, creativity and work. If you leave a bucket under a slightly dripping tap, the drip is so infrequent that you can hardly be bothered to tighten the tap. You go to bed and are amazed the next morning to find . . . the bucket is full! How did a little drip do this? It was simply given a few hours to do its work.

Richard Koch is rare in the self-development and business field for taking time itself seriously. He notes:

'. . . in thinking about time as a separate dimension of our lives, we rapidly slide into the view that time is finite and short, that it is in some sense our enemy, or at least a commodity in extremely short supply. Yet time is none of these things. Time is a dimension of our life and experience. Time is an integral part of what we do and who we are.'

Einstein's theory of relativity totally subverted our familiar existing understanding of space and time as separate hard realities. The way business and society is now organised is based on time as being separate to space. We do things, and then there is the time it takes to do them. But following Einstein, Koch suggests we should appreciate time as all wrapped as part of a product or service, one of its attributes.

Genuine success is the result of 'rich time', or deep thought given to a work or a problem. The *result* of this thought may be a sandwiching of time (for instance, a great book that can be read in an hour may have taken seven years to write; or a product like instant noodles may be ten years in the making). What we can do quickly or easily is what will be the greatest value to others, yet invariably this speed, or 'knack' at something is the product of practice, refinement, love, thought and skill over several years.

While it may seem obvious to say that we are each the product of how we have spent our time, accepting this fully means we have an advantage over others who are constantly battling against time. The simple act of thinking in terms of years and decades will mean that quality is invested in whatever it is we are offering the world. For anything that has had years of love poured into it is by nature more valuable than what is churned out with stress and hurry.

Before we begin

As far back as Aristotle, philosophers have sought to define what it means to live the 'good life'. Today, with the increased number of years, resources and choices that many of us enjoy, we expect nothing less than the 'great life'. That is not as unrealistic as it sounds. The chapters ahead will show how the adoption of reasonable timeframes can make achievement of even the most ambitious life project more predictable than you might think.

With a broader view of time you can be re-energised to discover or embark on the great projects of your life, whether these are a new career or a business, starting a family, becoming a master at something, or having some big adventure involving travel or social enterprise. Crucial to the success of such projects is a realistic understanding of the time it will take both to get the ball rolling and/or reach completion.

You may not be totally happy with what you have achieved so far, but this book aims to bring you to an interesting realisation: you do not have to race against time, because everything is unfolding as it should. The best is still ahead of you, and whatever you have done so far in life, chances are you have just been warming up.

CHAPTER TWO

LIFE ISN'T SHORT

*How increasing longevity is giving us
multiple chances to succeed*

Just over a century ago, a boy born in America could have expected to live, on average, to 46. A girl born in the same year, 1900, might have reached the grand old age of 48. Yet by 1950, a dramatic rise in life expectancy, due mainly to better nutrition and improved detection and treatment of disease, meant that an American baby boy would probably make it to 65, and a girl to 71. By 2000, this had gone up to 74 for males, and almost 80 for females.

Britain's longevity figures tell a similar story, except the statistics go back further. In the Britain of 1800, the average lifespan was 40 years. Today it is 80. This fact is remarkable when you consider that, between Roman times and 1800, there was no change at all in human longevity. The leap in lifespans in the early 19th century came through things we consider basic today: large-scale sewage systems and clean water supplies that drastically reduced people's exposure to deadly germs. The end of the 1800s saw the first vaccines come into use, protecting people from smallpox and other death-causing illnesses, and after the Second World War, antibiotics such as penicillin again saved millions from dying in youth or middle age.

In a little over 100 years then, life expectancy in wealthy countries has risen an astonishing 40 per cent, and it continues to rise at a minimum of two years per decade.

The new (time) rich

Life may sometimes feel short at a philosophical level, and there is always the chance we may die young. But for most people in well-off countries today, life is not, as the 17th-century political philosopher Thomas Hobbes famously put it, 'solitary, poor, nasty, brutish and short'. Compared to our ancestors, we are *awash* with time.

Millions are discovering that they can be active and reasonably independent into their nineties, living to see great-grandchildren come along who statistically can see turning 100 almost as a birthright. The Danish researchers (Kaare Christensen et al) who pointed out this probability also noted that increasing life expectancy is not being accompanied by severe disability. We are not only living longer, but better management of the ageing process means we can enjoy, and be relatively independent in, the extra years we are given.

Experts are fond of saying that the increase in lifespan will have to slow because longevity rises will be dragged down by rich country maladies such as obesity and diabetes. Oxford University biochemist Dr Lynne Cox is one who has predicted a slowing in lifespan increase, but also admits, 'It is a question of whether obese teenagers choose, in their thirties, to change their ways and become healthy adults . . .' Tom Kirkwood, a professor in charge of Britain's Institute for Ageing and Health, notes that through the 1970s and 1980s, the UN was predicting a slowing down of the rate of lifespan increase because it was thought that medicine had done all it could to reduce the causes of early death, and therefore lifespans would reach their 'natural' limit. 'That has not happened', he notes. 'Lifespans have continued to rise at the same rate and still show no sign of stopping . . . My feeling is we will see another ten-year increase in average lifespan [from 80 to 90], but no more this century. However, we are in unknown territory.'

Unknown territory indeed. Generally, the forecasts of a slowdown in longevity increase in rich countries takes little account of education, social influences like peer pressure or, crucially, people's self-directed motivation to change. True, some obese kids will stay obese as adults, but many others will experience personal health revolutions brought on by the realisation that if they start to exercise and eat better, they could prolong their healthy lifespan by an extra 20 years.

No one predicted a 40 per cent rise in life expectancy over a 100-year period, because although you can safely say that the installation of municipal sewage and water infrastructure will save lots of lives, you can't predict discoveries in medicine (like penicillin) that will save and prolong millions more. Even less are we able to foresee the effect of social and societal factors on health. For instance, few people saw coming the personal fitness boom when jogging, aerobics and weight training caught on in the 1970s, and the kind of hard-core exercise that was once done only by sportsmen – marathon running, lap swimming, road cycling, body building – is now a routine part of the lives of millions of men and women, fitted in to busy work and family schedules. Who knows what level of fitness the average person will rise to in another 50 years?

What's more, the forecasts of an increase of two years a decade in rich country lifespans, as we noted above, is only the *conservative*, incremental picture of our future. It is based on existing science only, takes no account of the likelihood that vigorous exercise and good diet will become ever more fashionable or socially accepted, and crucially does not factor in personal motivation to lead longer, healthier lives.

On the first point, it appears that medical technology and disease prevention are not simply improving at the rate they have done in the last 40 years, but are speeding up, with multiple breakthroughs promised that will enhance and extend life. With the pace of technological discovery accelerating, the surge in life expectancy experienced between 1900 and 1950 is likely to seem modest in comparison.

This longevity revolution involves an array of new and forthcoming technologies that will extend the healthy lifespan and increase knowledge on how environmental and personal factors (e.g. diet, exercise, familial and psychological factors) affect our ability to live long and fulfilled lives. Advances in longevity medicine will mean: instead of risky and expensive organ transplants, we will grow new organs from our own stem cells; instead of struggling with dementia, we will be able to restore perfect memory through brain cell manipulation; instead of crude metal hip replacements, we will be able to regenerate bone, joints and muscle; and in order to look younger, in place of using clumsy Botox we will have gene replacement therapy. A race is on to be able to produce commercially new tissues, organs and bones from stem cells. With a possible worldwide market of $5 trillion, the incentives are massive. Some scientists and futurists believe that if we can just stay alive for another 25 years, such predictable medical advances will mean that people can be kept alive in reasonable health for an extra 50 years, perhaps indefinitely.

Julian Savulescu, an Oxford University expert on human enhancement technology, notes, 'There is a significant chance that my own children will live beyond the age of 120. There-after we could be looking at two- or three-fold increases in human lifespans'. Although that brings with it its own challenges, personal, social and economic, imagine for a moment what becomes possible: the extra careers we can have, the skills we can perfect, the travelling we can do.

Too good to be true? Let's assume that it is, and that the promised advances do not materialise. But even staying with the incremental scenario of life expectancy – which is based on present, not future science – you may still be around much longer than you think. If you have not questioned the idea that you will retire at 65, pootle around your garden and play bridge for a few years then fade away, you may be in for a shock. Even at today's mortality rates, you may still have a third of your productive life ahead of you.

On a purely physical level, the average 40-year-old today would seem amazingly youthful to the 40-year-old of 100 or 200 years ago, and if you are a non-smoker, only a moderate drinker and exercise a few times a week, the chances of leading a mobile existence with all your wits about you well into your nineties is good, particularly if the life expectancy in the country where you live is above 75.

Longer lifespans have another interesting effect: the decreasing value of money compared to health. Who would you rather be, someone who becomes rich but dies at 45, or one who is only of middling means but lives until 85? Strangely, the longer we live as a society, the greater premium is placed *on* a long life. Anyone can make a fortune (and lose it too), but not everyone can enjoy a long, healthy, productive life. Most of us *will* have long lives though, and in doing so we are joining the ranks of the new *time*-rich.

The Schwartz exercise and its surprising results

If in doubt that your best years are still ahead of you, you may change your mind after doing an exercise devised by David J. Schwartz. Schwartz was a professor in psychology at the University of Georgia and also taught courses in career and life skills. He wrote the famous motivational book *The Magic of Thinking Big*, published in 1959 and still popular. In it, Schwartz points out that many people suffer from a disease called 'age excusitis', an ailment that is all in the mind, but which has crippling effects on the ability to achieve all we can in life.

He recalls that when participants in his courses complained that, at 40, they were too old to move into a different position or career, he would trot out the usual reassurances such as 'You are only as old as you feel'. These had no effect. But then he stumbled on a method of calculating current age in relation to productive lifespan. This would usually astound those who took it. Schwartz mentions an academic colleague who, after 24 years as a stockbroker, decided that he wanted to become a college professor. At 51, going against all his nay-saying family and friends, he enrolled at university, and within a few years was running the economics faculty at a liberal arts college. Not only did he have 20 years of productive life still in him, but the new career made him feel and act young. Schwartz also mentions a relative who, having never really enjoyed previous jobs, realised that the only thing that would make him happy was to become a church minister. At 45, with three children and little money, he entered a ministerial training programme, and five years later had his own congregation. Both men, Schwartz notes, had to overcome both their own worries about being 'too old', and the lack of faith of their family and friends that change was possible. Yet, having cured themselves of the disease of 'age excusitis', they had a new lease on life.

Do the exercise yourself

Schwartz would begin his exercise by asking those present to establish the span of an average person's productive lifespan.

Let's say that most people begin their working lives when they are around 20. How long will their productive life last? When Schwartz was writing in 1959, life expectancy was lower than it is now, so he settled on 70 as the average end age of a productive life. But as it has gone up around two years a decade since then, it is not unreasonable to think that we can lead a productive live until we are 80. Indeed, many people remain productive for another ten to 20 years after that, but let's settle on 80.

So this gives us a span of 60 years of productive life, six decades in which to make our mark.

How old are you right now? If you are 30, and the productive lifespan is 20 to 80, you still have 50 years of productive life left. That in itself is encouraging, but let's turn it into a percentage. Using a calculator, take the 50 years you have left and divide it by the span of productive life: 60. Then, multiply it by 100. So that's 50 ÷ 60 x 100.

Result: you have *83 per cent* of your most productive time still left.

As I write this I am 43, so counting the years until 80, I have 37 years of productive life ahead out of the total 60-year span we agreed on. So the calculation for me is 37 ÷ 60 x 100. The result? I have almost 62 per cent of my productive working life ahead of me. *37 years. 62 per cent.* These are encouraging figures, telling me not to worry too much about my pace of achievement, and to relax into my lifetime's work. I have time.

The numbers are equally surprising and inspiring for a 50-year-old, who still has *50 per cent* of his productive working life ahead. How different this is from the usual way of thinking, which goes along the lines of, 'At 50, I have only 15 years left until retirement, so most of my working life is over.'

For the Schwartz exercise to have a real effect, you need to do the sums yourself. Below, however, is provided a table giving an idea of productive lifespan percentages.

Productive lifespan

Current age	Productive years	Productive years by %
20	60	100%
25	55	92%
30	50	83%
35	45	75%
40	40	67%
45	35	58%
50	30	50%
55	25	42%
60	20	33%
65	15	25%

Note that even a 65-year-old, historically the average retirement age in wealthy countries, still has 25 per cent of productive time ahead of them. No wonder older people are staying on to work, and no wonder employers increasingly value them. Increasing longevity means that many are comparatively youthful at 65.

At this point in life, there's still going to be a lot you want to do, and can do, in the years ahead. In the year I discovered this exercise, for example, 71-year-old John McCain was entering the race to be president of the United States.

As Schwartz acknowledged, the exercise is counterintuitive because most people only count the years left until some official retirement age (e.g. 65), and then do not turn those years into a percentage. When you do, Schwartz noted, 'Life is much longer than you think.'

New life at 49

Though he never took the Schwartz exercise, Warwick Mayne-Wilson intuitively appreciates its liberating truth.

Warwick joined the Australian diplomatic service in his early twenties, straight out of a history degree. Over a career spanning more than two decades, he proved his value to his country, working his way up from graduate recruit to an appointment as Australia's ambassador to Sri Lanka. At only 42 he was listed in the Australian edition of *Who's Who*. By any normal measure then, a success.

Yet at a number of points, Warwick had contemplated leaving the service. He recalls that while he quite enjoyed the work, 'There were some aspects which were unsatisfying, and at times I felt I didn't quite "fit".' He had always been interested in architecture, plants and design, but only as hobbies.

In early 1977 he had signed up to do a short course in landscape design in London, but was offered an attractive posting in Rome, and then the Sri Lanka position came up. These postings kept him in the diplomatic service for another eight years, but after two and a half years in Colombo, at his own request Warwick returned to Australia. Finding the public service work in Canberra unrewarding, he was now keener than ever to make a transition to more fulfilling work.

At the age of 49, Warwick embarked on a four-year landscape architecture degree. Though he was a similar age, or older, than his university lecturers, he found he could relate to his fellow students since they were about the same age as his daughters!

Warwick started working in his chosen field just as a recession began, but still found a job in a landscape architecture firm. This didn't last long because the younger men in the firm saw this mature, knowledgeable older guy as a threat to their advancement.

A breakthrough came when he heard about a Master's degree course in heritage conservation. He applied and was accepted. This qualification, on top of his previous one, set Warwick apart from others in the field, and he set up on his own, quickly establishing a niche as a conservation/heritage landscape architect. Over two decades, Warwick built up a good reputation and established a healthy practice with many projects that helped to retain the unique historical character of Sydney.

Today, at 73, when his diplomat friends have long reached compulsory retirement, Warwick is still enjoying his work. He observes:

'The advantage [of my career change] has been that I have been able to continue working well beyond the age of 65, doing constructive work that helps "makes the world a better place" – even if only marginally. I aim to achieve

> something positive, a step forward in some area
> of activity or interest, each day. I have watched
> my fellow colleagues trying to cope with
> retirement at 63–65; all those with whom I've
> had contact have expressed envy that I'm so
> happy and busy.'

Financially, how was Warwick able to make his career jump? By his late forties, his two daughters had left home and were no longer dependent on him. Also, his degree course was in a different city, Sydney, to the diplomatic capital Canberra, where the family home was, so he was able to earn rental income from it. And though his wife had some misgivings about his change of direction, she was able to find work in Sydney. In addition, Warwick was only 'on leave' when he began his four-year course, and for the first year and a half eked out some pay in lieu of the long service leave he would have taken if he had stayed a diplomat. But when this leave expired, he finally burned his bridges and, in his early fifties, formally resigned.

It might be argued that what he did was not a giant leap of faith, that he had a cushion under him and was lucky enough not to have resistance from his family. And certainly, he did not go about his career change rashly; in fact, he was rather cautious about it. Yet Warwick reasoned that, if he had achieved success in one career, surely he had it in him to do so in another. He is a good example *because* of this caution; many people never change career because they are too worried it won't work out, but as Warwick's example shows, it is possible to do it in a way that minimises the risks.

It is not actually necessary or even wise to suddenly quit one's job and begin a new career overnight. Indeed it will probably work better, both psychologically and financially, to have a period of transition while we cut ties with the old life and develop skills, contacts and income in the new one.

This was my experience. I was on a solid career path not dissimilar to Warwick's, working as a government policy adviser, with great benefits and security, and the work was far from boring. Yet like him I felt that, ultimately, it was not really 'me'. I had also discovered the personal development field, and knew that this was an area I wanted to work in all the time, not just as a side interest. But like Warwick, there was quite a long lead time before this became my reality. I completed a Master's degree in London, which I had embarked on as the perfect next step in my government career, but on returning to Australia, instead of applying for a full-time job, I worked part-time for over two years to give me the space to study the personal growth literature. I worked as a 'temp' in offices while I was writing my first book. Like Warwick, I didn't much care about the drop in income and security because I was so excited to be doing this work. When I had been taken on as a graduate recruit in Sydney years before, my brother had remarked that I was now 'set for life'. But what regrets I would have had if I had stayed there! An outward success, making my way up a career ladder, but inside pining for a more meaningful life. And ironically, this 'insecure' path I chose has given me not only a good income, but the potential to earn much more than I ever did in my former life.

Today, Warwick tells others to follow their dream if what

they are doing no longer provides real interest or fulfilment. Reflecting on the new path that made him a much happier man, he notes: 'I'm not sure that I really considered whether it was too late to make a major career change. I just knew I had to do something else that would give me a "buzz", and I had the energy and enthusiasm to do it.'

When he began his degree course at 49, Warwick had, according to our version of the Schwartz exercise, almost 52 per cent of his productive life ahead of him. So what might have seemed like a rash move to his friends still in the diplomatic service was actually very rational and smart.

When told that the title of this book was *Never Too Late to be Great*, Warwick commented that he had reached conventional 'greatness' with his ambassadorship. However, it was a desire to be more fulfilled in work and life, and his subsequent career change, that made him genuinely great – on his own terms and in his own time.

Final thought

The 'life is short' maxim is spouted by anxious teachers and parents to spur recalcitrant teenagers into making solid career plans, and we also say it to ourselves to stop daydreaming and start taking action. The idea that your life is over before you know it is so ingrained in our cultures that it is rarely questioned. Yet the facts on increasing longevity should make us think again. You realise that 'Yes, I *do* have time', and with this extra time there can be few excuses not to pursue something remarkable, or something of great meaning to you.

Though David Schwartz's bestseller extolled thinking big as the secret to achievement, if he were writing it today (half a century later, and with the average person having over a decade longer to live), it is likely he would have given even more emphasis to his productive lifespan exercise, because the formula for success today is to combine the magic of thinking big with the power of thinking *long*.

CHAPTER THREE

THE LONG VIEW

A simple way to join the elite

In 1970, Harvard political scientist Edward Banfield published *The Unheavenly City*. It was ostensibly about urban planning and the failure of many of America's inner cities during a time of social upheaval, but Banfield's deeper aim was to identify what allowed some people to escape the cycle of poverty and become successful, while others stayed trapped in situations that had not changed much in generations.

To his shock, this apparently dull academic book blew up a tornado of controversy, with many accusing Banfield of trying to 'blame the victim', specifically the black under-class in the decaying inner cities.

In fact, the professor had been even-handed in looking at a range of factors, including intelligence, education and family situation, in his attempt to explain why some people were, or were not, able to climb out of poverty in their lifetimes. Ultimately he ruled each one out as being reason alone for social immobility.

Banfield came up with a different, surprising explanation, which he called *long time perspective*. 'Lower class' people are that way because of an extreme 'present-orientation', he argued. Their unwillingness to look into and provide for the future leads to lack of skill development, lower employment and income, and an inability to provide for the future. In contrast, the further you moved up the social scale, the more future-orientated people were, and the more likely they were to delay gratification in the present in the aid of some future goal. What separated the well-off in society (in every sense) from the poor was their *appreciation of time*. 'Class' was not simply a matter of material wealth, education or social status, but a set of values and attitudes relating to time which were being transmitted from one generation to the next.

Banfield's critics argued that people of the urban under-class were only in that situation because racial and social prejudice kept them there. A life in which you were pushed down at every turn *would* make you live moment to moment. What was the point of having some great vision of the future? He did not deny that the climb out of poverty was difficult, yet he noted that all underclasses eventually raise themselves up and become middle class, and they do so only having begun to factor the future into decisions made daily. The opening up of time horizons, he observed, causes radical changes in how people decide to live day to day. If, for instance, a couple decide to save for a child's future educa-tion, it guides their choices on how to spend their time (i.e. productively or not) and their daily habits. Such a long time horizon, over generations, creates confidence in the ability to chart one's destiny, which Banfield noted was a distinct feature of the 'upper class'.

Though he used a particular setting to illustrate his idea and was writing at a certain time in history, Banfield's work touches on something universal: our perception of time is a critical part of success in life. If you decide that the choices you are making today do not gear you up for a long-term successful future, you may decide to change them. You may decide it is not a waste of time to go back to university, train for a new career or start building up a savings account. You might be more willing to leave the job you hate and take a more risky employment path which, over the long run, will deliver you real satisfaction and/or material gain. In short, your long-term success depends on something quite intangible – how you perceive time.

The long view of your career

While engaged in an in-depth study of a metal manufacturing company in England, Canadian psychologist Elliott Jacques was once asked by an employee why lower-level workers were paid by the hour, whereas senior management received a monthly salary. The question, he recalled later, was 'the greatest gift I ever got'. It led him to a theory of hierarchy based on the fact that people are paid according to the timeframes in which they are expected to perform. For instance, a salesperson who must meet a weekly or monthly target is awarded much less than a department boss focused on one- to two-year goals, while the head of the company, who has to chart its direction ten to 20 years into the future, will be paid much more again.

In the zeal for 'flatter organisations' in the 1980s and 1990s, Jacques' work went against the grain and he was accused of wanting to 'keep people in their place'. Yet he was careful to note that a person's working time horizon could change during their career. By choosing to see further ahead and aligning their work with the organisation's long-term goals, they could leapfrog others and rise to senior levels. For Jacques, this ability to see ahead was the missing link in understanding success at work.

Jeff Bezos did not grow up in a decaying inner city; in fact his upbringing was rather upper middle class. But when the creator of the world's largest online retailer, Amazon.com, was asked to give career advice, his response echoed Banfield and Jacques: *have a different sense of time to your peers*:

> 'Always take a long-term point of view. I think
> this is something about which there's a lot of
> controversy. A lot of people – and I'm just not
> one of them – believe that you should live for
> the now. I think what you do is think about the
> great expanse of time ahead of you and try to
> make sure that you're planning for that in a way
> that's going to leave you ultimately satisfied.'

In the 1990s, Bezos had a good job in finance in New York City, but was drawn to the emerging online world. When he told his boss he wanted to leave his job to start selling books over the internet, his boss took him on a two-hour walk around Central Park to try to talk him out of it. Bezos agreed to think about it a bit more over the next two days before making a final decision.

How do we make really big life decisions like this? In his

geeky, mathematical way, Bezos began to look around for a framework that would give him the right answer. (Luckily for him, his wife said she would support whatever he wanted to do, so the choice was totally his.) What he came up with was a 'regret minimisation framework', which involved casting himself into the future, aged 80, and looking back over his life. As an 80-year-old, would he regret taking the leap and starting the online business, even if it failed? The answer was a clear 'no'. What he would regret was *not* having thrown himself into the internet, which he knew was going to be really big. Bezos recalls:

> 'You know, I left this Wall Street firm in the middle of the year. When you do that, you walk away from your annual bonus. That's the kind of thing that in the short term can confuse you, but if you think about the long term then you can really make good life decisions that you won't regret later.'

Through his framework, his decision was made easy.

If *you* adopt the Bezos framework, how would it change what you do? Chances are, it would shift your decision-making from a base of fear to an outlook of making the best possible use of your interests and talents. The career coach Brendon Burchard likes to ask three questions of people considering what to do next in life. The questions are not about the practical next step, but in fact philosophical prompts, things you will want to ask yourself at the end of your life: did I *live*; did I *love*; did I *matter*?

Most people don't consider these questions in the here and now, but they can be powerful sources of creativity and action. The great advantage of the long view (looking back in your imagination as well as forward) is the quality of decisions it generates in the present. Imagining yourself at 80, looking back, provides a powerful context that blows away confusion in the present.

Of course, human nature being what it is, we are all impatient to succeed as early in life as possible. It's a challenge to take a panoramic, wide-time view of your life and achievements, and it tends only to be obstacles and circumstances that force us into taking a long view of our careers. This is what happened with William Hague.

In 1977, the 16-year-old Hague gave a fiery speech to a Conservative Party conference that received a standing ovation. The young Tory was clearly a future leader, and even his middle name, 'Jefferson', suggested a certain destiny.

After finishing school, Hague trod the usual path of political ambition in the UK: a degree in Politics, Philosophy and Economics at Oxford University, then a job as a political adviser. Yet Hague was moving quicker than most. By 28 he had his own seat in parliament, and before he was 35 was a minister in the government of John Major. When, in 1997, Major was defeated in a landslide by Tony Blair, Hague was given the party leadership.

This time, things did not go according to the storyboard. Gaffe-prone and ineffectual against a resurgent Labour Party, Hague's time as opposition leader was a disaster, and he lost the 2001 election to Blair. In that year, a newspaper poll found that two-thirds of voters considered Hague 'a bit of a wally', and the majority believed he would 'say almost anything to win votes'.

At 40, not much was now expected of Hague. But he kept himself busy, taking on company directorships, learning to play the piano and writing a biography of the 18th-century Prime Minister, Pitt the Younger. Pitt was also an early starter, becoming PM, incredibly, in his twenties. A younger Hague must once have seen something of himself in Pitt, but perhaps no longer.

But wait long enough, and the winds of fortune often turn back in our favour. In 2005, the new Tory opposition leader David Cameron asked Hague to become Shadow Foreign Secretary. When Cameron's Conservatives formed a government in 2010, the 49-and-a-half-year-old Hague was back. As Foreign Secretary, Hague finally found his feet, and in a largely youthful cabinet, he had 'elder statesman' status, acknowledged as Cameron's deputy. The 16-year-old firebrand might have assumed he would become PM, not Foreign Secretary, by the time he was 50 – and yet the role perfectly suited his broad view of the world and appreciation of history. And he still has plenty of time to make a tilt at the party leadership, if or when the opportunity arises.

Early success is a double-edged sword. It makes you 'someone', but also creates a weight of expectation and typecasting that can prove almost too heavy to crawl out from under. Hague's story reminds us that getting noticed is one thing, but no matter how bright the promise, it is time and experience that in the end make us who we are.

Many years before, there had been another rising star in British politics. Winston Churchill had become a member of parliament in his mid-twenties after coming to the attention of the British public for his daring war escapades in Africa, and at only 34 he had been made a cabinet minister. Three years later, he was given the post of First Lord of the Admiralty to beef up Britain's army and navy.

But in 1915, when Britain was at war, Churchill commanded an ill-conceived campaign in the Dardenelles that led to the senseless death of thousands at Gallipoli. The failure plunged the 40-year-old Winston into depression, and an official report took months to come out. When it did, his name was cleared, but only just. Though he was given two more ministerial appointments between 1917 and 1921, Churchill fell out of favour, and compared to his fast, early rise, the 1920s and 1930s were a wilderness period.

Yet the Dardanelles debacle marked the beginning of a more thoughtful Winston who poured his energies into writing, painting, spending time with his wife, and clarifying his positions on various moral and policy issues. It was only with the Nazi threat emerging at the end of the 1930s that Churchill's uncompromising outlook came into its own. Compared to other political leaders, he seemed rock-like in his convictions. Yet by the time he became Prime Minister, Churchill was well into his sixties, and though he always considered himself a person of destiny, the post was still a long time coming, and the younger, cockier Winston would have been surprised at the 'old' age the office came to him.

Churchill's failure at 40 was the foundation of his success

at 60, but at the time, of course, it did not seem this way. It was only the older Winston, with greater moral courage, policy knowledge and standing among his peers, who was able to put up the fight to Hitler and save Europe from tyranny.

Henry Ford did not launch the motor company we know today until he was 40, and he'd had a long apprenticeship as a mechanic, inventor and failed businessman prior to his company's success. Yet he felt his achievements could not have come any earlier. 'I would like to communicate to others,' he told his pastor Samuel Marquis, 'the calmness that the long view of life gives to us.' Once he had this 'long view', Ford felt he could relax into his lifetime's work.

Robert Stigwood, the legendary music manager who guided the Bee Gees to superstardom, used to give this advice to the Gibb brothers on their songwriting: 'Write for forty years from now. Write for the future.'

Paradoxically, this aim of writing songs that were timeless, 'writing for the unborn' as Robin Gibb put it, led the Bee Gees to be wildly popular in the present.

Though few of us seem able to take the long view as a conscious strategy, it has many benefits, not least (as Henry Ford noted) a sense of calm that allows us to focus on the work at hand. A longer time horizon allows you to take in your stride the lead times that inevitably pass before you can make a mark, and to put obstacles into context. You are not thrown off track as much as someone with a short-term view, and instead of a wish, your success takes on an air of relaxed inevitability.

Yet the long view takes courage.

When Jonathan Franzen published *Strong Motion* in 1992, he was hailed by *Granta* and *The New Yorker* as one of the 'best new writers under 40'. But Franzen, who had already received a Fulbright scholarship for this perception of early promise, did not produce a new novel the following year, or the year after that. In fact, for the rest of the 1990s, in what might have seemed the best years to capitalise on his early high profile, there was a worrying lack of news.

In 1996, Franzen did make waves with an essay in *Harper's* magazine. In an age when movies seemed to be king, his article 'Perchance to Dream: In the Age of Images, A Reason to Write Novels', pointed to the lack of great contemporary social novels being written. A good point, but where was Franzen's? Even as the year 2000 dawned, there was no release scheduled. Instead, eating beans, rice and cheap chicken thighs, he continued to write in a tiny Manhattan apartment shared with his girlfriend, wearing earplugs to keep out the city noise.

In 2001, not long before the events of September 11, his big book *The Corrections* was finally published. Following the lives of a fractured family heading towards a reunion, the novel took a sharply satirical interpretation of modern life that also managed to be a page-turner. Receiving enormous publicity, the work clearly answered Franzen's own call for a great modern social novel, winning awards, becoming a book club favourite and selling frantically.

Yet over a dozen years had passed since his first title. In an interview, Franzen admitted he had taken his time with *The Corrections*, yet noted, '. . . all around me, I'm being offered evidence that you can take forever to write a book and still find a readership when it's done.'

Franzen's outlook was simple: he would work at his own pace and let his book ripen. For an author of integrity, there was no other way. And it did not harm him to wait.

We all want to get on quickly, but the 'get successful quick' schemes of our minds more often sabotage our chances at real achievement. Instead, try taking a long view of your career. You may find that it saves you heartache and disappointment, because if there is some setback, you will be able to pick yourself up quicker and focus on the opportunities at hand. Churchill's military failure and Hague's gaffes seemed to spell the end of their careers, but they turned out to be just steps on the way to a greater end. Jonathan Franzen didn't panic during his time out of the limelight, and neither should you. Keep working, and cultivate a relaxed feeling that your time will come.

The long view in business

It is easy for any big company – and for any small company or person for that matter – to get lost in the day to day, but great companies become great by their habit of looking further ahead than others. They must operate in the present, obviously, but their long-term view makes them a safer bet as an investment over several decades.

Josephine Esther Mentzer grew up in Corona, the site of a huge ash dump that was famously described by F. Scott Fitzgerald in *The Great Gatsby*, several miles outside of New

York City. Her immigrant Hungarian and Czech parents always called her by her middle name, or rather 'Esty' (which her father pronounced Estay).

Her father ran a grain and feed business, but the main influences of her youth were her sister-in-law Fanny, who ran a local department store, and her uncle John, a chemist who made and sold small batches of face cream and various lotions and fragrances. Already into beauty care, Esty enjoyed watching him work and thought his face cream was marvellous. She began making it on the stove at home, and was soon selling it direct to beauty salons.

At 22 she married Joseph Lauter, then in his late twenties, and three years later they had their first child, Leonard. But the ambitious and flighty Esty was disappointed with her husband's failure to make headway in business, and she began to regret the marriage. When Leonard was six, Esty (now calling herself Estée Lauder) divorced Joseph, and started dividing her time between New York and Miami. She sold her wares direct to beauty salons in both places, had a stand in a hotel in Miami, and worked the Jewish resorts on Long Island and the Catskills. She would give facials and provide demonstrations, and pioneered the giveaway of free samples with every purchase.

According to her biographer Lee Israel, in this time she also had a couple of relationships, the first with an English industrialist, Dr John Myers, 18 years her senior, and the second with Arnold Lewis van Ameringen, a big shot in fragrances who manufactured the scents for houses like Chanel. But van Ameringen was married and not willing to leave his wife. A friend says of Estée at the time: 'She thought she'd go out on her own and meet all kinds of millionaires. That doesn't happen so fast. And she was getting fed up with the kinds of people she was meeting. Different men. You know, people don't just hand things over. And so she said to me, "What am I knocking myself out for with other guys? Joe's a nice man. I don't know why I broke off with him." Estée decided she would be better off by reuniting with Joe, staying a family and building the business together.

In the years they were apart Joe had never given up on her, and they remarried in 1942. Estée was 31 and Joe 39. Estée later regretted their estrangement, noting 'You cannot fly on one wing'.

After the Lauders reunited they had a second son, Ronald, but before long, Estée was back working behind cosmetics counters in department stores selling her own line. But her real dream was to sell cosmetics in the glamorous Saks Fifth Avenue. In 1947, now in her late thirties and against the advice of their accountant, Estée and Joe formally began their business, Estée Lauder Inc., and a year or so later achieved the dream of selling into Saks. She used this as leverage to get into other stores, and the firm began to experience fast growth. For the next ten years, Estée criss-crossed America visiting department stores, becoming a minor legend for her force of personality and sales ability. Meanwhile, Joe was working seven days a week helping to make the products, literally mixing the ingredients and pouring them into jars, often with the help of young Leonard.

Though the pair was making solid progress, everything

changed with the 1953 launch of Youth Dew, the bath oil-cum-fragrance that took America by storm and soon represented 80 per cent of the company's revenues. The heady scent was Estée's creation, but she received lots of help from her old friend van Ameringen, who developed it for market and provided much-needed credit for its launch. With Estée at 47 and Joe at 55, proceeds from the scent enabled the Lauders to buy their first town house in Manhattan.

In 1960, the company hit its first million dollars in revenue, but it was still dwarfed by its competitors Revlon, Helena Rubinstein and Elizabeth Arden. It needed to become a mature company, and after becoming president in 1972, Leonard made it happen. According to one industry insider, Estée 'became like the Queen of England while Leonard became Margaret Thatcher'. The company's later successes included Aramis, the Clinique line and acquisitions such as Origins.

When the two Grande Dames of cosmetics, Elizabeth Arden and Helena Rubinstein, died, their empires were in financial disarray and had to be sold off to conglomerates. This left Revlon and Estée Lauder as the two titans of the market. But unlike Revlon (Charles Revson did not pass on his stake in the company to his two sons, and was divorced by his wife), Estée Lauder was determined to keep her company in the family. Though in 1995 she bowed to pressure and partly floated it on the New York Stock Exchange, it was so managed that the family stayed in control. Today, with various grandchildren involved in running the company, the Lauder family still has 70 per cent of voting shares.

How would the Lauder story have turned out if Estée had not got back together with Joe? Both the men she saw during the separation helped her, financially and socially, but ultimately she felt much more satisfaction from building something with Joe and the two boys. With Myers or van Ameringen she might have got ahead quicker, but by sticking with Joe, Estée Lauder stayed a family company and, despite huge later injections of public capital, is still controlled by the Lauders. It is one thing to build a great business empire, but even greater is the fact that Estée achieved it all with the love of her life alongside her. Following their reunion they doted on each other for the rest of their lives.

You have probably seen the advertisements for Patek Philippe watches that adorn the pages of glossy magazines. There are variations, but the scene is usually this: an urbane, good-looking, successful man in his mid-forties, greying at the temples and a master of all he surveys, is pictured in what looks like an elegant study next to his son. The boy is 16 or 17, a bit naive but with a bright future ahead of him, the apple of his father's eye. At the bottom of the image is the line: *You never actually own a Patek Philippe watch. You merely look after it for the next generation.*

As the ad suggests, the social and financial elite often have a different sense of time to the rest of us. They think not just in terms of years or decades, but *generations*. This very long view allows for deep investment in people that will be returned when the time is right.

As Banfield noted, people with a long-time horizon

tend to be more confident because they feel in control of their destiny. Writing in the 1970s, Banfield associated such confidence with the 'upper class', but today the benefits associated with long-time perspective are available to us all. You don't need the oak-lined study or the Ivy League or Oxbridge education to join this class. All you have to do is begin thinking in a similar way, and like Jeff Bezos, have a different time horizon than your friends or colleagues.

The following two stories, further prove this point.

In 1946, in the burned-out shell of a department store building in Tokyo, a group of people gathered to officially begin a new company, Tokyo Telecommunications Engineering Corporation. Masuru Ibuka, 38, had got the business going a few months earlier, his team repairing radios while they tried to come up with a profitable product. Now, Akio Morita, 25, joined him in the enterprise as a partner. The two had met during wartime service as researchers into heat-seeking missiles. In their love of electronics and wish to create new products that would help society, they bonded instantly.

The Moritas were one of Japan's oldest sake brewing families, going back 15 generations. They also produced soy sauce and miso paste for making the Japanese staple, miso soup. But when Kyuzaemon Morita took over the Morita company, it was not in good shape. His father and grandfather had been more interested in civic duties, the fine arts and collecting, and had put salaried managers in to run the company. As Kyuzaemon's son Akio recalls of his grandfather and great-grandfather, 'They did not carry the responsibility of the generations, of maintaining the continuity and prosperity of the enterprise.'

Kyuzaemon had to abandon his business studies to rescue the business, and raised cash by selling off many of the family treasures. But by the time his son Akio was born, the family was well off again, living in a large house on one of the best streets in Nagoya. Across the road were the Toyodas, the loom manufacturing clan who would soon plough their capital into car making. Akio was groomed to take over the company, and his father made him join in with many business activities, but what he loved most was tinkering with electronics, and he became increasingly interested in mathematics and physics. Instead of staying in the family business, Kyuzaemon gave his assent for Akio to go to university, to study engineering, and it was this open-mindedness that set Akio on the path to meet Masuru Ibuka, his lifelong business partner with whom he would create the Sony Corporation.

By 1955, the tiny concern that Ibuka and Morita created had established itself as a medium-sized company in Japan, but Morita had his sights set on the United States. It had tried to enter the US market with its pocket transistor radio, one of the first produced, but had mostly met with resistance; buyers did not see the market for such a small radio when people had large houses. But there was a buyer from the Bulova company who did like them, and wanted to order 10,000 units. This was a huge deal for Morita's young firm, worth several times its capital at that time. Part of the terms and conditions of the deal was that the radios would be sold under the Bulova name, not the new name that TTEC had come up with to sell its wares: 'Sony'.

Morita baulked at this, and despite pressure from the office back in Japan, came back to Bulova with a no. The Bulova purchasing officer was stunned and angry, saying: 'Our company name is a famous brand name that has taken over fifty years to establish. Nobody has ever heard of your brand name. Why not take advantage of ours?'

Morita could see the man's logic, but said: 'Fifty years ago, your brand name must have been just as unknown as our name is today. I am here with a new product, and I am now taking the first step for the next fifty years of my company. Fifty years from now I promise you that our name will be just as famous as your company name is today.'

Morita knew, even in the moment he said it, that it was the right decision, because he had always intended to create a proper brand name on the world stage. By avoiding the apparent attraction of the deal, Sony was now free and energised to pursue its real destiny.

Morita's long-range view of Sony's prospects in the US compelled him to set up Sony Corporation of America, the first Japanese company to do such a thing. Thanks to this, Sony became a leader in consumer electronics in the market that mattered most, and it was under Morita's watch that devices such as the Walkman (a brilliant precursor to today's music devices) were launched.

Though Morita did not take over from his father running the centuries-old Morita company, neither did he abdicate his role as head of the family, continuing to preside over family meetings even while he was running Sony. Though he had felt compelled to start something new (in Sony), he did not discard the natural Japanese understanding and respect for continuity.

We mentioned that the Moritas lived across the road from the Toyodas. What is their story? Sakichi Toyoda grew up in late 1800s Japan and became an expert at developing loom machinery. His invention of a loom that would automatically stop when a thread broke was just one of his innovations, and he became known as the country's 'king of inventors'. He was greatly inspired by a Japanese translation of Samuel Smiles' book *Self-Help* (1859), which glorified inventors such as James Watt, developer of the steam engine. What Toyoda got from Smiles' book was that success was not the result of natural talents or resources, but hard work, discipline and perseverance.

When Sakichi's son Kiichiro was sent to England to sell the patent rights to his 'mistake-proof loom' to a leading weaving equipment company, it netted the family £100,000. Sakichi did not see the family's future in looms, but in motor cars, and this capital was a foundation of Toyota Motor Company. He told his son:

> 'Everyone should tackle some great project at
> least once in their life. I devoted most of mine
> to inventing new kinds of looms. Now it is your
> turn. You should make an effort to complete
> something that will benefit society.'

Kiichiro Toyoda duly turned his family's company into a small car-making operation, but it was only when his cousin and confidante Eiji Toyoda took over the reins a few years later that Toyota (as it became known) emerged as a full-scale manufacturer, guiding it through great success with models including the Corolla and later the Lexus.

Jeffrey Liker, an engineering professor at the University of Michigan and author of *The Toyota Way*, characterises Toyota as a generally plodding company that is slow to make changes. On the other hand, it is intensely competitive and clear about its mission, and can stamp on the accelerator when need be. In 1990, Eiji Toyoda made an internal warning to the company that if it wanted to be number one in the 21st century, it couldn't keep making cars the same old way. He pushed for the company to start looking at alternative power sources to the conventional petrol engine, and despite some internal reluctance he got his way. In 1995 Toyota began testing a revolutionary new car. Its 'G21' research programme eventually yielded a car with a petrol/electric hybrid engine – the Prius – that has indeed changed motoring.

The Prius example shows us that as part of a generally slow-cooked nature, there is still the potential to move quickly if need be. Like a cat or a crocodile that sleeps for most of the day then suddenly leaps into action, power is reserved for when it is really needed. Toyota is a prime example of measured action that will not sabotage long-term success, of the truth that the further ahead your goals, the better able you are to spot opportunities *in the present* that match up to that long-term vision. This is how the Prius came to fruition, and it is also evident with Akio Morita's decision to forge ahead with creating the Sony brand. With a clear, long-range view of what you do and what you are about, decisions in the short term become easier because you know whether something does or does not fit into your vision.

Of Jeffrey Liker's '14 management principles from the world's greatest manufacturer', number one is *Long-Term Philosophy*. Without this, the investments Toyota makes in continuous improvement and 'adding value to society' would be meaningless. The press made much of a series of costly product recalls that hit Toyota in the late 2000s, and some even predicted they would permanently damage the company or even bring it down. But such alarmism fails to see the strength that lies in Toyota because of its long-term view. Yes, the recalls were expensive and embarrassing for a firm that rides on a reputation of bullet-proof engineering, but a company that also thinks in terms of decades is able to take such events in its stride[1].

Japanese companies are well known for their long-time horizons, but they do not have a monopoly here. General Electric was begun when Thomas Edison needed a corporate vehicle to sell his newly invented light bulbs. GE is now over 125 years old, and ranks as the world's largest firm, with its capitalisation and output dwarfing many states. Yet *Fortune* magazine noted that within its long history, the company has had fewer leaders than the Vatican has had popes over the same period. Indeed, former chief executive officer Jack Welch, who presided over a long and successful period at GE, provides a gripping account of the manoeuvring

---

1 A Toyoda is back in charge of the company. Akio Toyoda, grandson of Kiichiro Toyoda, became president and CEO in 2009.

to choose the next company head in his autobiography, and observes that it is not that different from the tortuous process that goes towards choosing a new pontiff.

Welch's successor, Jeffrey Immelt, put it this way: 'I run a company that is 125 years old. There's going to be someone after me, just as there was someone else before me.' For Immelt, whose father Joseph worked in GE's Cincinatti plant all his life, rising to manage an aircraft engines division, the company has a family dimension. When Immelt took over in 2001, he commissioned a study into the best-performing companies around the world. One of the key findings was that these firms value 'deep domain expertise'. They tend not to bring in outside managers to 'shake things up' or 'extract value', but instead place great store by the deep knowledge and expertise of people who have worked in their companies for years, and who have been groomed to be top managers. When Immelt looked at his own company, he found this to be true. As he noted to the *Harvard Business Review*:

> 'The most successful parts of GE are places where
> leaders have stayed in place a long time. Think
> of Brian Rowe's long tenure in aircraft engines.
> Four or five big decisions he made – relying on
> his deep knowledge of that business – won us
> maybe as many as 50 years of industry leadership.
> The same point applies to GE Capital. The places
> where we've churned people, like reinsurance,
> are where you will find we've failed.'

Is this your experience too? Any organisation that goes through lots of management or personnel changes is by nature unstable. In contrast, one that has had good people in place for a long time who know their stuff has an air of unhurried stability that naturally draws in more good people. Organisations only become like this through having clarity of purpose and giving themselves a longer time frame to achieve their goals. In business, as in life, seeing further ahead makes all the difference.

We have space for two final examples of the power of the long view.

Born in 1952 in India, in his early twenties Vikram Seth began doctoral studies in Economics at Stanford University in California, and for over a decade, no less, worked on his Economics PhD, studying poetry on the side. For a couple of years he was based at Nanjing University in China, in order to research his thesis on 'Chinese population planning', and in that time learned fluent Mandarin. After an overland trip from China into India, he wrote a travelogue and memoir, *From Heaven Lake: Travels Through Sinkiang and Tibet* (1983). It won the Thomas Cook award for travel writing, and sold well. Three years later he published *The Golden Gate*, a novel-length poem written in rhyming sonnets about a group of young professionals ('yuppies') living in 1980s San Francisco. Though not a bestseller, it was considered a success and received good reviews.

Seth returned to live in India to write his second novel, and took up lodging at his parents' house. He had not intended this book to be very long, but the project, based on the lives of four families in the period leading up to the first Indian national election in 1952, grew and grew. With a Proustian aversion to hurrying the book along, Seth spent years on it, and when *A Suitable Boy* was finally published in 1993, in his 41st year, it was a brick-like object running to 1,349 pages. The work is now known as the longest single-volume novel in the English language.

Despite, or perhaps partly because of, its size (John Steinbeck once said that if you wanted to make an impact with a book, make sure it was long), *A Suitable Boy* was a publishing phenomenon, selling over a million copies, and Seth became a literary darling courted by book festival organisers the world over. *The Washington Post* hailed him 'A Tolstoy – On His First Try'. He was no longer a 'promising young writer', but a major literary figure.

A person who spends a decade writing a book while living at his parents' house is not in a rush to 'get product out'.

Indeed, when you consider that it was written over ten years, Seth was averaging only 130 pages a year – not a huge amount for a writer. In pursuit of more frequent royalty cheques, he might have tried to sell *A Suitable Boy* in sections as they were written, but instead he was willing to wait years until this world within a book was released as one fat, fully ripe tome.

Seth has said that he sees himself as a conduit for his work, rather than its master, meaning that he must wait for a book to unfold almost as if it is an entity outside of himself. *A Suitable Boy* is such a rich, dense work because

Seth allowed it to cook on low heat over a long period. If had been whipped out of the literary oven much sooner, it may have had a weak structure or quite the wrong texture. But part of Seth's wisdom was sitting back and honouring the role of time in the creation of quality, of taking the long view in his life and work.

Antony Gormley is a British sculptor most famous for his huge *Angel of the North*, a winged figure that rises above a motorway in the north of England and is seen by over 30 million motorists a year. Yet his career took a long time to take off.

As a boy, Gormley would spend rainy Saturday afternoons wandering the British Museum, or be taken by his businessman, art-loving father to galleries. After attending the Catholic boarding school Ampleforth, where he won art prizes, he went to Cambridge to study archaeology, anthropology and history of art. But on graduating he didn't feel ready to become a full-blown artist, and so went travelling to India to learn about Buddhism. After three years away, during which he got typhoid and considered becoming a Buddhist monk, Gormley came back to Britain and enrolled in art school, living in a squat. He would spend the rest of his twenties in various London art schools.

Gormley's big break came in 1981, when he was given a solo exhibition at the Whitechapel Gallery. Now in his thirties, the newly married Gormley might have expected his career to move into the fast lane, but in fact it flatlined through the 1980s. More interested in getting his work shown in public galleries and in public spaces, there was not a lot that private dealers could actually sell. In a decade in which he also became the father of three children, there was little money and fading recognition.

But as the 1990s began, Gormley's work came into its own. He won the Turner Prize, the biggest in British contemporary art, for his work *Field*, a room of thousands of clay heads that he had got other people to make. He was also picked up by Jay Jopling, the White Cube gallery owner and the leading dealer of the BritArt movement who also represented Damien Hirst and Tracey Emin. At 43, money and acclaim finally poured in. Today, his metal body sculptures, often based on casts from his own body, are found around the world, and he has a team of people helping him to realise major commissions.

Of course, 43 is no great age in art. Many artists take much longer to achieve any kind of recognition, and in that respect Gormley was not really a late starter. On the other hand, given all his advantages – well-off family, Cambridge education, good art schools – he did take a while (20 years) to realise his potential. If this was the case with someone like him, why should we expect ourselves to get anywhere at a younger age? The paradox of art is that it is extremely competitive; for every prize, grant and dealer there may be hundreds, if not thousands, of suitors. *And yet*, what the art world most values is striking originality, which by its nature has no competition. Gormley doesn't have to bid for commissions or installations, they come to him. But that is only because he took the time, and carved out the space, to pursue his self-created artistic goals. Critics say he is a 'one-trick pony', doing little else but works involving metal casts of the human form. Yet it is precisely this focus that gave him renown. By choosing 'one big thing', the power of it – if relentlessly refined over many years – increases. This principle applies not just to art but any walk of life. It may take 20, 30 or 40 years to find your greatness in a job, a style, a project or a business, but if you have a relaxed expectation that it awaits you, that becomes a self-fulfilling prophecy.

Gormley could have derailed his career by making saleable, discrete works when he needed the money, but he wasn't interested in his work ending up in people's houses where no one would see it. He stuck to his interest in public spaces and public interaction, and eventually the public valued this commitment. As with Jonathan Franzen, Gormley's view paid off, not simply in acclaim or status, but in the knowledge that he had stuck to his artistic guns through difficulties and changing fashions. Paradoxically, in a world that demands everything by the minute, this kind of steadfastness is prized.

Final thoughts

There is an ancient proverb, attributed to the Chinese: *time and patience change the mulberry leaf to satin.*

When fed mulberry leaves, silkworms produce a shimmering thread that can be processed and woven into a black, shiny, luxurious material. It was reputedly the favourite saying of the French statesman Talleyrand, who held a remarkable degree of influence in his nation's political affairs. Over several decades, despite various periods in exile or disgrace, he always seemed to bounce back and play vital roles. Talleyrand was well born, well connected and intellectually brilliant, but even with these advantages, he recognised that one goes nowhere without a keen appreciation of time and timing. People come in and out of fashion too, he knew, so the intelligent had to be willing to hold tight, waiting again for their opportunity.

If things aren't happening for you now, despite the work you have done . . . *wait* – things will usually swing back your way again. As Fritjof Capra noted in *The Tao of Physics*:

> 'The Chinese believe that whenever a situation
> develops to its extreme, it is bound to turn
> around and become its opposite. This basic
> belief has given them courage and perseverance
> in times of distress and has made them cautious
> and modest in times of success.'

You can't measure success in a year or two. Speculating on a day-to-day or week-to-week basis is fraught with uncertainty and dangers, but someone who takes a long-term view invariably does well.

Take the long view of your life, career or business, and much worry and angst is removed from the equation. You may be no better than someone else at what you do at the outset, but if you let time and experience play its part, and have a willingness to build these into the 'product' that you offer the world (whether this is a thing, a service, or you yourself), you will set yourself apart from your peers.

Fashions come and go, but quality and originality are always recognised. Don't despair if you feel like a lone voice in the wilderness, or if people see what you do as being out of step with the times. Consider this radical idea: you do not have to depend on 'the times' for your success. Rather, by sticking to your guns, by being faithful to who you are and what you do, the times can be shaped *by* you.

CHAPTER FOUR:

LEAD TIME

It's the 'time in between' that matters

One evening in 2004, in tears, having spent yet another evening scraping a living serving drinks at a swish party, Erika Sunnegardh was about to give up on her singing career. For 16 years she had worked as a waitress and singer at churches and funerals and was beginning to lose hope. But at 38, Erika decided she should give her dream one last try. Though she was living in New York, a family friend suggested she audition for Sweden's Malmo Opera. The audition went well and she was given her first professional role, in a production of *Turandot*.

This experience in turn gave her the confidence to audition for the Met. She was taken on as an understudy, and one night in 2006 the singer for the role of Leonore in Beethoven's *Fidelio* was taken ill. The 40-year-old Sunnegardh filled in at the last minute, and it was a triumph: the performance was critically praised and the audience loved her. Finally, her career was established.

As the French philosopher Montesquieu, who did not produce his masterwork, *The Spirit of the Laws*, until his late fifties, said: *'Success in most things depends on knowing how long it takes to succeed.'*

And how long *does* it take? Naturally, everyone is different, but the actual age that a person makes their mark is less important than the fact that there must be a portion of time that elapses between the initial idea of something and its full implementation: *lead time*. Fully allow for this 'time in between', and you will find that your success not only comes when it is due, but in a seemingly perfect way – as the examples below illustrate.

Give me a decade and see what I can do

In *Self-Help*, his seminal treatise on personal development written in the same year as Darwin's *Origin of the Species*, Samuel Smiles remarked that people '. . . of the most distinguished genius have invariably been found the most indefatigable workers'. He admits that no amount of hard work could have produced from an ordinary person a Shakespeare, Beethoven, Mozart or Michelangelo, yet everyone has a kernel of talent, and with enough discipline and application it could become something very substantial. 'Facility will come with labour,' he observed.

His American counterpart, Orison Swett Marden, said:

> 'The slow penny is surer than the quick dollar.
> The slow trotter will out-travel the fleet racer.
> Genius darts, flutters, and tires; but perseverance
> wears and wins . . . The last blow drives home
> the nail.'

The great art critic and aesthete John Ruskin counselled:

> 'Never depend upon your genius. If you have
> talent, industry will improve it; if you have none,
> industry will supply the deficiency.'

Voltaire, who liked to prick the balloon of privilege and rank, remarked that there was a very fine line that separates the person of 'genius' from the ordinary man. 'Work', he said, 'banishes those three great evils: boredom, vice and poverty.'

Buffon, the 19th-century naturalist, simply said: *'Genius is patience.'*

Such are the views of 'old school' thinkers on the subject of genius, time and work. But what does the research say?

In the early 1970s, Nobel Prize winner Herbert Simon and William Chase made a study of top international chess players and noticed that none had reached the highest levels of their field without at least a decade of intense study and practice. The exception was Bobby Fisher, who by the time he became world champion was only 16. But despite the astonishingly young age of his supremacy, even Fisher was not a 'freak' but had more or less followed the law of lead time, having spent the previous nine years, since he was seven, in intensive study of the game. The 'ten-year rule', as Simon and Chase called it, was later confirmed by studies of people in a range of fields, including maths, music, swimming, tennis and literature.

In 1990, John Hayes of Carnegie Mellon University made a study into the age at which the great composers produced their masterworks. He found that hardly any of their great works were produced in the first ten years of their career. Out of 500 works analysed, there were only three exceptions: from Satie, Shostakovich and Paganini, produced in years eight, nine and nine respectively. 'Averaged over the group,' Hayes reported, 'the pattern of career productivity involved an initial ten-year period of silence, a rapid increase in productivity from year ten to year 25, a period of stable productivity from year 25 to about year 45 and then a gradual decline.'

Hayes noted the peak year of productivity to be around 40, and if Handel and Verdi died as young as Schubert, they wouldn't have been considered great composers at all. Many composers continued producing significant works past the 50th years of their career, such as Albeniz at 72. He concluded:

> 'The early silence observed in all three of these
> studies suggests that a long period of preparation
> is essential for creative productivity even for the
> most talented of our composers, painters, and
> poets.'

But does great work result from preparation (the years spent learning and studying music), Hayes wondered, or from age itself (life wisdom being critical to truly original work)? Assuming that age *was* the most important element in musical distinction, it followed that those composers who started really young would have to wait longer to achieve distinction than those who began their training later. The facts, Hayes found, did not bear this out. What mattered was the *time spent in persistent application*, whether this was initiated at five, ten or 15 years old. Whatever the age a person produced their first great work, or became publicly known, it was preceded by 'ten years of silence', a time of relative obscurity that allows the refinement of skills to an acute point.

What about Mozart, who produced so much so young? Surely he was a case of genius bypassing 'ten years of silence'? Hayes looked at which of Mozart's works were recorded the most (considering this a reasonable gauge of worth and esteem, both in a popular and critical sense) and found that the compositions done in the first ten years of his career (that is, from the time of his intensive musical training as a young boy into his mid-teens) were in fact little recorded. Moreover, when they were, it was often part of Mozart compilations that covered his whole career. On the whole, such early compositions were considered interesting, given who composed them, but hardly great or enduring. He recalls a remark of Harold Schonberg, the music critic:

> 'It is strange to say of a composer who started
> writing at six, and lived only thirty-six years, that
> he developed late, but that is the truth. Few of
> Mozart's early works, elegant as they are, have
> the personality, concentration, and richness that
> entered his work after 1781 . . . 1781 marks the
> period of Mozart's maturity, and virtually every
> work thereafter is a masterpiece.'

In 1781 Mozart may only have been 25, but he had been composing since he was five, and virtually made to do so by his father. By 1781, Hayes notes, Mozart was 21 years into his career. Thus, the works we think of when we hear the name 'Mozart', are those created by someone who had spent *two decades* mastering his art. Mozart may have been very lucky to have the father he did, a musical teacher intent on making his son a star, but there is no evidence for other-worldly genius that just came from nowhere. If that were true, we would be listening to his early compositions as much as his later ones.

Like anyone, Mozart had to spend many years at his craft to fulfil his potential. But because he had started so young, he had the *appearance* of genius. Even when we look at the greats of music and sport, areas in which youth is often seen to be at a premium, this holds true. Consider Michael Jackson being made to perform on stage at five, the Bee Gees singing professionally through their childhood, or Tiger Woods being put on the golf course at two. Svetlana Khorkova, who won two Olympic gymnastics gold medals and had new manoeuvres named after her, rose to prominence in her mid-teens, but in the tradition of many Russian gymnasts, had been practising since the age of four. Lady Gaga, in some minds the epitome of overnight success, in fact learned the piano at four and was writing songs and performing at open mike nights by her early teens. Celine Dion was singing from a very young age at her parents' wine bar in Montreal.

Thomas Edison famously said, 'Genius is one per cent inspiration and 99 per cent perspiration.' Less often recorded is the rest of Edison's statement: 'Accordingly, a "genius" is often merely a talented person who has done all of his or her homework.' A boy once asked the great violinist Felice Giardini how long it would take to learn to play. 'Twelve hours a day for twenty years together', was his reply.

Practice does make perfect, and the younger you start refining your skills, the more remarkable you will seem.

Yet Anders Ericsson, a world expert on expertise itself, notes that practice as we normally think of it is not enough to get you to the top of your field – it must be *deliberate* practice, involving constant work to be slightly better every day in very specific skills, using feedback and measured against pre-set benchmarks. This is exactly what the golfer Ben Hogan did, and it is what Donald Bradman, generally acknowledged as the greatest cricketer ever, was famous for. As a boy, Bradman would hit a golf ball against a water tank in his back yard, hour after hour, not with a cricket bat but with a cricket *stump*, to 'get his eye in'. Today's sporting heroes can't replace deliberate practice either. Even football's flashy David Beckham, for instance, is well known for his love of practice.

Ericsson, like Simon & Chase and Hayes, noticed that there were no real shortcuts in the time it took to become great. No matter the depth of raw talent or the ardour for practice, it always took top achievers years to reach the top. The only 'shortcut', if there was one, was starting younger than your peers. But again, and as we will see, even this is no requirement for success.

Down the mineshaft, working in the mud

Examples of 'ten years of silence' and wilderness periods

The pioneering anatomist and surgeon John Hunter was typical of original people, Samuel Smiles said, in that he 'worked for a long time as it were underground, digging and laying foundations'. The same could be said of Sigmund

Freud and Martin Luther, who both had 'ten years of silence' before doing something unique.

Sigmund Freud was a star student at school, and his parents gave him special privileges, including a room of his own. He was all set to study law at the University of Vienna, but changed his mind at the last minute, enrolling in medicine. He then took a full eight years to complete his degree, and when he entered the world of work, was again in no hurry. He had wanted to become a medical researcher, and did in fact write several excellent scientific papers, but he also wished to marry and knew he would have to have a secure job to start a family. So Freud started work at Vienna General Hospital in the area of brain anatomy, and a few years later set himself up in private practice.

Over the next 13 years, through his daily interaction with patients and his own research, Freud laid an intellectual foundation for what he would later call psychoanalysis, shifting his attention beyond the physical brain itself to psychological issues. His workload and family obligations were not too onerous, allowing him to mull over big questions, collect Egyptian statuary and read from his voluminous library in philosophy, mythology and literature. Although he had some involvement with other doctors, Sigmund basically worked on his own for over a decade. He likened this period to time down a mineshaft.

The result was that the work which made his name, *Die Traumdeutung*, was not published until he was in his mid-forties. After finishing it, he wrote: 'Insight such as this falls to one's lot but once in a lifetime'. Yet only a few hundred copies were printed, and these took several years to sell. It was only after the book was translated into English, 12 years later, as *The Interpretation of Dreams*, that Freud's fame began to grow. By then he was in his late fifties.

Martin Luther, the great religious reformer, stood up to the excesses and corruption of the Catholic Church, sparking off the Protestant Reformation. His nailing to the door of a German church his '95 theses' (points which spelled out the need for reform) was a bombshell which, thanks to the new invention of printing, was felt throughout Christendom. Rebellion is usually manifested in one's younger years, but Luther was 34 by the time he spoke out – which in those times was decidedly middle age. What took him so long?

Although his father had wanted him to be a lawyer, Martin was set on joining a monastery, but once there felt like an outsider. It was in the monastery that he had his famous crises about his vocation. Despite these doubts, his sharp mind and ability helped him move up the church ladder quickly. By his mid-thirties he was in charge of 11 monasteries, by any conventional standard a 'success'.

Erik Erikson, the Danish-American psychiatrist who wrote a famous biography of Luther, argued that great figures in history often spend years in a surprisingly passive state, wanting to believe fully in whatever they are involved. Yet it is only having been through this stage that truly personal convictions begin to emerge, which often run counter to what they have been taught. 'An original thinker,' Erikson said, 'often waits a long time not only for impressions, but also for his own reactions.' In Luther's case, he could only come out against the Church *after* having been fully committed to it.

Erikson observed that both Luther and Freud were willing

'. . . to do the dirty work of their ages'. That is, looking for the truth even if it meant offending the social and religious mores of the time. If Freud had described the years prior to writing *The Interpretation of Dreams* as his time 'down the mineshaft', Luther used a similar phrase to describe the ten years in which he quietly developed the views that would lead to his coming out as a reformer. He described this time as 'working in the mud'.

We tend to look on such times in a negative way, yet for Freud and Luther they were periods of freedom to explore exactly what interested them and who they were, before fame and its pressures closed in.

Have you had wilderness periods, 'times in the mud' or stints 'down a mineshaft'? The key to these periods is to settle into them and enjoy them for what they are. By trying to move quicker, you can miss out on the richness of insight that they bring.

Pamela Travers, the Australian who created the strict, spritely and mysterious English nanny, Mary Poppins, knew this. In her teens she dreamed of becoming an actress, and toured as an actor in a Shakespearean company. But she also loved to write, and began having poems and stories published in magazines. With her earnings she saved to buy a ticket to England, intending to meet some of the great literary names of her day. After her arrival in 1924, she struck up a friendship with George Russell, editor of the *Irish Statesman*, who published some of her work, and also got to know William Butler Yeats and T. S. Eliot. When recovering from an illness, Travers moved to the Sussex countryside, and it was there that she began jotting down her first story of a 'flying nanny'. Echoing J. K. Rowling's remark about her Harry Potter character, Travers would later say that she did not feel she invented Mary Poppins, rather that 'Mary Poppins had invented her'.

Her breakthrough success did not come particularly early – roughly the same age as Rowling's first Harry Potter book (34), yet she had been writing in a public capacity for ten years, her craft now well refined, and had been creating worlds in her imagination for much longer.

Mary Poppins was only the beginning of a series numbering eight books whose writing spanned 54 years. The second Poppins book came out a year after the first, but the third followed nine years later; the rest were spaced at intervals of between eight and 12 years. This pacing meant that Travers never had to rush out work she was not happy with. Partly due to Travers' role in its making, the film *Mary Poppins* was not released until 1964, a full 20 years after Disney had begun talking to her. It was worth the wait. Consistently rated one of the most popular movies of all time, its quality was in part due to Travers' insistence that the project should not be rushed. After all, if the Mary Poppins book had needed years to manifest, why shouldn't a movie also have its appropriate lead time?

What about the wunderkinds?

But if it is true that we need a lot of lead time to do great things, how do we account for the young stars of the computer technology world who, in what seems like a few short years, notch up incredible achievements? Aren't some people, and some industries, just different?

Consider the Google founders, Larry Page and Sergey Brin. Page grew up with a computer science professor father and a programmer mother in a house filled with computers and science magazines. From an early age he wanted to be an inventor, and dreamed of one day starting a technology company. Brin's parents were immigrant mathematicians from Russia, and as a boy he loved nothing more than knotting out mathematical problems. Instead of charting a future as a video game designer, he wondered how computing power could be made truly useful to people. When the two met on a PhD programme at Stanford University, their mutual interest in making meaningful use of huge amounts of data led to the development of their famous search engine. They were only in their early twenties when Google took off, but by this age had already been long apprenticed to the problem of intelligent internet search.

Michael Dell (Dell Computing) and Bill Gates (Microsoft), also both had an early immersion in technology, and Gates was fortunate in that his school in Seattle had unusual access to the early teletype computers. Along with the technology obsession, both also had a strong interest in business strategy. Gates and Dell's early experience in technology and business meant that, by the time they started the companies that would make them famous, they were effectively 'old hands', with at least a decade's worth of experience in their chosen areas.

So even though it may appear that young computer whizzes are a freak of nature, in fact they exemplify what Simon & Chase, Ericsson and Hayes have told us: that the laws of lead time and success are never broken. Look more closely at every apparent wunderkind, and you find that each in fact had a long lead time before they made their early mark, and generally the younger they started on their career journeys, the earlier success happened for them.

Having said this, it is also a myth (as we will discover next) that success in the technology world has to happen when you are barely out of high school.

'I don't know of any time when there are not great possibilities'

On lucky years and missing boats

In contrast to Brin, Page, Dell and Gates, there was nothing particular about Larry Ellison's upbringing that set him up for success.

Given up for adoption by his mother, he was raised by his aunt and uncle in Chicago. He loved his Aunt Lilian, but her husband Louis was curmudgeonly and liked to tell his nephew that he would never amount to much. After graduating from school, Larry enrolled at the University of Illinois, but after Lilian died of cancer during his sophomore year, a heartbroken Larry missed the exams and dropped out. Then, after a summer in California he started again at the University of Chicago, taking physics and mathematics classes; this time, he dropped out after a semester. Uncle Louis was turning out to be right, after all. But in his brief time at Chicago, Larry did learn one valuable skill: computer programming.

Ellison moved to California and began working as a journeyman technician and programmer, choosing San

Francisco because it was where he thought 'all the interesting people were'. Yet through his twenties, he moved from one company to another without making a real impact. At an age when Steve Jobs of Apple, Bill Gates and the Google guys had long since graced the cover of *Time* magazine, Larry was doing weekend and night shifts doing data backup work.

He met his first wife Adda at an employment agency in Berkeley. What little money they had Larry spent on hiking trips to Yosemite and sailing boats, always spending more than he earned. In 1974, the year Larry turned 30, Adda divorced him, fed up with his debts and lack of focus. Trying to persuade her to stay, he agreed to see a psychologist, and apparently came out of the experience a changed man. He promised her he would become a millionaire, but she saw no evidence of it ever happening.

At this time Larry was working as a programmer for a company called Ampex, creating a database for the CIA with the codename 'Oracle'. He was also becoming interested in the idea of relational databases, which promised to make real, practical use of reams of complex data. While one day routinely leafing through the *IBM Journal of Research and Development*, he saw an article by Ted Codd, a computer scientist working for IBM. The company was developing a relational database and had announced a release date, but it was worried the new software would cannibalise its existing database revenue, and the project was given the go-slow. But Larry was seized by the potential of the new type of database, and essentially copied the workings of it from papers picked up at conferences. With his supervisor at Ampex, Bob Miner, and co-worker Ed Oates, the trio raced to get a product out to market before IBM brought out their own.

The first version of the famous Oracle database was soon created, and despite being famously unreliable and hard to work in the early years, was still the best of its kind. In the years to come, it would experience explosive demand, becoming a mainstay of businesses and organisations. A huge advance on IBM's hierarchical data-processing models, Oracle's system provided what everyone wanted: intelligent answers in a split second. True to his word, Larry Ellison not only became a millionaire, but through his shares in the company, one of the wealthiest people on the planet – in the computing world, second only to Bill Gates in size of fortune. (He and a surprised Adda remain good friends.)

Yet when Ellison put in $2,000 to join his friends in starting the company, he was almost 33. Miner was 36 and Oates 31. At the age when Gates, Dell, Brin and Page had long since founded their companies and made billions, Ellison, Miner and Oates were sitting in their offices at Ampex complaining about management. Ellison had long talked big about what he would do, but most people just thought he was just full of s***. And Miner and Oates, though talented programmers, had not shown any particular streak of ambition; none of the projects they had worked on until then had amounted to much.

Everyone knows about the great duos of modern computing, usually involving a visionary and a nuts and bolts implementer (think Steve Jobs and Steve Wozniak of Apple, Bill Gates and Paul Allen), but much less is known about the huge role that Miner played as Ellison's sidekick. While the tall, debonair Ellison was out there talking up the company, short and bald Miner was the one back at the office actually creating and refining the product. Like Ellison, Miner had worked as a programmer for various firms through his twenties, one stint giving him an enjoyable three years in Europe where he met his English wife. But no project he had worked on had been a great success, and when he met Ellison in his mid-thirties was still a middle manager. Yet when Oracle went public in 1986, he netted at least $300 million – pretty good for the son of a hotel clerk who had emigrated from Iran. Miner's early death at 52 is symbolic of his unsung role in creating one of the great modern companies, but his story is worth mentioning because it, along with Ellison's, goes against the conventional wisdom that you have to be 22 to do something great in the technology world.

As do the stories of Jimmy Wales and Craig Newmark.

Wales had spent his twenties teaching at universities and working in finance, and at 30 he founded Bomis, a racy search engine with adult content for men. With the funds from this very commercial enterprise he launched Nupedia, an online peer-reviewed encyclopedia. However, the difficulty in managing new articles led to the introduction of a 'wiki' system, in which users themselves directly input and manage the content. Nupedia, the child of pornographic profit, had given birth to today's most famous non-profit website: Wikipedia. In the year it got under way, Wales turned 35.

At college, Craig Newmark had taken a couple of degrees in computer science. He then worked for 17 years at IBM in Boca Raton, then Washington DC, mostly involved in PC and Unix development. While living in Boca the short, nerdy

Newmark took ballet and jazz classes to meet women, but ended up in hospital with a hernia. But in 1995 Newmark moved to San Francisco to work for Charles Schwab as a consultant on the newly emerging internet. Just like Larry Ellison, the move was less a calculated career step than a desire to live in a happening place. Keen to do something online himself, Newmark could only think of starting a mailing list to friends about upcoming events in San Francisco. But this ultra-simple, local service became popular, and people started wanting to post and exchange information on jobs and apartments on 'Craig's List'. Before long, Craigslist.org was expanding to just about every other city in America.

In the year it really got under way, Newmark turned 43. Even then, he kept working as a software contractor, only going full-time in 1999 when Craigslist began bringing in money from job advertisements. It was still running on Newmark's personal computer before expansion to other cities required the purchase of a server. Although the company now employs 50 people and makes a profit, the site has kept its trademark, ultra-basic layout which looks like it has been put up by an amateur. Newmark, now well into his fifties, is still in charge.

Let's finish with a word on Jack Dorsey, one of the co-inventors and founders of Twitter. Dorsey was 30 when Twitter actually launched, but this is what he had to say about the journey that got him there:

> 'Although it may seem so, simple technologies
> like this don't happen overnight. What looks like
> a story of one to three years actually has a

shadow of over 15 years of work, dumb
mistakes, false starts, late-night frenetic insight,
and patient distillation.'

An overnight success that took 15 years? Again, even in the computer world the laws of time and success hold true.

In his book *Outliers: The Story of Success*, Malcolm Gladwell includes a chapter looking at the relationship between luck and success that focuses on the stars of computing. His idea is that the phenomenal success of people like Bill Gates and Steve Jobs was not just due to their being smart and seizing opportunities, but the result of being born at the right time. Gates and his partner Paul Allen, and Jobs, for instance, were all were born in 1955, as was Eric Schmidt, the former CEO of Google. Bill Joy, a founder of Sun Microsystems, was born in 1954, and the other founders of Sun were all born in 1954 or 1955.

Gladwell does not say that you had to be born in these years to be successful in computing, but that having come into the world in the mid-1950s would make you the perfect age to take advantage of any opportunities around at the time to learn programming. Born any earlier, and if you were talented you probably would have been snapped up by IBM to work on its mainframe computers (and stayed there as an executive with all the comfy perks, not wanting to leave). Born a few years later, and you would have missed being part of the software and personal computer revolution.

Gladwell includes in his chapter a list of the richest people of all time, including Gates and other American software billionaires, to point out a link between certain birth years and the creation of fantastic fortunes. The list includes Larry Ellison, but Gladwell chooses not to discuss him, apparently because he does not fit the thesis, being born 'too early' in 1944, not around the 'lucky year' of 1955.

Circumstances and logic might have suggested you could rule out someone of Ellison's age doing something great in computing, but do 'the times' really shape human action to that extent? Ellison and Miner may have missed the personal computer revolution, but their timing was just right for another one: databases. As Ellison's biographer Mike Wilson notes, many people thought that Ellison had just been in the right place at the right time, that all he had done was find (or copy) a good idea and implement it. Yet there were lots of people who knew about the work that IBM was doing on relational databases (they had, perhaps unwisely, published the results of their work); it was only Ellison who saw the new kind of database as a massive commercial opportunity, something companies would cry out for once perfected. As Ellison said to Wilson: *I don't know of any place or time where there aren't great possibilities.*

Exactly. You miss one revolution, another one happens.

Michael Dell is also worth mentioning in this respect. Because he was born in 1965, Dell was indeed 'too late' to be an important player in the emerging personal computer and software revolution, but no matter; another opportunity came along to do something equally hi-impact: filling a huge market by selling computer hardware for less through mail order.

Ascribing people's fortune to some lucky year of birth

can blind them to what's happening *now*. Ellison and Miner may have grumbled about not having their worth recognised, but they did not panic or conclude they had 'missed a boat'.

Moreover, even big opportunities may not be fully appreciated at the time. Neither Jimmy Wales nor Craig Newmark was sure their enterprises would work. In the early days of Wikipedia, Wales constantly worried about the nature and standard of new entries, but decided to publish anyway. Newmark, as we've noted, kept his day job.

You don't, obviously, have to follow the 'take off like a rocket at 22 and never look back' trajectory that we hear is the norm in the technology world. You don't need to have massive intelligence or Napoleonic ambition. Watch, wait and learn, and success can come in surprising ways. Finally, you don't need to have a neat, linear career. Consider, in a few lines, the Steve Jobs story. Though born in the 'right' year (1955), like Ellison he was adopted out because his mother was unmarried. His parents encouraged his fascination with electronics, and they saved enough for him to go to college. He found classes in calligraphy and philosophy interesting, but dropped out to go travelling in India. On returning, the 21-year-old Jobs started Apple Computer in his parents' garage with friend Steve Wozniak. They launched the Apple 1 and Apple 2 computers, and by 25 Jobs was worth $200 million. At 26 he was on the cover of *Time* magazine.

What an amazing story of youthful success! Yes, Jobs did create Apple very young, but his poor management and people skills later led to him being ejected from his own company, forcing him into a long wilderness period in which he started ('out of revenge', says the Silicon Valley pioneer Don Valentine) other companies including Pixar. Though successful, it was only when he came back to Apple some years later, older and wiser, that Jobs really came into his own. The comeback is one of the great modern business stories, and its moral is this: raw talent goes only so far as character allows. Jobs may have burst onto the scene young, but all his enduring creations (the iPod, iPhone and iPad) came from the older man. Like Mozart's early compositions, Jobs' early work is of interest to scholars, but we only listen to the later symphonies.

Done other things

Life experience and the slow development of character count for something

The film critic Joe Morgenstern was once having breakfast at a restaurant in Santa Monica when he eavesdropped on a conversation between two young screenwriters. One was telling the other about a film he was pitching to the studios. 'It's, like, *Kill Bill* meets *Napoleon Dynamite*.' Other screenwriters he knew of were fond of 'pie chart' pitches (e.g. 'Imagine one-third *Wedding Singer* and two-thirds *Wedding Crashers*.')

This way of selling a new film only in relation to other films, Morgenstern commented, showed the malaise in Hollywood filmmaking: 'Many . . . of today's filmmakers know very little, and care less, about the real world. Their movies derive from other movies. Clever with shorthand, they've never learned longhand.'

Look at the great movies, Morgenstern suggested, and you

will find they are nearly all the product of filmmakers 'who have been out in the world, doing more than making films.' Worldliness, in fact, was once the norm in Hollywood. Billy Wilder (*Double Indemnity*, *Sunset Boulevard*, *The Apartment*) worked as a reporter in his native Austria and then Berlin, then lived in Paris before making his way to Hollywood. In his early twenties, John Huston (*The Maltese Falcon*, *African Queen*) tried his hand at scriptwriting in Hollywood but got nowhere. After killing a female pedestrian in a car he was driving, a shocked Huston went to live in London and Paris for several years, drifting and dabbling in painting, before returning to Hollywood at 31. Preston Sturges (*The Great McGinty*) worked in the family cosmetic business before becoming a successful playwright, and only then started his film career. George Miller (*The Witches of Eastwick*, *Happy Feet*) was a doctor in Australia before making his first feature film, *Mad Max*. John Boorman (*Hope and Glory*) was first a journalist; and Pedro Almodovar worked in a Spanish telephone company. Robert Altman was a bomber pilot in the Second World War, worked in a company developing a dog tattooing system, and then made a long line of educational and industry films before getting into commercial features. Even the great David Lean (*Lawrence of Arabia*, *A Passage to India*) spent over a decade as an editor before getting a chance to direct a feature film.

Great films arise from the combined insights and life experience of the writer, actors, director and producer. A great film says something, not about other movies, but about *life*. And if you haven't lived a bit, what really can you have to say?

When Erika Sunnegardh went for her audition at the Met, its artistic administrator Jonathan Friend was amazed at her voice. But he was also drawn to her beauty and maturity. 'She was, as a human being, grown up,' he said. 'She had had another life, and knew what she didn't know.'

A man once asked James Joyce, who could not get his first book, *Dubliners*, published for many years, if he could kiss the hand that wrote *Ulysses*.

'No', Joyce drily responded, because '. . . this hand has done a lot of other things.'

The passing of time has a way of revealing truth. It lifts up to recognition those who stick to their guns, even when they face lack of recognition or opposition. It also puts in their proper place people who once seemed invincible and ubiquitous, and whose true merits can now be properly judged. It is never enough to be excellent or even extraordinary in terms of talents, technical skills or ability to motivate and command people. For a person to reach his or her potential, there must be a certain amount of self-reflection and willingness to correct character flaws or rackets. Self-reflection may not be compatible with the go-getting nature of fast success, but it *is* compatible with real, slow-cooked success.

Early success

It makes a splash, but do we ever know what is really there until the water settles?

A 'hit' when young can make it seem one is set up for life, but in the creative field nothing is further from the truth.

When he was barely 25, William Styron's *Lie Down in Darkness* won the American Academy's Prix de Rome, making him an overnight literary sensation. Flushed with success, Styron moved to Paris where he enjoyed the company of Romain Gary and James Baldwin, and helped to establish the legendary *Paris Review*. The future was bright.

But it took Styron almost another decade for his next major work, *Set This House on Fire*, to be published, and the reviews were not good. In fact, the critics savaged it. Lesson learned, Styron spent years researching, drafting and perfecting his next work, the fictional memoir *The Confessions of Nat Turner*. Despite, or thanks to, a whirlwind of controversy around it, the book was a commercial hit and won Styron a Pulitzer Prize. After years of 'promise' following the success of his first book, Styron's talent had – at 42 – finally been fulfilled. Another 12 years passed before, in his mid-fifties, he wrote *Sophie's Choice* (1979), which sold millions and became the film starring Meryl Streep.

'Wisely and slow; they stumble that run fast,' Shakespeare said. Early success can be dangerous, setting up an expectation that, if not soon fulfilled, can lead creative types to self-destruction.

Keith Urban grew up on a small Queensland farm, his parents keeping cows and pigs. Urban Snr loved country music, and his eldest son did too. In 1992, the 25-year-old Urban won the Star Maker contest at the Tamworth Festival, Australia's largest for country music. In its wake he released a string of top-selling country records. His success as an Australian musician was assured.

But Urban hungered for recognition in the United States,

and decided to move there in 1992. He worked as a session guitarist, as a busker at Dolly Parton's estate, and started a band (The Ranch) that had only modest success. Things were not turning out as he had hoped, and Urban developed an addiction to cocaine. In 1998, now past 30, came his nadir. While fellow Australian Nicole Kidman had reached the height of fame as an actor and as the wife of Tom Cruise, Urban was battling his demons in a Nashville rehab centre.

Pulling himself together, the following year he released his first solo American album, *Keith Urban*. It went platinum, and Urban was properly launched as a solo country music star. A few years later, he married Kidman; they live with their two daughters in Nashville. What does this story tell us?

When he won the Tamworth competition, in the eyes of most onlookers Urban was surely 'set for life'. Actually, it was only the beginning.

Born in Canada, high school drop-out Peter Jennings was, in his early career, an outsider in the American media world. At only 26, he became the evening news anchorman for the ABC network. Anchor positions usually went to much older men who could project gravitas, but Jennings was suave, good-looking and serious, and seemed a good candidate for what was hopefully a long-term position. ABC was considered a poor cousin to the bigger CBC and NBC networks, and was chasing a younger audience.

This was the theory. In fact, American audiences did not take to his Canadian accent and phraseology, and apparent ignorance of American affairs, and within three years he was out of the job. Hived off to the Middle East, Jennings established a television news bureau in Beirut, and in 1975 came back to the US to become morning news anchor with ABC, and in 1983 – at 45 – finally moved back to the evening news anchor position. He would hold the job for the next 20 years, becoming one of the 'big three' anchors (along with Tom Brokaw and Dan Rather).

Jennings' early 'prize' of the anchor role came at about the same time as Styron's and Urban's early recognition. Like them, he found that being raised to a height when young can be both a blessing and a curse. An early success or award is simply a message that says 'You are good, given how young you are'. But that quality then takes many years to be properly realised – and this is as it should be.

When we try to identify universal laws of success, rock 'n' roll turns out to be no different. For most of the 1980s, REM toured America constantly in small venues. They were popular on the college circuit but were still an underground act. Then in 1987 came the *Document* album with its breakthrough hit 'The One I Love'. The following year, after signing with Warner Bros, REM continued to express their strong political concerns with the album *Automatic for the People*. With hits like 'Losing My Religion', they began playing large arenas around the world.

Peter Buck, the band's founding member, did not get on stage when he was 15 and start wielding a guitar. Instead, he studied the patterns of success and failure in his chosen field. The observations he made helped determine the mode of operation of REM (for instance, no members' faces on albums, no use of their songs in advertising), ensuring that it would live on as long as the members wanted it to.

In the early days, when they were slugging it out doing small gigs across America, the band lived on five dollars a day. On the benefits of slow-cooked success as opposed to very young, quick stardom, lead singer Michael Stipe commented:

> 'I know that I would not be alive today if my
> first record had sold five million. In those days,
> I did everything in the extreme. I was in self-
> destruct mode back then, and that kind of
> big success would have been extremely
> dangerous.'

In the context of *genuine* achievement, what seem like glories when we are young are only hors d'oeuvres before the substantial courses to come. It is no bad thing to earn recognition over time; when it does come, we are better able to handle it, enjoy it and maintain it.

First, do the old things well

We get creative when we master a domain

After interviewing many individuals considered to be highly creative and successful in their fields, creativity researcher Mihaly Csikszentmihalyi's finding was that people rarely become truly creative in their field until they have first assimilated all its rules and passed all its tests – a process which takes at least a decade. Only after we have fully 'mastered a domain' can we begin to create new rules or genuinely new ways of doing things.

We like to believe in techniques such as 'brainstorming', but *genuine* creative breakthroughs, Csikszentmihalyi says, are almost always the result of years of hard work and close attention. Many creative discoveries, particularly of the scientific type, are lucky, but usually the 'luck' comes after years of detailed work in the area in which the discovery is made. He tells of the astronomer Vera Rubin, who discovered that stars in some galaxies do not all rotate in the same direction – some go clockwise, and others anti-clockwise. She would not have made the discovery if she had not had access to a new type of clearer spectral analysis, and this access came from her already being known for her substantial contributions to the field over many years of work.

Rubin was not out to 'make a big discovery'. Rather, it was the result of close observation of stars and a love of her work. Her goal was recording data, but it was her *dedication* that yielded the surprise findings. Truly creative people work for its own sake (every day they get into what Csikszentmihalyi calls a state of 'flow' in which time seems to stand still while they are absorbed in their work) and if they make a public discovery or become famous, that is a bonus. What drives them is the desire to find or create order where there was none before.

Robin Warren's story is similar. In 2005, Warren was one of the pair of Australian doctors who won a Nobel Prize for proving that peptic stomach ulcers were not caused by stress or acid or spicy foods, but by bacteria. In 1979, when he was in his early forties, Warren was working at Royal Perth

Hospital's pathology department analysing suspect gastric biopsies. Looking into his microscope one day at the cells from a stomach lining that was severely inflamed (a condition which usually precedes ulcer growth), he was surprised to see millions of bacteria growing. 'It was not supposed to be there,' he recalls. He obsessively developed staining techniques to reveal that patients with gastritis all had the corkscrew-shaped helicobacter bacteria in their gut. The implication was clear: ulcers developed in response to the helicobacter germ, so the way to treat ulcers was not through the conventionally accepted means of antacids, but through killing the bacteria (through a combination of antibiotics and the chemical element bismuth). It would take years for the medical establishment and the drug companies to accept these findings, because they had a lot to lose in giving up existing treatments (they eventually did).

As with Rubin and her access to new types of spectral analysis, Warren could not have made his discovery without the more advanced kind of gastric biopsies, which had only become possible late in his career thanks to flexible endoscopes which could be pushed down a patient's throat into their stomach to take tissue samples. He combined the biopsies with an unrelated obsession with improving staining techniques on microscope slides, which finally revealed the heliobacter germ to be the 'missing link' in gastritis and ulcer formation.

Today, Warren wonders: 'Did I find the bacteria because of brilliant research work? Was it just luck? It's sort of the fact that I was the right person in the right place at the right time, with the right interests.' Despite his modesty, the fact is that his discovery, like Rubin's, was the result of close observation over many years. Would a young scientist have been as willing to take all the steps he had, over a long period, to find out what he did? Perhaps, but what experience gives one is an eye for anomalies, for things which 'are not meant to be there'. You might also say that Warren's findings were not 'creative' in the conventional sense, yet surely work which obsessively takes up all our attention, concentration and ingenuity – as was clearly the case with Warren and his staining techniques – *is* creative.

Warren had achieved 'mastery of a domain'. All people who create genuine change need to have first mastered their field, soaking up its rules and learning the necessary skills. It is only then that they can truly make a creative mark, bending or breaking these rules to create something new. Only with a huge mental database of information on their subject can a person move more adroitly into new intellectual territories or draw novel connections. In short, *to do new things, you first have to have done the old things well*. And this can't be done in a few weeks or months.

Of course, you cannot discount the role of chance in significant discoveries or creativity, but 'chance' is a relative term. Marie and Pierre Curie's discovery of radium (one of the most useful elements ever) would not have happened if they had not already had deep knowledge of the other elements and their properties. They discovered radium only because they noticed that the mineral they were examining was more radioactive than it should have been, based on the known elements that composed it. This is the sort of 'chance' discovery that only happens to those who know their stuff to begin with. As Louis Pasteur noted: '. . . chance favours only the prepared mind'.

Final thoughts

'Overnight success' is usually just the rest of the world's perception catching on to something that has, in fact, had long germination and suddenly bursts forth. While gestation time for anything good is nearly always long, the actual *expression* of a successful idea can happen relatively quickly, usually when a sudden new clarity of purpose is found. Success either takes a while to happen or, if it does come young, we find that the person concerned has been at it since a very young age. In both cases, time may be condensed through experience, but never shortcutted. You can expose yourself to a greater range of experiences, or practice your craft or skill more intensively, but you cannot get around lead time and character development as a fact of life.

For every celebrated case of a prodigy, wunderkind or star that bursts into the limelight comparatively young, there are at least 40 or 50 more who did it the longer, slower way. And for every company or movement that experiences early dramatic growth, many more will have been around for a long time before they came to prominence.

While it can be hard to accept the law of lead time – or the period between having an idea of something, and its actual fulfilment – awareness of it allows us to focus on our goals instead of bemoaning how long it takes to reach them. From first being perceived as an obstacle, we can begin to see lead time in its true light: as the *friend* of success. And the good news is that, across a longish lifespan, most of us are given not just a second chance, but possibly a third or even a fourth to succeed at what we really want to do.

Success may only look or feel like success with hindsight. At the time, there is rarely much glamour. The mistake most people make is to see a fully formed success and compare themselves to it. Instead, we should be comparing ourselves to how that person was *before* they were successful. What were they doing in the early years? Chances are, they were doing very humdrum things, fighting everyday battles the same as everyone else, until they got some kind of break. When you find yourself saying, 'At my age, I should be . . .', or 'Why aren't I like . . .?', focus on your own domain of experience and do what you possibly can within it now. A rule of life is that we never seem to progress until we have first fully lived out the possibilities in the situation we are in *now*.

It's natural to seek shortcuts and dream of overnight success, but these are like basing a strategy for wealth creation on buying lottery tickets. Understandable, but there's a better way. At the outset, it may seem that by admitting the fact of lead time we are surrendering some of our power. In fact, only by doing so do we put ourselves on the path of real achievement.

Extras

More examples, thoughts, quotes and aphorisms on lead time, work and success

William Holden had his Hollywood breakthrough with *Golden Boy* at only 21. Then the Second World War intervened. He served in the US Air Force, acting in training films, but on returning home his career stalled. It was only with Billy Wilder's casting of him as a struggling screenwriter in *Sunset Boulevard*, at 31, that his real (second stage) career began.

Harrison Ford was put on the payroll of Columbia Pictures in his early twenties, and despite a variety of supporting film and television roles, for many years his main income came from work as a carpenter. A role in *American Graffiti* increased his profile, but his career only took off at 35 with *Star Wars* (1977), after more than a decade in Hollywood.

Paul Gaugin, the French Impressionist, worked as a stockbroker for 12 years, collecting paintings in his spare time, before in his mid-thirties finally deciding to devote himself full-time to art. After a flash of early success, fellow Frenchman and painter **Theodore Rousseau** endured a 12-year wilderness period before coming into artistic fashion. As the painter and soldier **Xavier De Maistre** said: 'To know *how to wait* is the great secret of success.'

Piet Mondrian, born in 1872, did not produce his iconic coloured grid works until 1919, when he was in his late forties. **Francis Bacon** was an interior designer first, before friends convinced him to get serious about painting. **Mark Rothko**, born in 1903, had his first one-man show in 1935, but he remained a financial failure throughout his thirties. Things began to look up when, at 42, he had a show at the Guggenheim, but the reviews were bad and he didn't sell many works. This prompted him to break away from surrealist imagery and move towards total abstraction (large works involving intense, glowing blocks of colour with blurred edges), and only then did things begin to happen. His 1949 Betty Parsons show was well received, and his direction as one of the twentieth-century greats was set. **Hans Hoffman**, **Jackson Pollock** and **Roy Lichtenstein** all arrived at their signature style relatively late into their careers, after decades of experimentation with other styles. **Claude Monet** worked as a painter for decades, but did not start his famous water lily paintings until he was an old man. **Vasily Kandinsky** first studied to become a lawyer in Moscow, then went to Munich to study art. Thirty before he began painting, he was 44 before he did the watercolour that was said to be the first work of abstract art.

Ann Mary Robertson Moses had ten children, five of whom died in childbirth. She had spent decades doing embroidery, but due to arthritis in her seventies she took up painting; she had two prices for her works: $3 for small, $5 for large. When a New York art collector saw her work in a shop window, he bought everything and included her in an exhibition of 'American unknowns'. She soon became one of the country's most celebrated artists. 'Grandma Moses' as she was known, kept painting up to her death at 101.

Gordon Moore, famous for 'Moore's law' concerning the doubling of transistors on an integrated circuit every two years, was not 21, 25 or even 30 when he co-founded the computer chip giant Intel, but 37. **Andy Grove** was one of the first employees at Intel, but did not come into his own there until he was made CEO in his fifties.

Microsoft's **Windows** computer software revolutionised personal computing, but 80 work years went into its building and testing, involving hundreds of programmers (and screaming fits by Bill Gates). The first version of Windows didn't do well, and it took until Windows 3.0 in 1990 to really deliver on its initial promise. All up, the successful Windows was seven years in the making.

As the hotelier **J. W. Marriott** put it, 'success can be boring'. Slow-cooked success recognises the 99 per cent of time that you have to be at your desk, in your studio, on the factory floor, dealing with your staff – the 'drudge work' that you must do to achieve something marvellous.

Earl Nightingale said: 'Don't let the fear of the time it will take to accomplish something stand in the way of your doing it. The time will pass anyway; we might just as well put that passing time to the best possible use.' The seed of the creativity flower may lie in each of us, but it grows best in the mud of work.

David Ogilvy, regarded as one of the great advertising minds of the 20th century, was '. . . expelled from Oxford, slaved in a hotel kitchen in Paris, sold stoves in Scotland, and farmed in Pennsylvania, among many other apparently random occupations that consumed the first 17 years of his career. Predicting that he would make his mark as an advertising legend would have been difficult, considering that he presented precious little evidence that he would make any mark at all.'

William Styron, as we noted, had to wait at least fifteen years after his early prize before similar success revisited him. But he had the character to put his head down and work when things did not go as expected. He once remarked: 'I am solaced by the belief that if my work has any quality at all, it has this quality because of its long germination time. Had I written with a composition to get books out, they would not be very good.'

Stephen King once said: 'Talent is cheaper than table salt. What separates the talented individual from the successful one is a lot of hard work.' **David Foster Wallace** wrote in *The Pale King*: 'True heroism is minutes, hours, weeks, year upon year of the quiet, precise, judicious exercise of probity and care – with no one there to see or cheer. This is the world.'

A woman once came up to a particularly virtuoso musician after a performance, and breathlessly announced, 'I would give half my life to play as you have done tonight.' The musician replied, 'Madam, that is exactly what I have given.'

'Those who look into practical life,' **Orison Swett Marden** noted, 'will find that fortune is usually on the side of the industrious, as the winds and waves are on the side of the best navigators.'

Isaac Newton, everyone knows, was a 'genius'. Yet when Newton was asked how he came to solve some of the great problems that had perplexed others, he simply said: 'I thought about them a lot.'

The modernising preacher **Harry Emerson Fosdick** wrote: 'No steam or gas drives anything until it is confined. No life ever grows great until it is focused, dedicated, disciplined.'

Naturalist **Rachel Carson** worked for many years at the US Bureau of Fisheries in charge of publications, while on the side writing articles for magazines. Her first book, *Under the Sea Wind*, was several years in the making, got good reviews, but sold poorly. Seven years later, as she entered her forties, she decided to leave her safe employment and write full-time. Her next work, *The Sea Around Us*, sold well. But it would be another decade before the release of *Silent Spring* (1961), the book on the dangers of the pesticide DDT to the ecosystem that made her famous when she was in her mid-fifties. Less well known is that for most of her working life, Carson (after the death of her father in her twenties) was the breadwinner for her mother, sister, nieces, and a niece's orphaned son.

In his novel *Freedom*, **Jonathan Franzen** questioned the assumption that freedom is always a great thing. We celebrate democracy and open societies, but when it comes to our own lives, the truth is that many of us don't know what to *do* with all the possibilities before us. To have a meaningful life, we have to restrict some of our freedom. Big commitments in work and love may give us less 'time to ourselves', yet their effect is to make us into a person who really stands for something.

CHAPTER FIVE:

THE 40 FACTOR

*Why many people never do anything remarkable
until their fifth decade*

In researching the specific ages at which people begin to
achieve, I noticed a real spike around the age of 40. Was
there was some special significance to this point in life? And
was there some weight attached to the number 40 itself, a
symbol that could be a powerful catalyst for action?

In her book *Passages: Predictable Crises of Adult Life*, Gail
Sheehy described our thirties as the 'deadline decade', in
which we suddenly realise we will not live forever. Having
lived through the 'anything is possible' twenties, we begin
to wonder whether we do, in fact, have all the answers. Not
only are we forced to identify priorities and narrow focus,
but demand authenticity of ourselves. Until well into their
thirties a person can exist on the 'spin' of what they present
to the world, but close to 40, the truth inevitably emerges.
In the process, they become a powerful person. Shedding
personal illusions about life may be painful, but it can also
unleash tremendous energies.

The Swiss psychologist Carl Jung noticed that in nature,
religion, myth, history and culture we find quaternal (or '4')

symbols everywhere, such as the four seasons, the four elements, the four bodily humours, the four Evangelists, the four letters in the sacred name of God (YHVH), not to mention the number 40 itself (for example, the Biblical days in the wilderness, symbolising a time of preparation). In a psychological sense, for Jung the 'quaternity' meant the fourth (decade) bringing three-dimensionality, or depth, to a person, in place of the two-dimensional. As the bridge between youth and middle age, the years around 40 took on a special importance. By this point, our 'sides' and complexes are seen for what they are and incorporated into a single, stronger personality. Jung called this process 'individuation'. If youth was associated with extraversion and libido, the onset of middle age was marked by greater self-examination, and the bridling of the sex drive.

With Jung's idea of the quaternity, turning 40 is best seen as a completion, paving the way for new life, interests, priorities and achievements. The successes that come now are likely to be richly deserved, not just in terms of making use of what we know or can do, but in the stronger, unified self that emerges. Awareness that we will not live forever naturally leads us to focus our energies on things that matter, on where we can make a difference – whether with our children, a cause, a business or an organisation.

Many of the people discussed or mentioned in the following pages experienced such an 'explosion of purpose'. To begin, we look at three people who came to be known as great forces for good. The others come from a variety of fields, places and times, but a similar pattern can be observed in their stories.

The point of this chapter is not to suggest that we all must succeed by 40, or that it is some 'magic year' when everything falls into place. However, it can be a marker with real symbolic power that can cause you to act. If you will not be 40 for many years yet, and still haven't figured out what you want to do with your life, you will discover that many others did not find their calling until at least this age. If you are past 40, you may recall it as an important turning point which led you to where you are now. But even if you did not, read on, as the examples also highlight the general truth of slow-cooked success.

The first people we look at are admittedly capital-G 'Great' figures from history, but if even they had not alighted on their true mission in life until they were in their forties, why should you be fretting now?

Agnes, Mohandas and Eleanor

Agnes Gonxha Bojaxhiu was born in what is now Macedonia in 1910, her father a building contractor. When he died, Agnes's resourceful mother started a business selling cloth and making embroidery. She brought up Agnes not in the Orthodox Church, but as a Catholic.

In her teens, Agnes was a pious girl and felt a call to become a missionary. She joined the Loreto Sisters in Ireland as a novice, knowing they had missions in India. Having taken the name Teresa, after St Therese of Lisieux, in 1929 she was transferred to Calcutta, where she began teaching geography in St Mary's, a school run by the Loreto order.

In September 1946, Agnes was on a train to Darjeeling, where she had been sent by the order to recover from a suspected case of tuberculosis. On this journey she had her famous 'call within a call', a virtual divine instruction, as she described it, to go and work with the 'poorest of the poor' in Calcutta.

Her superiors in the order did not instantly take to Teresa's idea of leaving the convent and working with the destitute, and in fact made her continue teaching for some time. However, in 1948 she was permitted to leave, and in the same year received medical training in Paris and became an Indian citizen. She admitted in a diary that the first year away from the convent was hard, and she felt tempted to return to the security of her former life. Without a home herself, and having to beg for food and supplies to continue her work, it took all her courage to stay true to her new calling.

Yet her work soon came to be recognised, and in 1950 – her fortieth year – the Vatican granted Teresa permission to start her Missionaries of Charity order. Within the next decade it established 25 orphanages and homes for the sick and dying across India, and through the 1970s and 1980s overseas expansion included hospices, homes for drug addicts, alcoholics, prostitutes, people with AIDS, abandoned children and leprosy sufferers. The order's 500 missions saw Mother Teresa become one of the 20th century's great spiritual entrepreneurs, bringing comfort and care to millions. Yet like her namesake, Therese of Lisieux, who was 40 by the time she founded her first convent,

Mother Teresa was a relatively late starter. Her call to work with the poorest of the poor only came when she was 36, and by the time the Missionaries of Charity was officially launched she had spent no less than *19 years* as a teacher and head teacher.

A spiritual calling may be something that comes from the eternal realm, yet it still has to be carried through in time and space. Perhaps God is a realist: the command Teresa heard on that train journey came at 36, not 26 or 56. A twenty-something Teresa would not have had the courage to implement it, perhaps scurrying back to the convent after a few days on the Calcutta streets. A fifty-something Teresa may have felt herself too old to begin a religious enterprise that would draw on all her physical and mental energies. But at 36, Teresa had developed the mental and spiritual strength to achieve what she believed was her destiny, and had plenty of energy and years ahead of her to carry it out. Maybe it was coincidence that her order officially began in the year she turned 40, but it neatly recalls Jesus's 40 days in the wilderness before he began his adult mission, or Moses' 40 *years* of time in the desert. Like Moses, by this time she was truly ready to serve, to be a 'pencil for God' as she described herself.

Where and how did Mohandas Gandhi develop his famous moral conviction and strength, enough to undermine the rulers of whole nations?

The image most people have of Gandhi is of a white-robed man in his sixties, travelling around India preaching peace and independence from British rule. In fact, Gandhi did not actually return to live in India until 1915, when he was in his mid-forties. Then, he was not the monk-like figure called 'Mahatma' (great soul), but a lawyer in a suit with a family. While biographical dictionaries devote most of their entries to Gandhi's political work in India, he had actually spent 21 years of his adult life working for the rights of Indians in South Africa.

One of the key events in Gandhi's late thirties was the British administration's attempt to force all Indians in South Africa's state of Transvaal to be registered under the terms of The Black Act. Gandhi and others refused. This was his first use of *satyagraha*, or non-violent non-cooperation principle in action. As a result of the protest, he was sentenced, at 39, to two months in prison. It was a defining experience, and in the following year, the 40-year-old travelled to London to highlight the plight of South African Indians. Thanks to his campaigning, the Transvaal registration law was repealed, a success which gave him the taste for more non-violent protests that would later be so crucial to his leadership role in India.

Eleanor Roosevelt's well-off background and connection to power (her uncle was Teddy Roosevelt) did not save her from having a largely miserable childhood. Her mother was a society beauty who was cold towards her plain daughter, and her much-loved father was a drinker who died when she was only nine. Both her mother and her four-year-old brother also died when she was a girl.

Just before she turned 21, Eleanor married her distant cousin Franklin Delano Roosevelt, and for the next 12 years she relished the role of devoted wife and mother, raising five children and giving moral support to her husband in his role as an emerging political leader.

However, in her mid-thirties this contented domesticity was shattered when she discovered that FDR had been having an affair with her social secretary. Pressured by her family, particularly her domineering mother-in-law, she decided to stay in the marriage. Wanting a life of her own, she began working as a hospital volunteer, helping war veterans, and began her lifelong involvement in women's issues, joining the League of Women Voters and the Women's Trade Union League, and helping out at the International Congress of Working Women. By her early forties, Eleanor had discovered her leadership passion – social reform – and began to create her own circle of like-minded friends. Among other things, she helped establish a furniture factory and co-founded and taught at a school for girls in New York.

Her grass roots campaigning to encourage women to vote became an important factor in FDR's election to the governorship of New York, and would also prove invaluable in his becoming president in 1932. Eleanor became a significant force in her husband's administration, during the Depression becoming his 'eyes and ears' to report back on the grinding poverty and joblessness that overwhelmed America. In bonding with housewives, struggling farmers and soldiers, and befriending Black and Jewish Americans, she was considered by some to be a traitor to her class, but to ordinary people she was a breath of fresh air. She supported the emerging civil rights movement, and after FDR's death in 1945 became instrumental in developing the UN's Universal Declaration of Human Rights. Her campaigning and writing attracted the tag 'First Lady of the World'.

Eleanor's story exemplifies the pattern of 'crisis and completion' that psychologist Erik Erikson identified as the experience of many people between the ages of 35 and 45. Specifically, she endured a painful crisis that cleared the ground for greater clarity of purpose, allowing her to move from one important phase of life to another. Yet this harrowing period was a blessing in disguise that compelled her to become independent and make the most of her considerable talents. By the time she turned 40, most of her children were in their teens and she could begin to think about what she would do for the rest of her years. By this point, Eleanor was able to express her true self, free of others' expectations. Biographers have noted that her life could be divided into two phases, almost two people: the protected upper-class wife and mother, a persona which had been fully expressed and spent by the end of her thirties, and the political force that she became until her death in 1962, aged 78.

The ability to have a dramatic impact on the world only comes after a person has, paradoxically, been through intense personal changes. In Roosevelt's case, a private metamorphosis unleashed personal moral convictions that made her efforts at social change seem credible to others.

If you had made studies of Mother Teresa, Gandhi and Roosevelt in their mid-thirties, it is doubtful you could have predicted the impact they would have. By the time each had reached 40, they had certainly achieved significant things (Teresa's teaching career, Gandhi's work in South Africa, Eleanor's children), but in fact they were only getting going. Though Gandhi was clearly a rising star in the social reform stakes, Mother Teresa was relatively obscure prior to her 40th birthday, and Eleanor was only just emerging in her own right. When they entered their fifth decades neither of their life paths had been set, yet with deep self-knowledge and the discovery of a mission, at 40 they were free to become vehicles for the greater good.

You may be nearing 'the big four-0' yourself and are frustrated by the pace of your achievements, or have yet to find your calling. Though it is normal to fret about the pace of one's progress, a key to long-term success is (perhaps paradoxically) to focus fully on the present. You never know when a chance encounter or sudden realisation may come along that may change everything. Your own explosion of purpose may not be far away. As the following examples illustrate, be aware, be open to opportunity, and bide your time until the right moment appears.

Second life metamorphoses

The explosion of purpose and resulting success that happens to many around 40 is frequently the product of years of close attention to a problem (artistic, social or scientific), and many thousands of hours' work trying to solve that problem. Sometimes, however, a person is hardly even aware they have been mulling over something until an answer appears.

At school in Queens, New York, Jean Slutsky's group of friends had one thing in common: they were overweight. United by their size, they envied girls who never seemed to put on weight however much they ate. Thin girls almost seemed like they were from another caste, they were so different, and Jean and her friends hardly even talked to them. By the time she was in her late teens, her worldview had solidified: there were only really two types of people in the world – the fat and the thin.

At 24 she married Marty Nidetch, an overweight bus driver whom she had met in a diner. Jean had two sons, and despite constant effort, the pounds seemed to pile on as the years advanced, not helped by a self-confessed addiction to cookies. When one day she was shopping at the supermarket and a neighbour greeted her with 'Hey Jean! You look great . . . when are you due?' (she wasn't pregnant), she knew something had to be done. At 39, she weighed over 15 stone.

At that time the only diet class she knew of was an obesity clinic run by the New York City health department. She attended it religiously every Wednesday, and the programme helped her lose weight rapidly, but it occurred to her that the real power of the programme was in the regularity of the meetings and the camaraderie with others fighting the same battle. Her friends, noticing her new figure, wanted to join her, but they were not keen on travelling into Manhattan every week. She offered to have them over to her apartment every Thursday, where she would relate what she had learned in the clinic the day before. These get-togethers were popular, and when it reached a point where there were not enough chairs in the living room, she began renting a loft above a cinema and holding weight-loss meetings three times a day, after breakfast, lunch and dinner, for the price of a movie ticket.

As her enterprise grew, Jean Nidetch began holding additional meetings outside of New York City. With a businessman friend she hatched the idea of franchising out the idea so that people could run their own meetings without her. In 1963, now 40, Jean quit her job as a clerk at the local tax office and incorporated her little business as Weight Watchers International.

Ten years later, there were thousands of groups across America, Canada and Europe, and Nidetch was a wealthy woman. With her shock of blonde hair and expensive clothes, the glamorous new Jean could not have been more different to the pudgy office worker of before.

It might be argued that Weight Watchers happened by accident (Nidetch did not at the time realise how big her organisation would become, and did not have any long-term goals), and was borne more of desperation than design. Yet when a successful path opened up unexpectedly, she did not hesitate to follow it. Not everyone would have thrown caution to the wind, quitting their job and taking out a lease for loft space, but she did and reaped the benefits.

Most of her life she had wondered why it was so difficult to lose weight, but the clinic she had gone to offered real answers: diets alone did not work because there was no one to be accountable to for your weight-loss efforts. A sensible diet was important, but even more so was getting weighed each week in front of an instructor who had once been overweight themselves. The other missing link in dieting she drew from her own life experience – the fact that, at school and as adults, the fat people always seemed to hang out together. She turned this into a powerful positive, making group camaraderie an important element in Weight Watchers' success.

Nidetch had to wait until she was 39 to discover these answers, and until then there was nothing unusual – in fact, nothing remarkable at all – about her life. She became remarkable when she saw that a personal breakthrough could be replicated on a universal scale, and by 40 she was ready to devote her life to the cause. Her husband, used to plump Jean, never came to grips with his wife looking more like Marilyn Monroe, jetting around the world as the evangelist of a growing empire, and they divorced amicably.

Nidetch still serves as a consultant to the organisation she gave birth to. Living comfortably in Florida, she looks back on a life almost divided in two: the fat office clerk before 40, and after 40, the thin, rich, famous figurehead of a worldwide movement.

Another perfect example of a 'second life' metamorphosis is Bill Wilson.

Wilson was a precocious child and always wanted to be 'number one' in anything he put his mind to, but his family life was less than happy. Because of his father's drinking, his parents divorced. It was a big shock for Bill, and he didn't see his dad for another nine years.

With his mother away at college, Bill's grandparents became his substitute parents, and he flourished in school as president of the senior class and fullback on the football team.

But then came another shock: the girl he was in love with died suddenly after an operation and he was depressed for the next three years. He made it through college, and then entered military training. In the town where he was stationed, wealthy families were having parties for young officers. Bill had never been in 'society' before and felt very insecure and out of his depth. To be different to his father he had always been teetotal, but a cocktail was put in front of him. 'So I took it, and another one, and then, lo, the miracle!' he remembered. From this point on, he could rely on drinking to stop his feelings of inferiority, and if he had the opportunity when in war service he would drink heavily, hiding it from his wife Lois.

After the war he became one of the first 'securities analysts', visiting companies on the road and writing reports. He was very successful at this, and subsequently in his work as a margin trader, and the couple enjoyed the affluence of the Roaring Twenties. But Wilson started to drink more and more, every night after work, despite numerous pledges to Lois. Then, in the 1929 crash they lost everything.

In his mid-thirties, after being fired from another Wall St job after a bar-room incident, Wilson was $60,000 in debt. But he was taken on again because of his unusual stock acumen, even though most people knew he was an alcoholic. At this time, alcoholism was not seen as a disease, but as a sin or a minor crime, but he began receiving treatment from a Dr Silkworth who believed that it was an illness that could not be cured by willpower alone.

Wilson kept up a pattern of sobriety for a few months, then had drinking bouts followed by suicidal depression. He had one last great drinking bout after a visit to a golf club on Armistice Day, 1934, and for months afterwards stayed home drinking gin and pineapple juice.

Then, an old drinking friend, who had actually become an alcoholic too, visited. He first surprised Bill by refusing a drink, then flabbergasted him by stating that he had 'found religion'. The friend had become a part of the Oxford Group, a non-denominational evangelical and very open Christian movement that encouraged absolute honesty with one's self, and restitution to those one has hurt. Most importantly, his new faith had cancelled out the desire to drink. It was as if God had taken over the problem, and he was free, productive and happy.

Despite being a non-believer, opposed to organised religion, Wilson couldn't get his friend's visit out of his head. He went along to a mission that his friend was connected with, which helped the homeless, drunk and destitute. He continued drinking for a few days, then admitted himself again to a hospital for alcoholics. As he grew sober, there seemed nothing ahead now other than death or insanity. It was then that Wilson had his famous spiritual experience.

At this lowest of lows, Wilson totally surrendered to anything that might rescue him, crying out, 'If there be a God, let Him show Himself!'

He recalled the next moment: 'Suddenly, my room blazed with an indescribably white light. I was seized with an ecstasy beyond description. Every joy I had known was pale by comparison.'

He saw himself on a mountain in which spirit was blowing through him, then had the clearest thought: 'You are a free man.'

Wilson had just turned 39, and never had a drink again. Ever the reasoner, he read William James' classic *The Varieties of Religious Experience*, which seemed to validate what had happened to him. With this, and reassurance from Dr Silkworth that he had not been hallucinating, a new life lay ahead.

Though he felt massively blessed by what had happened, Wilson wondered why thousands of other drunks had to miss out on it and die terrible deaths. The thought began to grow on him to start a movement for recovering alcoholics. But even his Oxford Group friends thought that alcoholics were a lost cause. It would take Wilson's characteristic drive and determination, mixed with missionary zeal, to prove them wrong, ironically turning that movement's spiritual principles, which were drawn from all the world's religions, into the famous 12 Steps, one of which involved giving one's problem with alcohol to a 'higher power'. In this, Wilson was echoing Carl Jung's view that only a major spiritual experience could save most hardened alcoholics.

Such was the beginnings of Wilson's Alcoholics Anonymous, officially begun when he was 43 with his writing of its Handbook. His experience must make anyone wonder, who has been plagued by some negative experience for half their life, how it might be turned into a positive. The experience of Nidetch and Wilson show, that even the worst things can be used as the raw material for our greatness. For both did not simply survive their struggle, but went on to benefit millions who were in the same predicament. Moreover, there was nothing in the first 40 years of their lives that would have predicted their later influence.

Since we are on the subject of movements, let's look at one more.

Chance reading that changes a life

In May 1961, a 39-year-old British lawyer in a suit and bowler hat was on his way to work on the London Underground.

Opening his newspaper, he read a very small piece about two students who had been jailed for seven years by the Portuguese government for raising their glasses in a toast to freedom. *Seven years for raising a toast*. Peter Benenson was shocked, and not least because the story had been relegated to the back pages. Why wasn't there more fuss being made of this?

Benenson's first instinct was to go to the Portuguese Embassy and make a protest, but instead, on alighting at Trafalgar Square, he went into the church of St Martin's-in-the-Field and had a quiet think. There, a plan of action took shape.

Within a few weeks he managed to get *The Observer* (a Sunday newspaper) to publish an appeal, 'The Forgotten Prisoners', which urged public action for political prisoners. It caught the public's imagination, and later that year he formed an organisation to co-ordinate letter-writing campaigns to political prisoners. Within a year, letter-writing groups had formed in over a dozen countries. From a chance reading of an article, Amnesty International was born.

As Amnesty itself said in an obituary for its founder: 'He was born into a world without the United Nations. Not a single international human rights treaty was in existence. The Universal Declaration of Human Rights was yet to be written.' Indeed, few of the big human rights organisations we have today had come into existence, so Benenson was really going out on a limb. But all his legal education and experience to that point, he realised, had simply set him up for this vital task. As with the others in this chapter, the first 40 years were just a platform on which the real life's work could begin.

Keeping your oar in the water

For every person whose name becomes a brand there are thousands of others who make equally remarkable, if lesser known, contributions, and many do not come into their own until at least 40.

Unless you work in her particular field of mathematics, for instance, you are unlikely to have heard of Joan S. Birman, a leading expert in topology and 'braid and knot theory', who has made a number of important solutions and discoveries.

Born to immigrant parents who had settled in New York, in pre-school Birman was fascinated with patterns and 'the way things fit together'. Throughout her school years, mathematics was her favourite subject. At college she majored in maths and physics, but when the time came to graduate, the idea of becoming a full-blown mathematician, with its deep commitment of time and energy, seemed less appealing. Instead she sought work that would still allow her to also have a family, and the result turned out to be a 'fifteen-year detour' working in systems analysis in the aircraft industry, which then had few, if any, women working in professional roles.

When she had her first child, even though she would have liked to continue working there was no day care available then, so for a time she did not work at all. For the next few years she juggled part-time work with raising her children. However, not long after her third child was born, she enrolled in graduate school at New York University and began taking evening classes towards a Master's degree in Pure Mathematics. Financially this was possible because her very supportive husband, who had moved from industry to academia, was on the faculty and she was able to get free tuition. It was 1961, and Birman was now 33.

With the demands of family life, it was years by the time she received her PhD (at 41), and getting there was not easy. One teacher she approached to guide her doctoral work told her bluntly, 'You're too old and you don't know enough topology.' The mathematician who did take her on noted that he was fond of 'picking up strays', which is exactly what Birman, an older woman in what was then considered a young man's game, felt like.

Having not worked as a mathematician for a decade, at 41 Birman was hired by the Stevens Institute of Technology, then its first female maths faculty member, but had to take a year of absence when her husband took a sabbatical in Paris. Though the year should have been fun, Birman felt intellectually isolated. She amused herself by doing a calculation which, several years later, other mathematicians proved correct.

On her return to America, she began giving lectures on work she had done with a colleague on the role of braids in knot theory. This was not a fashionable area, but some mathematicians at Princeton University took an interest. 'This was when my career really began to get going,' Birman recalls. The lectures would lead to her book *Braids, Links and Mapping Class Groups*, published in her late forties, and she became a visiting staff member at Princeton concurrently with her job at Stevens Institute. There also she was the only female maths staff member.

While the trajectory of Birman's life is not uncommon for a female academic, it does not make it any less remarkable. At college, courage was required to major in mathematics in the first place, then almost exclusively the domain of the male student. Then, when she had children, she wondered if she would ever have a career again, but was willing to take the risk, and happily put up with being the only woman in the companies where she worked. Courage was required again when, in her thirties, she went back to graduate school to take her PhD, where a thick skin enabled her to quietly prove her abilities again and re-enter the competitive world of academic mathematics.

On her return to graduate school, she commented:

'I was rusty, but that did not seem
insurmountable because, as a compensation,
maturity had given me an ability to focus and to
concentrate in a way which had seemed
impossible fifteen years earlier.'

Anyone who has looked after young children knows that
when you do get an hour or two to do something on your
own, you make the most of it. Strict time limits breed efficiency.
In career terms, Birman's colleagues may have viewed her time
raising a family and working in industry as lost years when
her brain was at its sharpest. But as she notes, the greater
maturity, focus and judgment that developed in the meantime
arguably made her better at her work when she finally had
the time to devote to it. In addition, thanks to family life and
having worked as part of teams in industry, she had developed
advanced skills in collaboration and co-operation. As opposed
to the myth of a brilliant lone mathematician, much of her
career success, she is keen to note, has come through working
closely with others. With invitations to conferences and seminars, after 40 Birman's life opened up. Though having children
had set her career back a few years, when opportunities came
to re-enter the stream of academic life she plunged right in
and, she suggests, as a better mathematician than the one she
might have been if her career trajectory had been smoother.

Of her love of mathematics, Birman comments:

'I learn things about how people think, and I
find it very moving and interesting. Mathematics
puts me in touch with people on a deep level.

> It's the creativity that other people express that touches me so much. I find that, and the mathematics, very beautiful. There is something very lasting about it also.'

The willingness to bide one's time is an attribute many mothers have had to acquire. Yet for Birman, the timeless nature of mathematical equations perhaps helped her put her own years of obscurity into perspective.

The Harvard-educated babysitter

Tony Mendoza had read somewhere that by the age of 40, most people have either succeeded or failed in life. If not successful by then, the overwhelming odds were that they never would be.

At the time he came across this 'fact', Mendoza was 41. For a decade he had never earned more than $10,000 a year, and professionally his work as an art photographer had gained little recognition. His personal life, he notes, was a 'mini-disaster'. He had never married and none of his relationships with women had lasted more than a couple of years.

On the plus side, he had degrees from famous institutions – engineering at Yale, architecture at Harvard – but now had little interest in these areas. He joked with his father that he must be the only Yale and Harvard graduate in America who earned less than $10,000 a year. His father would reply that he must be the only person *in America* who earned less than $10,000 a year.

'Somehow', Mendoza notes, 'I never got depressed.' He knew he was getting better at his work and was happy to 'pay his dues', even if things were taking longer than he thought. For all of the 1970s he lived in an urban commune, whose low costs enabled him to pursue his art. The only problem was that his 'art' was photographing dogs, not a subject the art photography world took seriously. His father thought if he was going to make any money from photography, it should be taking pictures of beautiful women. His mother just wanted him to settle down and have a family.

Others may have thought him aimless or lazy, but Mendoza saw things differently: he was simply a late achiever. He had been cheered up by reading articles on Grandma Moses, who took up the brush when she was 76, and Colonel Sanders, who didn't turn Kentucky Fried Chicken big until he was of pensioner age. Mendoza rationalised his professional life this way:

> 'I turned full-time to photography at age 33.
> It takes ten years to get really good at anything,
> including photography, and so I have 'til I'm
> 43 before I need to start worrying.'

When 43 came around, he had plenty to worry about.

He had moved from his commune into New York City, but unable to afford the rent, found himself living at his sister's house across the river in Brooklyn. There he cooked and babysat to pay his way. 'I was the only Yale and Harvard graduate who babysat for a living,' he recalls. With nothing much happening in his professional life, by any conventional measure he was not a success.

Then things began to change. His work began to get featured in magazines, he started having exhibitions, and he even had a show at the Museum of Modern Art. He hired his first lawyer and bought his first necktie. A book he had published got great reviews, and he started to earn proper money. With his first royalty cheque he moved to Florida, and there fell in love and got married.

Ironically, for a photographer of dogs, it was some pictures he had taken of a cat called Ernie that tipped him towards success. The first printing of his book of Ernie pictures sold out in three months, which led to funding from a Guggenheim fellowship for a second book. Today, Mendoza is a professor of photography at Ohio State University, and he and his wife have two children.

The gas station owner who loved chicken

Since Mendoza looked to Colonel Sanders for inspiration, let's briefly consider his story.

Harland Sanders' father was a coal miner, and died when Harland was only six. When his mother went out to work in a shirt factory, the household chores fell to Harland's responsibility, including the cooking. In later life he claimed to have mastered a variety of Southern dishes before he was ten.

Harland dropped out of school, got jobs as a farmhand and then as a tramcar conductor. During his twenties and thirties he worked with a fire-fighting crew on the railroads, studied law by correspondence, became a Justice of the Peace, enlisted as a soldier in Cuba, was a midwife, sold insurance, and ran a steamboat ferry on the Ohio River.

In his late thirties, Sanders found himself selling tyres, dealing directly with gas station owners. This job made him think he could run a gas station himself, and at 40 he started operating his own Shell station in Corbin, Kentucky. He started to notice that motorists were asking where they could get a good meal, and with the thought of an extra line of income Sanders seized the opportunity of offering his first love – Southern-fried chicken – to the hungry travellers. He began serving meals in the couple's own dining room that was part of the gas station, and soon people started visiting for the food alone. The couple added more chairs and tables, but it wasn't enough. Sanders took over a 142-seat restaurant and motel across the street, working as its chef and perfecting his '11 secret herbs and spices' chicken recipe.

By 1935, Sanders' local fame was such that Kentucky's governor Ruby Laffoon made him a 'Kentucky Colonel', an honorary title given to people who have made a significant contribution to the state. Making the most of it, Sanders began calling himself 'The Colonel' and dressing as a Southern gentleman, complete with white suit and black ribbon tie. But just as his restaurant was taking off, an inter-state highway made Corbin a backwater. Sanders auctioned off his restaurant and its effects. After paying all his bills there was not a lot left over and he began claiming social security benefits.

At this point, most in his situation would have given up, but rather than settling into a life of elderly penury, Sanders took his first benefit cheque of $105 and went on the road, selling his secret chicken recipe to restaurants around the country who gave him a nickel for every chicken they sold using the recipe.

Ten years later, there were hundreds of franchised Kentucky Fried Chicken outlets, and in 1964, Sanders sold his operation to a group of businessmen for $2 million (about $14 million in today's money).

Sanders only discovered his vocation at 40, did not begin to really exploit the commercial potential of his secret recipe until his sixties, and only became rich in his seventies. Given these facts, Mendoza was right to be inspired by the Colonel when his career was going nowhere.

Where are you at with your career right now? Chances are you have more going for you than Sanders did when he entered his sixties, and if that is so, what excuses are there for not seizing the day and doing what you've always wanted to? Or, if you enjoy your work, what is preventing you from ramping up your career and moving your life to a new level? If you look closely, it's probable that nothing is really stopping you.

Before they were famous

Stephen Fry, the English author and wit, was once having coffee with some young, emerging comedians in Chicago. He said to them:

'From the vantage point of my "elderly" position of a fifty-year-old . . . if I could offer any advice, it is that it is never too late, that the idea that the door closes and "Oh gosh, I'm already 30, nothing's happened" – it's complete nonsense. Actually almost the reverse is true. A lot of the stars . . . George Clooney . . . who is that guy from *House*? He had to wait until his late forties . . .'

Fry was being ironic, as 'that guy from *House*' was his old friend Hugh Laurie with whom he had done television comedy shows with in their younger years. Laurie became one of America's highest-paid television stars in his role as the genius, quirky doctor in *House*, but this success was hardly preordained. When invited to audition for the show's pilot Laurie was in Namibia working on a film. But he made a video of himself doing the part in his hotel bathroom, 'because it had the best light'. The show's director, Bryan Singer, had wanted a quintessential American for the lead role, and instantly felt Laurie was what he was looking for (Laurie's accent was so good Singer didn't know he was British). At 43, he had the part. Fry goes on to mention George Clooney, who didn't get his famous *ER* role until his mid-thirties, and until that point had had only minor parts.

The actor Hugh Grant fell into acting by accident, but enjoyed it enough to keep plugging away with small television and film roles. However, as he entered his thirties, what enthusiasm he still had began to desert him. After watching a clip from an early stage performance, a BBC interviewer pressed him as to whether he always believed, in the early part of his career, that he would 'make it'. He replied:

> 'I didn't think anything great was going to happen . . . I did very bad television for a number of years.'
>
> *Interviewer:* 'But then it just took off.'
>
> 'Just when I was about to give up, it took off, yeah. I remember going to the audition for *Four Weddings* and saying "This is the last one I go to. I'm 32, I'm bored of this, it's humiliating." And then I got the job.'

To the interviewer's question, Grant's response is hardly a rousing *Of course I believed!* In fact, the prospect facing the later-than-normal succeeder almost always includes some perceived humiliation, but Fortune often requires us to try *one more time* before she opens to us her heart, connections and coffers. Grant did, and as anyone knows, *Four Weddings and a Funeral* was a huge hit that made him a star. But the star Grant is in some ways less interesting than the pre-fame actor, who felt he might still do something even when the odds told him that great things had probably passed him by.

When someone becomes famous, we feel as if we have known them all along, and that their rise was inevitable. Yet in his book *Focus*, Al Ries provides a rather counterintuitive tip for becoming a remarkable person:

'What you need to do is to study what leaders
did before they became leaders, not what they
did after they became leaders.'

Television programmes and popular magazines like to point
out amusing or embarrassing things the stars did before they
'made it'. They do not highlight the serious amounts of work
or refinement of character and skills that would lead to their
'lucky' break.

In studying successful people, it is much more useful to
look at the steps taken and the years lived prior to such
breaks. What were they doing that prepared them for later
success? How were they refining themselves and their powers
of judgment in such a way that they would be ready to take
on a greatly expanded role?

There is no point 'trying to be a remarkable person'.
Instead, we must seek remarkable insights or wisdom, which
in turn, at some later date, will open the door to doing or
being something truly significant. When a group of nuns
who had lived with Mother Teresa during the 19 years she
spent as a teacher were interviewed, none could remember
anything about her that stood out, save for her fragile health.
Outwardly she may have seemed just like the other sisters,
but the tectonic plates inside were obviously moving. She
sought first the insights, and the personal and public results
came in due course.

Never get too discouraged by the apparent gap between
what you believe you are capable of and what it seems you
are now. Don't ever be afraid to entertain thoughts of yourself doing something or being someone of real impact. Part

of the work of achievement is arriving at strong self-belief. But more importantly, give yourself the *time* to do the thing, or become the person.

Careers going nowhere . . . and then

Brown, Lichtenstein and Grant

The son of a mathematics teacher at prestigious Phillips Exeter Academy, a school in New Hampshire, and a professional church organist, Dan Brown was born in 1964, the oldest of three. At college (Amherst) he was a keen singer, and as part of a Glee Club sang his way around the world. He also won a degree in Spanish and English. But his ardent desire was to be a successful singer-songwriter.

In the mid-1980s, Brown released a cassette of children's music, but it sold only a few hundred copies. In 1990 he released his own CD of adult music, but again this did not do well. Persistent, Brown moved to Los Angeles, hoping to make it big. He taught in schools to earn money, and got involved in the National Academy of Songwriters. Through its activities he met its director of artistic development, Blythe Newlon, and as romance blossomed between them she began to help him with his career. After the release of another poor-selling album, the couple left Hollywood and moved back to Brown's New Hampshire, where he fell back on teaching, this time Spanish classes at a local school. Not yet giving up on his music, he released another CD, *Angels & Demons*, which again made zero impact. As he entered his mid-thirties, no one, aside from family and friends, cared much whether Dan Brown succeeded or failed.

But in 1994, while on a vacation in Tahiti, Brown read a Sidney Sheldon thriller. Thinking he could do better, he began writing *Digital Fortress*, set in the code-breaking section of the National Security Agency and in Seville, Spain. At this time he also penned, with his wife, *187 Men to Avoid: A Guide for the Romantically Frustrated Woman*, and another humorous book. Two years later, coming to terms with the fact that his music career was going nowhere, Brown decided to focus on writing full-time.

By the time he managed to net a publisher for *Digital Fortress* in 1998, Brown was 34. *Angels and Demons* followed in 2000, and *Deception Point* in 2001. Though not flops, they were not big bestsellers either, and he remained a small player in the world of thriller literature.

However, in March 2003, a few months before his 39th birthday, *The Da Vinci Code* was published. Opening with a murder in the Louvre Museum in Paris, the book was a racy occult mystery involving revelations of secret societies and an alternative history of Christianity. The publisher, Doubleday, was more excited about it than his other books and expected it to do well, announcing a first printing of 85,000. Even they, however, could not have dreamed of its reception. Selling millions of copies in its first year of release, and many the next, as he entered his 40th year Brown's life changed forever. Three years after publication, *The Da Vinci Code* had sold over 60 million copies, and had shot Brown into the *Forbes* magazine celebrity rich list. While the book was hardly high literature, Brown brought millions of adults back to reading who had not picked up a book for years.

The time between Brown's first book and the phenomenon

of *The Da Vinci Code* was nine years. Considering he had come to writing late, this was quite an achievement. Yet he had been chasing success as a creative person since leaving college in 1986, so in truth his journey towards real recognition was a 17-year one.

Why did Brown keep ploughing away at music when he was much better at writing? Despite high ambitions, it obviously took him time, and a degree of self-awareness, to come to terms with the fact he would never make it in music – and to see that there was still time to begin and succeed in another field.

If at first you don't succeed, try something different.

Brown had the self-awareness to realise that his music was not leading anywhere and that he had better try something else. Every motivational book crows about the power of persistence, but the attribute only has power if you are persisting along the right path. Brown is a textbook example of how persistence combined with *experimentation* is needed to make the most of your talents. He always knew that he had 'something' – it was just a matter of finding the right vessel into which it could be poured. It also made a huge difference that Brown's spouse was his champion. Blythe Brown worked tirelessly to promote her husband's music career, wrote two books with him, then became the chief researcher for his thrillers when he decided that was his best chance for success.

It is difficult to give up a chosen path that you believe will lead to glory (in Brown's case, music), yet paradoxically, this sacrifice often leads people to their true calling. Brown was 30 when he discovered his, Mother Teresa 36, but each would take some years before they began to make real public progress. Yet their crucial moment had happened. If Brown had not stayed open to opportunity, today there would be no *Da Vinci Code*, only a pile of mediocre music CDs no one wants. Yet having been open to a change of course earlier in his thirties, by the time he neared 40, Brown was able to seize success with strong hands.

Roy Lichtenstein always knew he wanted to be an artist, but this certainty did not shorten his road to success. Born in 1923 into an upper-middle-class Manhattan family, the private school he was sent to had no art instruction on the curriculum, so he began attending Saturday morning painting classes. Following his school graduation, he attended the Art Students League of New York before enrolling in one of the first fine arts degree courses in Ohio.

When the Second World War intervened, Lichtenstein was sent for basic training then shipped off to Europe, where he made the most of his military service by taking time out to visit exhibitions in London and Paris. Towards the end of his service he began taking art classes at the Sorbonne, but in 1946, on hearing news of the death of his father, came back to the United States. Under the GI Bill he finished his degree at Ohio State, and was then invited to teach art there.

Through the 1950s Lichtenstein blended family life (he married Isobel Wilson and had two sons) with attempts to earn money. Despite various stints as an art teacher, he was unable to get a tenured teaching position, taking on other jobs including engineering draftsman, store window decorator and maker of architectural models. He had his first small solo exhibition in New York in 1951, but income from his art was almost non-existent, and his wife's interior design work made her the breadwinner. On trips to New York he would visit the Cedar Bar where Jackson Pollock, Franz Kline and Willem de Kooning, emerging as famous names in modern art, were hanging out. But he was too shy to introduce himself. The sculptor Lee Csuri noted of him at this time: 'Roy was very despondent about what he was doing. And feeling he was nowhere.' Nothing particularly original was happening with his painting; he was just doing the 'muddy abstract expressionism' that was in vogue, and remained an art-world outsider.

In 1957 he took up a position at the University of New York, Oswego, near the Canadian border. A dead-end post he felt forced to do just for the money, it was a long way from New York, the centre of the art world. The couple hated the freezing winters, and Isobel, unable to get good work, started drinking. Oswego marked a new low point. Though he had had half a dozen solo exhibitions, and had been painting for 20 years, Lichtenstein's career had conked out.

Then, in 1960, he scored a teaching job at Rutgers University in New Jersey. Here, a vibrant faculty brought new hope, and he felt encouraged to experiment. He had earlier done some ink drawings of Donald Duck, Mickey Mouse and Bugs Bunny, and in the summer of 1961 completed his first large painting in the style he became famous for, of Mickey and Donald on a jetty. His son can be partly credited for this shift towards 'pop' art, as he had pointed to an image of Mickey Mouse in his comic, and challenged his dad with, 'I bet you can't paint as well as that, eh, Dad!' He also began doing paintings in the style of advertisements, of gym shoes and a washing machine.

In 1961 the Leo Castelli gallery in New York had begun showing Lichtenstein's new work, and the following year he created the famous 'Whaam!', and 'The Kiss', huge paintings depicting images from comic strips rendered in thousands of coloured dots using commercial techniques. The works could not have been more different than the muddy abstracts he had been labouring on all these years. In the same year, his 39th, the gallery put on a solo exhibition that sold out almost immediately.

His fortunes had changed. 'At 37', as one art critic put it, 'Roy Lichtenstein had a dead-end job and a studio full of paintings that no one wanted. By 40 he was a celebrity.'

He resigned from his teaching post and moved back to New York, where over the next decade there was a clamour for his paintings, and where he could virtually name a price for his works. Along with Andy Warhol, Lichtenstein is now considered the pre-eminent exponent of Pop Art, his paintings providing the perfect combination of cultural irony and visual brilliance, a superb reflection of 1960s consumer society.

Was his success simply a case of being in the right place at the right time?

The work of every artist is certainly shaped by the *zeitgeist* (the spirit of the times), but ultimately all great artistic advances must involve courage. It is easy to forget that, in the 1960s, people were shocked by Lichtenstein's new style of painting, and for the painter himself, in terms of concept, style and technique, it was a true leap in the dark. Yet even though he was as surprised as anyone by the direction his work had taken, Lichtenstein wisely chose to stick with what was having the most impact.

In attempting to identify the elements of Lichtenstein's rise, we note again the classic combination, so common to the 'slow-cooked success', of hard work combined with experimentation. Recall that he toiled away doing abstract paintings for years before making his radical departure to the imagery of the comic book. Yet as with Dan Brown, his fortunes began to change when he combined natural persistence with an openness to the new. In Lichtenstein's case, when the world began to tell him that what he was doing was fascinating and valuable, he listened, even if it was a path that at first seemed alien to his own cherished style.

There is another important aspect. His second wife Dorothy noted that, unlike the macho abstract expressionists like Jackson Pollock and de Kooning who were always getting into drunken fistfights, the pop artists were *disciplined*. They had to be, given the technical virtuosity of the work, and Lichtenstein was known as an obsessive worker who would often not come out of his studio for two or three days, so intent was he on getting it right.

A popular image of the artist or writer is a shambolic figure who rises at noon, paints or taps away for a couple of hours and then goes out drinking for the evening. There have been many like this, but if they achieved anything it was despite such a routine, not because of it. When writing *The Da Vinci Code*, Dan Brown rose at four each morning and worked through until lunchtime, virtually every day for several years. Lichtenstein found success through *focus*, both in terms of a daily work routine and in a conscious choice to follow through in a direction that held promise. Brown and Lichtenstein's mental discipline allowed them to take full advantage of the creative breakthroughs that came their way, giving them the ability to really *implement* ideas. At 30 they would not have had the skills, but by 40 the right blend of imagination and execution was in place.

We have mentioned one Englishman called Grant; another is worth noting.

While Brown and Lichtenstein's careers might have stalled, Jim Grant's was actually taken away from him. Not long after he turned 40, Jim Grant lost his job as an in-house director for Granada, a British television company. In his 18 years in the job, he had been quite successful, part of the team that created a number of primetime dramas including *Brideshead Revisited* and *Cracker*. But with a young family to support, this 'corporate restructure' could hardly have come at a worse time.

Refusing to panic, Grant bought some paper and pencils and settled down to write a book. Though hardly a promising career move, Grant 'wrote with a fury that was a perfect balance of creativity and financial necessity'.

Grant was already thinking big, and set a goal to be the number one thriller writer in America. 'Dream on' would be the acceptable reaction to such an ambition, but when in March 1995 he submitted his manuscript, *Killing Floor*, to an agent (Darley Anderson), he was bowled over.

In the early weeks of writing the book, Grant had still

not thought of a name for the main character. The 6'5" Grant was in a supermarket one day with his wife, who said, 'Hey, if this writing thing doesn't pan out, you could always be a reacher in a supermarket.' His protagonist became Jack Reacher, a politically incorrect cross between a hero from a Western and James Bond, who travels across America getting into violent confrontations and righting wrongs.

You may be thinking, 'Well, I have never heard of Jim Grant; his second book probably flopped.' But Grant is better known by his pen name Lee Child, and his Jack Reacher books, including *Bad Luck and Trouble* and *Nothing to Lose*, have sold over 16 million copies. The Reacher character is set to star in Hollywood movies. Today, the 55-year-old Child lives in Manhattan and has properties there and in St Tropez.

As a Brit with no writing experience, it took tremendous gall and self-belief for Child to think he could become a bestselling author in the US, beating American writers at their own game. But before you dismiss this as a fairy-tale success story, perhaps it is worth seeing if there are any generic success lessons we can draw from it. The first one is obvious: many a writer or painter will excuse their lack of success on the basis of 'I am an artist' – and therefore do not stoop to such things as establishing clear goals for their career. Of course, it is possible to succeed without articulating where we want to be in, say, five or ten years' time, but if we do succeed it is likely to have come *despite* lack of a clear direction, not thanks to it. Financial necessity and pent-up creativity powered Child to hammer out his first, powerful novel. But if he had not had a long-term goal to reach the pinnacle of his field, and stay there, his career may have petered out after one or two books.

The second lesson is more universal. Most people made redundant at 40 would, in a panic, start searching around for similar work in their field, hoping they find something before their pay-out dries up. But calmly ask, 'What opportunity does this event [being careful not to label anything a 'disaster'] give me?'

Note that Child, even though he was taking a leap of faith, was not irresponsible or unrealistic. He knew that his new path had to pay, and was willing to take a calculated risk that took into account the welfare of his family. Child clearly did not believe he was over the hill or too late to start something great. He knew it would take years to achieve what he wanted, but it didn't stop him. There are always more options than we think, but they are not open to us if we are in the wrong state of mind. Beyond panic lies possibility.

An interviewer asked Child: 'You came to writing fairly late in life. How important is it to have lived some life before getting the words to come out right?' He responded:

> 'I think it's vital. I know that's true in my own
> case, and by looking at my colleagues. All of us
> did something else first. I think writing is truly a
> "second-phase" career. I know there are
> occasional successful books by 20-somethings
> . . . but how many of them do successful second
> books? I was 40 when I started, like Raymond
> Chandler, Robert Ludlum and all kinds of other

people. I don't personally know any successful writers who haven't worked half a lifetime doing something else first.'

How true, but it can't just be correct for one field (writing), and it isn't. Have you 'worked half a lifetime' doing something, and are now ready for the second, better half?

Life begins at 40

In the 1930s, philosopher Walter B. Pitkin published a book that went to some lengths to convince Americans of his generation that they were very lucky; even in tough economic times, they were much better off than their parents and grandparents. In the second part of their lives they could actually begin to think about *life*, instead of simply 'making a living'. He noted that, before the Machine Age, most people were worn out by 40 thanks to the drudgery of physical labour. At the outbreak of the First World War, for instance, the British government had to find many of its recruits from the mill towns and mining villages of England. When the chairman of a medical board was asked to report on the physical quality of these recruits, he wrote that they were '. . . already ageing at 35. Most of the industrial classes around Manchester were, for military purposes, old men at 38 . . . The list of their disabilities was appalling.'

Pitkin's bestselling *Life Begins at 40* (yes, it was he who coined the phrase) attempted to convince readers that this age was more of a beginning than an end. Yet what may have seemed like excessive optimism in Pitkin's day is now, with our greater life expectancy and prosperity, almost an uncontested truth. If your four-decade milestone is looming, if you passed it this year, or even if you wish you were still 40, and are not happy with what you have achieved so far in life, don't despair. As the stories in this chapter suggest, Walter Pitkin's phrase – usually meant in jest and the basis of many greeting card jokes – has never been more correct.

Most 40-year-olds still have 65 in mind as a retirement age, which leads them to think, 'I only have 25 productive years left.' But if you take a broader view of the span of lifetime productivity, something interesting happens. Suddenly 40 is not the beginning of the end in a productivity or achievement sense, but a genuine beginning. You have only used up two decades, or a third, of your productive span, and you still have four decades, or two-thirds of your life, to fulfil your ambitions.

Final thoughts

Whether or not you accept the theories surrounding mid-life, it is difficult to argue that having spent four decades on the planet has no effect in terms of the ripening of personal character and skills, or the execution of successful ideas. By 40, we usually know what we are good at, but we may be more open to changing our ways if it leads to greater success. By this age we know the value of persistence, but are wise enough to keep experimenting in order to find 'what works'. Finally, whatever pressures we felt when younger to conform to expectations of peers, teachers or parents, we are now our own person.

The high-minded will recoil from the idea of mentioning Gandhi and Mother Teresa in the same breath as Colonel Sanders, who gave the world nothing more than an increased availability of fried chicken, or Dan Brown, yet such figures were just the same in this respect: they did not come into their own until around 40, and like the others kept searching for what would give their lives the most impact. Have the same kind of openness, and you too can be led to something that gives your life an extraordinary impact.

A few more . . .

Brief examples of those who didn't really hit their stride until well into their fourth or fifth decades

Julia Child, the television chef who raised the culinary skills of millions of Americans from the 1960s to the 1990s, didn't even start learning to cook until she was 37, and did not become well known in her field until her late forties.

When her charismatic husband committed suicide, at 46 the inexperienced **Katherine Graham** took over the reins at *The Washington Post* and, through its superb coverage of events such as the Watergate scandal, turned it into an opinion-making powerhouse.

In her early thirties, **Betty Friedan** was dismissed from her job as a journalist for a union newspaper when she became pregnant with her second child. She managed to do some freelance writing, but it was difficult with three children, and through her twenties and thirties juggled as best she could. When she was 35, Friedan was given an interesting project: a survey on her Smith College classmates 15 years after graduation. Her interviews revealed many unhappy, unfulfilled housewives, and this sparked the research that would lead to *The Feminine Mystique*, the multi-million bestseller that burst upon an unsuspecting public in 1963, launching the feminist 'second wave'. With her children at school and growing up, Friedan found more time for writing and research, and after the publication of the book in her early forties, she became a public figure.

After a period of depression, in his 40th year the sociologist **Max Weber** penned his famous essay *The Protestant Ethic and the Spirit of Capitalism*. **Thomas Aquinas** began the great *Summa Theologiae* when he also was 40. **Thomas Kuhn** was an obscure academic until, in his 40th year, he wrote *The Structure of Scientific Revolutions* (1962), one of the most cited non-fiction works of the twentieth century. Having spent most of his university career in physics, he was a latecomer to the philosophy of science.

After years as an assistant to other couturiers, the 40-year-old **Christian Dior** established his own fashion house. Against a background of post-war austerity, his first collection, the luxurious 'New Look', was an instant success.

The French painter **Rousseau** did not really begin painting until he was in his forties, and then stayed a customs officer for many years.

Danny Trejo, drug addict and armed robber, spent 11 years in and out of jails before, at 41, turning his life around with a 12-step recovery programme. When visiting a friend on a movie set he was offered a part as an extra, beginning a remarkable Hollywood career with tough guy/convict roles alongside the likes of Clooney, Depp and De Niro. **Samuel L. Jackson** was a heroin and cocaine addict through his forties, before Spike Lee offered him a bit part in a film that resurrected his career.

Sam Walton spent over two decades honing his knowledge of the retail industry before, at 44, opening his first Walmart store.

Psychiatrist **M. Scott Peck** worked in relative obscurity until, at 43, he wrote *The Road Less Travelled*. Expected to interest a small self-help audience, it went on to sell ten million copies.

After years as a teacher in Britain and the Far East, **Anthony Burgess** had his first book published at 39. His most famous work, *A Clockwork Orange*, was written at 45.

Tropic of Cancer, one of the twentieth century's

great novels depicting **Henry Miller**'s bohemian life in Paris, was not published until he was 43.

Raymond Chandler worked as a bookkeeper, soldier and oil company executive well into his forties. Fired from his job for drinking, womanising and absenteeism, with dwindling funds he turned his hand to writing pulp fiction. Though Chandler had his first short story published at 45, *The Big Sleep*, his first novel featuring the hard-boiled private eye Philip Marlowe, was not published until he was 51.

Lech Walesa, a Polish tradesman unknown to the world, was 37 when elected leader of his country's free trade union, Solidarnosc. His defiance of the communist powers helped to bring an end to the Soviet era, and at 47 he was president of a free Poland.

Joseph Campbell, the American mythologist who told people to 'follow their bliss', spent most of his twenties living in a shack, reading every day. His first real job, a minor post at a newly founded women's college, did not come until well into his thirties. He never cared much for the academic maxim of 'publish or perish'. The work he is best known for, *The Hero With a Thousand Faces,* which inspired George Lucas to make *Star Wars*, was published when he was 45.

At medical school in Australia, **Howard Florey** routinely topped his class and won three scholarships. But he was over 40 by the time he conducted the experiments with an anti-bacterial mould that would make him famous. Though it was Alexander Fleming who actually discovered penicillin, Florey and his partner Ernst Chain made it useable on humans, in the process saving millions of lives.

Love him or hate him, it's a fact that **George W. Bush** didn't really do anything with his life until he gave up drinking for good – at 40.

The mock documentary television series that made **Ricky Gervais** famous, *The Office*, first aired a few weeks after his 40th birthday.

Benjamin Graham, the legendary value investor who mentored Warren Buffett, spent 20 years on Wall Street before writing a book. His classic *Security Analysis* was published in 1934, his 40th year. One of the great modern investors, **George Soros**, started his famous Quantum Fund at 39, after 14 years learning the ropes as a broker and analyst.

Poet **T. S. Eliot** had published *The Wasteland* in his 40th year, having worked on it for the previous seven. After failing, in his early twenties, to be accepted into the Foreign Office, **Ian Fleming** worked as a journalist, banker, stockbroker, naval intelligence officer and senior manager of a newspaper group. He only wrote full-time for the last decade of his life. *Casino Royale*, which introduced a character called James Bond, was published in 1953, in his mid-forties.

In his 45th year, **Nicholas Evans** was an unemployed film producer with a family to support. The banks were closing in, and he was crying himself to sleep when his novel sold for $350,000. *The Horse Whisperer* (1995) went to number one in many countries and became a successful film.

Ruth Handler, 43, and her husband Elliot had been running a small toy company for over a decade when she premiered the 'Barbie' doll (named after her daughter) at the American Toy Fair. At a time when dolls resembled little girls, the adult-looking Barbie made their Mattel company into one of the great post-war corporate success stories.

CHAPTER SIX:

MID-CENTURY MAGIC

'Now for my next half-century'

Many oak trees wait 50 years before, in a burst of creative power, they produce their first crop of hundreds of acorns.

It's the same for many people: nothing major happens for several decades, and then it all happens. We use the phrases 'late starters' and 'late bloomers' as if there was some problem or delay in a person's flourishing, but surely this is a tautology. The point of ripening is that it happens when it does, and not before.

To use another analogy, if the forties are the decade in which people gather steam, the fifties see them on their full speed run. In this decade many find they are at the height of their powers, combining good health with heightened skills and wisdom. A career can be crowned, or equally something new started. Age itself, we come to realise, matters little next to readiness and enthusiasm. With many people now living in reasonable health until their nineties, it is no longer ridiculous for a person to say to themselves, on turning 50, 'Now for my next half-century.'

We never know when a calling may be revealed

At 48, the gift that changed a life

Julia Margaret Pattle grew up in a family celebrated for its female beauty. Julia's stunning mother, Adeline, was the daughter of French aristocrats, and with her husband James, an upper-class Englishman who worked for the East India Company, they had seven daughters. Julia was the fourth.

Writing about the girls, their great niece Virginia Woolf recalled a trio of similar age in which one was Beauty, one Dash, and the other – Julia – Talent. In the social confines of her time, Julia's wit, creative instincts and energy were certainly assets, but she was considered, if not quite the ugly duckling, certainly the plain one.

After an education in France and England, she returned to India to marry a man 20 years her senior, Charles Hay Cameron, who would later help to write British India's penal code. For a decade, Julia enjoyed bringing up her children and being hostess in an important colonial household.

When Charles retired, the family moved to England, where one of the Prattle sisters had created a salon at Little Holland House in London. The salon attracted some of the leading lights of the time: writers and poets including Thackeray, Tennyson and Browning, painters George Frederic Watts and Edward Burne-Jones and painter turned photographer David Wilkie Wynfield. Julia revelled in its relatively bohemian atmosphere. Later, the Camerons helped create another cultural centre when they bought a couple of cottages next to the home of their friends the Tennysons at Freshwater on the Isle of Wight. It was named Dimbola Lodge, after their former home in India. Artists, intellectuals and writers (including Lewis Carroll) visited, and the photographer Oscar Rejlander photographed the family.

One Christmas, when Julia was alone at Dimbola (Charles was visiting, with two of their sons, a coffee plantation they had bought in Ceylon), her daughter and her husband came to stay. Hoping it would ease her loneliness, they gave her a camera, noting on the card:

> 'It may amuse you, Mother, to try to photograph during your solitude at Freshwater.'

Instead of 'amusing' her, at 48 the gift changed her life.

Today, getting a camera for a present is of no great moment, but then it was a large and expensive piece of equipment that required substantial technical knowledge and skill of its user, and this was even before the difficult process of making prints.

Julia had previously created elaborate photo albums as gifts, but having a camera of her own suddenly gave her a vessel into which she could pour her prodigious energies. The coal store at Dimbola became a darkroom, and its chicken house a studio. Having discovered her passion late in life and, with the advice of David Wilkie Wynfield, she now worked constantly, and within a few months was creating albums and individual photographs for sale and exhibition. Cameron became a member of the Photographic Society of London, and convinced the British Museum to acquire some of her work. 'Talent' finally had an outlet, and it wasted no time.

Though she produced elaborate images on religious themes, it is the intense, close-cropped portraits of family, friends and notable figures that became Julia's trademark. Haunting images of Charles Darwin, Alfred Lord Tennyson, the celebrated astronomer Heschel, actor Ellen Terry, the essayist Thomas Carlyle, and Pre-Raphaelite painters Millais, Rosetti and Burne-Jones were among her subjects. Her style is still mimicked today.

The great Victor Hugo once wrote to her: 'No one has ever captured the rays of the sun and used them as you have. I throw myself at your feet.' A great tribute, but even more remarkable was the fact that Cameron did not even discover her art form until she was close to 50.

Living in an Annie Proulx age

Another who naturally ripened is Annie Proulx (pronounced 'Proo'). Born in 1935, in Connecticut, the oldest of five sisters, her father was a French Canadian who had moved to the United States. He became a vice-president of a textile company, and because of his work the family moved around from state to state. Her mother was a painter and keen naturalist whose family had lived in Connecticut since the 1600s, and her grandmother a great storyteller.

Proulx went to school in Portland, Maine, then attended college briefly, but in 1955, as often happened at that time, she left to marry. The marriage lasted only a few years, and the daughter it produced grew up with her father.

She only returned to college in her thirties, where in 1969 she graduated from the University of Vermont with honours in History. While there, she married again. Of this turbulent second marriage, Proulx wrote 'the less said the better', but it produced two sons. Her third union, although lasting 20 years and ending amicably, led her to the conclusion that she 'was simply not well suited for marriage'.

In 1973, she received a Master's degree from Sir George Williams University (now Concordia University) in Montreal, and got as far as her oral examination for a doctorate. Not relishing a future in academia with its scarce job opportunities, in 1975 the 40-year-old Proulx abandoned her doctorate and became a journalist. For the next 13 years she was a magazine writer covering a range of practical topics. Not many now know that in the 1980s she published several works of non-fiction, with titles like *Plane and Make Your Own Fences and Gates, Walkways, Walls and Drives* (1983), and *Sweet and Hard Cider: Making It, Using It and Enjoying It* (1984). She lived in an isolated shack in rural Vermont, and had difficulty supporting her two sons.

Proulx's first published fiction was some stories in *Gray's Sporting Journal*, a literary magazine focused on the outdoor life of hunting and fishing, but it was 1988 before she first saw her fiction published in book form. When *Heartsongs*, a collection of short stories, was issued by the prestigious Scribner house, she was well into her fifties.

The second book, *Postcards* (1992), was critically acclaimed, and won the PEN/Faulkner Award for Fiction, but it was *The Shipping News* (1994), a novel she had first had the idea for during a fishing trip to Newfoundland in 1988, that first brought Proulx fame. Selling over a million copies, it won both the Pulitzer Prize for Fiction and America's National Book Award, and was later made into a film directed by Lasse Hallström. In the year of its release, Proulx was almost 60.

But Proulx was just warming up. In 1997, one of her short stories, 'Brokeback Mountain', a tale of love between two cowboys in Wyoming (a state she had loved since she first set eyes upon it, and where she now lives) appeared in *The New Yorker*. It was included in a book of short stories, *Close Range*, in 1999, and then in 2005 the story was made into a film. Nominated for eight Academy Awards, *Brokeback Mountain*, with Jake Gyllenhaal and Heath Ledger as the cowboys, was a surprise hit.

When, in her fifties, Proulx emerged into the public eye a fully formed writer, delighted readers must have wondered what she had been doing all these years. But of course part of her attraction is the fact that she was *not* young, and had lived a life.

Ten years can bring us to mastery in a particular domain, but in some ways this is just a minimum – many people do not really make strides until they are closer to 20 years into a career. Though this sounds long, the flipside, as the author of *Talent is Overrated* Geoff Colvin has pointed out, is that in year 19 'you are still getting better'. It also explains why people who first had some level of success in their thirties often do not produce more enduring work until their fifties.

*　　*　　*

What great benefits might flow to our societies if cases of slow-cooked success such as Proulx's could be multiplied by the millions? Her example does not promise that every amateur can follow the same path to professional renown, but it does suggest that if you have the talent, and the discipline to make something of it, time may be more on your side than you think. The fact that people are healthier in mind and body to a later age than in the past creates opportunities. A hundred years ago, the chances of someone like Proulx being able to launch a writing career in her fifties would have been small. Now, with women in the richer countries living on average well into their eighties and nineties, it is no great issue to begin fulfilling a vocation so late.

No greatness without foundations

'Now you are going to operate on his head'

During the Second World War, many Polish Jews fled the Nazis and journeyed to Russia. Among them were Dora, from Warsaw, and Nachman, from Lodz. Both were captured by the Red Army and put in hard labour camps in Siberia. When freed in 1942, they made the long trek south to Kyrgyzstan. Here, the two refugees met and fell in love.

But Kyrgyzstan was gripped by famine, and they had to survive on insects and weeds. After a daughter was born, and Dora had become pregnant again, in 1946 they decided to make the journey back to Poland. Nachman stayed in Warsaw to try to sell a bag of salt he had dug from an old mine – their only source of income. Dora went to Lodz to locate relatives, hoping to stay with them. A shock awaited her: 85 of the couple's immediate family members had been killed.

A distraught Dora begged a Red Army guard for help. He took pity on her, and let the eight and a half months pregnant woman sleep in a metal cot in the guardhouse. The following morning, her son Daniel was born.

The young family moved to America on one of the last immigrant boats, and growing up in New York, Daniel watched the World Trade Center being built. He loved drawing and wanted to be an artist. When his mother tried to drive him away from the idea, he would mention Andy Warhol as an example of a successful, well-off artist. But his mother would say, 'For every Warhol there are a thousand penniless waiters. Be an architect. You can always do art in architecture, but you can't do architecture in art. You get two fish with the same hook.'

Daniel Libeskind duly took an architecture degree, and in his twenties took his new bride, Nina, on a 'honeymoon' visiting Frank Lloyd Wright buildings across America. But instead of becoming an architect, Libeskind fell into architectural theory. Over the next 25 years the family, including three children, lived in many places around the world, following Dad's next university teaching post. For the most part it was a happy, interesting life, but Libeskind felt very aware that his full creativity was not being expressed. Each time he made an attempt to get one of his building designs erected, they were considered unbuildable or too confronting. He did win a design competition for a housing complex in West Berlin, but the fall of the Berlin Wall in 1989 saw it cancelled.

But almost a decade later, in 1998, Libeskind won a

competition to design a small museum in Germany to honour Felix Nussbaum, the artist who died in Auschwitz. 'Imagine', Libeskind said, 'that you've been trained as a surgeon but you've never had your hand on a scalpel, and someone says: now you are going to operate on his head.' At 52, the museum was his first actual building, and its success led to a commission to design the Jewish Museum in Berlin, a much bigger project that would make his name.

Were the years Libeskind spent in university teaching in vain? Hardly. The decades he was in theoretical architecture meant that the buildings he did finally design were rich with meaning, not put up for the architect's vanity but with people and their unique histories in mind.

Though today Libeskind is known for his buildings rather than his academic work, the point is that the former could not have happened without the latter. As it was, he enjoyed his years on the theory side, and only by filling this role completely did other avenues open up (a success law we observe in many others).

Today, Libeskind oversees dozens of major projects around the world, but perhaps his most important project has been the master plan for rebuilding the World Trade Center, whose original form he watched going up as a boy.

Transferring expertise

You never know where your experience can take you

Another example of the success law of filling one role completely before another can open is Alfred Kinsey, author of the ground-breaking Kinsey Reports into human sexuality.

Until well into his forties, Kinsey was known as a world expert on gall wasps – a classic narrow-focus academic. But fate took him in a different direction when, at Indiana University where he worked, its Association of Women Students made a petition for a course for married students or those contemplating marriage. The job fell to the slightly aloof Professor Kinsey to run it. The students had questions such as: what would the effect of premarital orgasm or sex have on later married life? What is normal or abnormal in sexual activity? The little knowledge they did have had been shaped by religion, philosophy or social mores, and Kinsey quickly found out that there was more scientific information on the sexual behaviour of small insects than there was on people.

Kinsey launched a massive research programme involving questionnaires and interviews with thousands of Americans, and in 1948, in his mid-fifties, Kinsey and his team published *Sexual Behavior in the Human Male* which, written for a university audience, became a surprise bestseller (over half a million copies). He became a national figure, and the Kinsey Institute for Sex Research became famous. It was followed five years later by the 800-page *Sexual Behavior in the Human Female*, and in the year of its release, 1953, Kinsey appeared on the cover of *Time* magazine. The two volumes, probably because their titles were embarrassing to ask for in a bookshop or library, became known simply as the 'Kinsey Reports'.

Over a period of 20 years, Kinsey became the world authority on human sexual behaviour, but he could not have achieved this without the research skills gained from having spent years studying an obscure insect.

* * *

When we become an expert in our field, often we do not realise at the time just how many generic skills we have developed along with specialised knowledge, and that these can be put to good use in a totally different area. You may not like everything about your current job, but a particular skill or knowledge it gives you may become the key to your success in something else.

What are you doing now that is setting you up for your real glory? What 'extra project' might you begin in the next year or so that draws on already honed skills? What idea, excitedly scrawled on the back of a napkin late one night in a restaurant, may end up as your defining achievement? The simplest ideas are often the most powerful, and what may seem too obvious to you could, with proper execution, powerfully affect many others. Equally, do not dismiss proposals that come to you which, like the request to Kinsey to teach sex education, could totally change your course.

Finally, take the time to dream, muse, meditate or just play around. When work becomes play, it can have surprising power. A mind consists of millions of memories, thoughts and impressions, all of them unique to you. Don't waste them. In the years you have, find something that draws together everything you have ever seen, done and learned. 'Gather up the fragments, so that nothing is lost.'

In their spare time

Hours here and there can add up to something great

Momofuko Ando could not forget the scenes, just after the Second World War, when Japan was still experiencing severe food shortages and long lines of people shivered in the Osaka streets to buy hot noodles from black market sellers. For the rest of his life he would associate the elimination of hunger with peace, and felt it his mission to provide cheap, convenient hot food to the masses.

Ando started a company producing salt, but through the 1950s faced various financial difficulties, including the bankruptcy of a credit union of which he had been the chairman. But in his spare time, in a hut in his back garden, he began experimenting with noodle production. Having watched his wife make tempura (deep fried fish or vegetables), he realised that when fresh noodles were immersed in hot oil, their water content was leached out and they became a noodle 'brick'. Yet if you simply immersed them in boiling water again for two or three minutes, they came back to life, with flavouring added, as a marvellous hot snack.

With his 50th year not far away, and after countless kitchen experiments, Ando perfected his recipe for the instant noodle. Launched in 1958, this humble innovation made him a household name in Japan and the patron saint of busy non-cooks the world over. A few years later, he would also invent the cup noodle, and continued going into the office and innovating until he was 96.

Ando's story is one of great progress achieved through spare-time tinkering, and the message of his life could be boiled down to this:

If you perceive a problem or a need, chances are it is a problem for many other people (even if they have not articulated or expressed it).

If a solution is required, who better than you to work at it and deliver it? You have probably thought about it more than anyone else. Take the time, or make the time, to work on it. Remember, you probably have more time than you think.

Chester Carlson's story exemplifies this. After a poverty-stricken childhood in which virtually every minute was taken up working, Carlson made his way to college to study chemistry and physics. Graduating in the Depression, there were no jobs but he eventually found his way into a position in the patent office at Bell Labs.

Carlson had always wanted to be an inventor and thought constantly about a machine that would easily copy documents, but that would involve no costly and messy chemical or photographic process. At 29, he remembers, 'I was just living from hand to mouth . . . and I had just got married. It was kind of a hard struggle. So I thought the possibility of making an invention might kill two birds with one stone; it would be a chance to do the world some good and also a chance to do myself some good.'

In his spare time he experimented in his apartment, slowly developing the process that would become xerography. But Carlson could not interest big companies like IBM in his process, and it would be another decade before the Haloid company (which later became Xerox) licensed his invention and created a commercial product. So counter-intuitive was Carlson's process, bringing together a range of unconnected methods and technologies, that (rare among inventions) it was truly original. But the complexity of the process, the difficulty in use and the expense of these machines meant there was only a small market for them.

It was only in 1959, when Carlson was in his fifties, that the release of the relatively simple Xerox 914 changed office copying forever. The Xerox company began to double in size every year or so, and even though the agreement with Xerox only netted him a sixteenth of every cent Xerox made from each copy, the explosion in photocopying would make Carlson a rich man. Sensitive and humble, he would give away most of his money before his death in the late Sixties.

If looking at people who made the most of their time, we should also mention Eric Hoffer.

After both his parents died while he was still in his teens, New York-born Hoffer took an inheritance of $300 and moved to California. Through his twenties and thirties he supported himself as a travelling labourer, odd jobs man and gold prospector, getting to know the hard-working underside of the Californian dream. But Hoffer was different to your average labourer; in his spare time he visited public libraries and read everything from Montaigne to Hitler's *Mein Kampf*. After this itinerant life, in his forties he finally 'settled down' to a permanent job as a longshoreman, loading and unloading cargo on the San Francisco docks.

Never marrying, Hoffer found a tiny flat near the docks and continued to read and think in his spare time. Though totally unconnected to the literary and intellectual world, he met a woman who worked on a magazine, and she encouraged him to write.

Just shy of 50, Hoffer found a publisher for his book,

The True Believer. A compelling look at mass movements and their power to shape minds, the book shows how spiritual hunger or lack of self-esteem leads people to jettison their old selves in order to become part of something apparently greater and more glorious. It became a sociological classic, and though it had particular meaning in the wake of the Second World War, and the attractions of fascism, it could equally apply to the terrorists and suicide bombers of today, and so has found a new audience.

How was it that a dock worker could suddenly burst onto the world intellectual scene, a fully formed philosopher? Though it might be supposed that you have to go to university and know the right people to make a mark in the world of ideas, perhaps the cliché is true that there is no better teacher than the 'university of life'. If Hoffer had taken a conventional path in academia, he may never have had the free time for his voluminous reading and to develop his own ideas. As the archetypal working-class intellectual, Hoffer showed that our day jobs do not define us, and that spare time reading and thinking can really add up to something. Are you in a similar position? If you are ever tempted to bemoan your lack of opportunities, look to people like Hoffer, who did great things despite their apparently limited work or life situations.

The books that waited for their writer

It may seem like forever, but the time comes

The world is full of unpublished manuscripts of fiction, and if we are honest, most of them should stay that way. For a field built on supposed creativity, it is actually very hard to say something truly original, or which fills an unmet need for readers. Most writers stick to their day job, and those who do make a career out of the novel often find it takes them much longer than they had imagined. Consider the life of Bryce Courtenay.

Courtenay was born in 1933 in South Africa's Northern Transvaal. His seamstress single mother put him into an orphanage, where because of his small size, and having an English rather than Afrikaaner background, he was frequently bullied and beaten.

Life got brighter when, as an 11-year-old, he won a scholarship to a top private school in Johannesburg. He excelled, and his wish to become a writer led him to apply, and be accepted into, a journalism course in London. He worked in the copper mines to raise his fare.

In London, Courtenay met an Australian woman. They married in 1957 and settled back in Sydney, where Courtenay found work in the emerging television industry. He later moved into advertising, and with his skills at writing and persuasion went from a position as junior copywriter to creative director of a large agency in under five years.

Though he had never wanted to make a career out of advertising, his youngest son, Damon, was a haemophiliac, and with two more children the family needed all the money he could bring in. So Courtenay, without much choice, spent his thirties, forties and into his fifties climbing a ladder that he didn't really want to be on (even if by conventional measures he was a success).

When Damon died, at only 24 from an AIDS-infected

blood transfusion, Courtenay was 55. With the other children now older, it was finally time to begin what he felt was his real calling: writing. In 12 months, he hammered out a long novel which he did not actually expect to get published; it was practice. When finished, the heavy manuscript was used to keep the kitchen door in place.

But in 1989, Courtenay's epic story of a South African boy growing up in the Second World War who makes something out of his life, despite tough circumstances, was published. Unforgettable characters, plus its uplifting message that just one person can change the world, turned *The Power of One* into a bestseller in Australia, and its success was then replicated around the world. In 1992 it was made into a Hollywood film, and has sold more than seven million copies.

Another author in the popular style, the previously mentioned Dan Brown, wrote this piece of advice to students at his old university, a few years before *The Da Vinci Code*:

> 'Follow your dreams and do what you want to
> do. Be creative. Do something you can be proud
> of. The key to happiness is doing what you want
> to do every day.'

How true, and yet, for many, how impractical. When writing his first four novels, Brown did not have to worry about children; Courtenay did. For over 25 years he nursed a burning ambition to be a writer, but was not in any position to make the break. When an interviewer asked him about the long road he had taken, he replied:

'[It] was always going to be my life. It's just that
. . . things got out of hand, as they do in life.
You know, things happen and I just couldn't do
it. But every morning of my life I'd wake up and
say there's another day I've gotta spend not
being what I want to be.'

Courtenay never considered leaving his wife and children
to write in a hut next to the sea. He loved them and always
put them first. Damon's condition, in particular, required a
huge amount of attention. But as the years passed, he might
have privately wondered if he had sacrificed too much.

When the time came, he made up for the lost years of
creativity. In the decade and a half following *The Power of
One*, Courtenay wrote another 14 novels, and is still writing.
Even now, he has noted, the long days he is able to spend
at his computer seem a fantastic luxury.

To believe yourself to be something, yet not be able to express
it, is a cruel place. It doesn't matter if you are successful
in another career. Yet the slow-cooked success learns that
whether you are able to begin 'doing your thing' at 30,
40, or 50 matters less than the fact that, when the opportunity does come, it is seized. If *The Power of One* had
been written when Courtenay was 40, it would not have
been the same book, and probably not quite as good. As
it was, the work waited another 15 years before it came
into being, and thanks to the incredible stored-up energy
of its author, then only took a year to get onto paper and
was perfect.

If something is worth being created, nature has a way of making sure it is – but according to *its* timescale, not our own. In cases like Courtenay's, it is perhaps wrong to say that 'He waited until he was 55 to write his great book', and more correct to note that 'The book waited until he was 55 to be written.'

The same could be said of Lionel Shriver, who in 2005, after 20 years of struggle, won the prestigious Orange Prize for fiction by female authors. Though the prize money itself is very welcome (£30,000, or around $45,000), its winner earns much more through extra book sales.

Her book, *We Need to Talk About Kevin*, released without fanfare in 2003, is a brutally honest story of a woman's despair about her own feelings of disinterest towards a difficult child – a child who becomes a Columbine-style classroom killer. Word of mouth helped sales grow, and crucially, some influential figures in the New York literary world also got behind the book. Yet the work also generated negative reviews, perhaps understandable given its controversial subject.

We Need to Talk About Kevin was Shriver's seventh published novel. Rejected by 30 publishers, even her agent didn't like it. Despite having written half a dozen novels, some of which got good reviews, none had sold in great numbers and she had continued to support herself by writing pieces for *The Economist* (fittingly, a magazine whose contributors are kept anonymous). In no way was she an insider in London's literary scene, and when she did get invitations to book launches or parties, she recalls, '. . . no one would talk to me, and I would end up hanging out with the catering staff and then I'd sneak home.' At 47, the future didn't look bright.

Shriver had long coveted the Orange prize, knowing it would transform her career. Yet she also felt ready to give up after two decades of toil without much recognition. 'I'm not an overnight success', she noted. 'I never thought I would get to this point. I was so tired . . . I was just so drained. I never got anything back. And even when something seemed to go really well, you get your hopes up and it's just very tiring.' But in winning the prize, there was no going back to oblivion. Her future writings would be at the top of reviewers' piles, and she would now have ready, appreciative audiences.

Shriver grew up in a household with lots of books. Her mother was an academic (in theology), a poet and political campaigner, and her father a Presbyterian minister; both shaped the preoccupation with touchy moral issues later expressed in her work. You could argue this background gave her a real head start in becoming a writer, yet there was never any expectation or encouragement to that end from her parents. She was certainly no 'outlier' – Malcolm Gladwell's term to describe people freakishly ahead of the pack in their chosen field like a Bill Gates or a Tiger Woods. Though the outlier idea is interesting in the way it shines a light on high achievement at a young age, it leaves little room for consideration of the rest of us. For not only are most people who succeed in life not outliers, they are often, like Shriver, *outsiders*. Between her leaving school in North Carolina and winning the Orange prize 30 years later, Shriver went to college in New York, worked in catering, taught freshmen's and remedial English courses, and lived in

Nairobi, Belfast, Israel, Thailand and London. Her first novel was not published until she was 30. In short, by the time she finally received due recognition she had lived half a lifetime. There was nothing 'outlier' or 'insider' about her. She simply kept plugging away, and got somewhere. Though society may be set up to advance those who look the part or who know the right people, quality and imagination do eventually have a way of getting noticed.

Of her pre-prize life, Shriver noted: 'It's really humiliating to be an aspirant at 48.'

It is, but you have to go on anyway if you believe your work is worth something. A writer of mature years is tortured by the thought, 'By this point I should be . . .', perhaps brought on by seeing a magazine feature on a much younger author. These thoughts grow darker the longer the time one works without recognition.

Motivational gurus are fond of telling us that 'Persistence always pays', yet in the artistic world there are no certainties as to how, or if, one's work will be recognised. What *is* certain is that for those who do 'break through', along the way they find no shortcuts.

The most interesting thing about Shriver is the divided nature of her mind just before her breakthrough: on the one hand, still plugging away and desperate for some kind of recognition, still believing that she might crack one of the big literary awards; on the other, so beaten down by lack of recognition that she is about to give up. Winston Churchill's famous line, '. . . never give in, never give in, never, never, never, never' is all too easily thrown into after-dinner speeches or yelled at hapless players in the locker room at half-time, but the reality is, most of us are just not able to sustain such a constant attitude through the normal trials and grind of everyday life. In truth, we can express both sentiments almost simultaneously. The flame that we hold for some particular outcome may be small, but seemingly against reason we keep it alight. And so we should.

Final thought

Julia Margaret Cameron could have conformed to the mores of her time, the unobtrusive Victorian wife and mother. Bryce Courtenay could have rested on his laurels as a successful executive. Annie Proulx and Lionel Shriver might have given up on creative writing altogether, such was their invisibility to the literary world. And Momofuko Ando and Chester Carlson could have dismissed their ideas as a crazy dream or an unproductive hobby. Instead, each said to themselves, 'I have something real to give,' and made a decision to keep at it.

Many people do experience a kind of mid-century magic in terms of achievement, yet it often comes only after years of reasonable expectations have been quashed. At the time, circumstances often seem to hold us back from what we really want, and it is only in hindsight that we see they actually strengthened us, or provided just the right conditions and timing for genuine success. When fearful or in doubt about the rate of your progress, remember the stories above. Recall the oak tree, biding its time and drawing up its energies for a summer explosion of acorns, decades after its initial sprouting.

A few more . . .

Henry Steinway hand-built 492 pianos before, at 56, launching his own company and creating the famous piano brand.

Fritz Perls, pioneer of gestalt therapy, was at 32 still living with his mother. Only in his fifties did he begin to branch out on his own, and was in his sixties by the time he became influential in counterculture America.

Leo Sternbach was 51 when he invented Valium, a safe tranquiliser that for over a decade was the world's highest-selling pharmaceutical. He created a number of other important drugs, and continued to work until he was 95. **Norman Borlaug**, the agricultural scientist credited with saving the lives of a billion people through his high-yield grain varieties, was 56 when he won the Nobel Prize.

Chaucer, 'the father of English literature', wrote his unfinished masterwork, *The Canterbury Tales*, between the ages of 54 and 61. After three decades as a journalist and editor, children's author **Mary Alice Fontenot** wrote her first book at 51 and proceeded to publish another 30 into her eighties and nineties.

Charles Bukowski, the 'lowlife laureate of Los Angeles', spent decades doing odd jobs and living in rooming houses, drinking and writing poetry in his spare time. At 49 he was a post-office worker, at the end of his tether, when a publisher agreed to fund his first novel. He delivered the manuscript for *Post Office* three weeks later, and the book established his reputation. **Richard Adams** worked as a civil servant for many years in Britain's Ministry of Housing and Local Government, writing in his spare time. He was 52 when *Watership Down* was published. The American poet **Wallace Stevens** had his first collection of poetry published in his mid-forties, but to pay the bills he sold insurance into his fifties.

Leonardo da Vinci began the *Mona Lisa* in his fifties and was still painting well into his sixties. **Charles Darwin**, spurred into action by Alfred Wallace's paper on the introduction of new species, hurriedly wrote up his own ideas, publishing *The Origin of the Species* in his 50th year. **Adam Smith** published his famous *Wealth of Nations* at 53, after over a decade of work.

Despite a famously intensive education, and the publication of a major work of philosophy in his thirties, **John Stuart Mill** did not produce his most famous work, *On Liberty,* until he was 53, and then with much help from his wife.

Immanuel Kant only became a professor of philosophy at 46, and even after this milestone there was a 'silent decade' in which he hardly published anything. Much of what he had written in his earlier books wasn't right, he realised, and he had to go through a long period of re-examination of his basic positions before arriving at what he thought was the truth. But in a burst of insight, at 57 he wrote the famous *Critique of Pure Reason* in a few months.

Contemporary philosopher **Mary Midgley** didn't publish her first book, *Beast and Man*, until she was 59. 'I wrote no books until I was a good 50,' she noted, 'and I'm jolly glad because I didn't know what I thought before then.' With her three sons growing up, she was finally able to devote her time to writing and speaking. **Murray Walker**, the English Formula 1 commentator, spent most of his working life in advertising, only becoming a full-time commentator in his fifties.

At 53, **Mary Whitehouse** was an unknown high-school teacher with a set of convictions about moral standards in the media. Her beliefs about what was acceptable for children to see on television before bedtime became a movement that she herself felt unprepared to lead, particularly in the face of derision and torrents of hate mail. But Whitehouse pressed on and had a significant influence in shaping Britain's broadcasting policy – and all this at a time when she might have been coasting towards retirement. Her prudery may have been out of step with the modern world, but even her detractors had to admit that she stood for something.

Taikichiro Mori grew up in pre-war Japan, and became an economics professor at Yokohama City University. When his father, a rice farmer, merchant and landlord died, Mori inherited two buildings in central Tokyo and at 55 launched himself on a second career as a property developer, replacing thousands of wooden structures with earthquake-resistant steel and glass buildings. When Mori died in 1993 he was the richest man in the world.

CHAPTER SEVEN:

THE 30-YEAR GOLDMINE

*How many, usually without intention,
save their best for last*

In 1992, an Australian miner who had been brought up in Egypt found himself back on home turf investigating an ilmenite and zircon deposit near Alexandria. Visiting the offices of the Egyptian geological survey one day, he noticed something intriguing on the wall: an ancient papyrus depicting the mines of the Pharaohs along the Red Sea Hills. It turned out to be the oldest geological map in the world.

Sami El-Raghy dropped everything and headed out to the desert south-west of Cairo along the Red Sea. Apart from an attempt by the British to mine the area a few decades before, it had been left largely untouched for over 2,000 years. The Egyptian government had stifled any attempt at foreign mining investment, and its own mining authorities believed the Pharaohs had exhausted the deposits.

In fact, El-Raghy's modern equipment revealed that the Pharaohs had only really scratched the surface. There were still vast gold reserves in the Eastern Desert. Having battled to convince the authorities, his company took out a 30-year lease on areas covering old mines, and in 2009, at its Sukari Project site, it again began bringing gold to the surface.

From one desert to another:

Alice Springs in the Australian Outback is one of the more isolated towns in the world, over 800 miles from the nearest capital city, Adelaide. One hundred and forty miles north-east of Alice is Alhalkere, a landscape of red earth, stunning rock formations and wild grasses that is the clan country of the Anmatyerre people. Here, probably around 1910, Emily Kame Kngwarreye was born.

For the first ten years of her life, Emily did not see a white man, or a horse, but within a few years she would be working on cattle stations and leading camel trains carrying supplies between settlements. When, in her mid-sixties, land rights were granted to her people, she moved off the pastoral properties into a settlement called Utopia, the name the cattlemen had given her ancestral lands.

She had painted on women's bodies and drawn in sand all her life, but a government-sponsored batik project allowed Emily to express herself in a new medium. She founded a women's art group, which a little later began working with canvas and acrylic paint. Her very first painting, *Emu Woman*, attracted attention, marking the beginning of an explosion of demand for her work for the remainder of her life. Emily's paintings were bought by museums around the world, and her *Earth's Creation* was the first work by an Aboriginal artist to fetch over $1 million. Until her death in 1996, she continued to live simply, sharing any earnings with her community. Close to 80 when she began painting, in her brief career she produced 3,000 works.

Kngwarreye is perhaps an extreme example of a late flowering life, but it tells us that the so-called 'sunset years' can actually be a dawn of power and creativity. Precisely because we are at a time in life when no-one expects much of us, we are free to truly be ourselves.

You may feel you have done your dash in life, dwelling on former glories. Perhaps you feel your mines of creativity and energy are spent. If so, remember the Red Sea gold deposits that the authorities 'knew' were mined out, yet were anything but. Perhaps you too have a potential 30-year goldmine in the waiting, a time in which to start a new career, follow your heart's desire to travel, intensely pursue lifelong hobbies or interests, or explore new dimensions of your life's work.

As I write, average life expectancy in rich countries is in the early eighties. But that is only the average. Once you enter your sixties you may well have another 30 years of productive life before you. You can take out a new 'lease' on your life, extracting raw material from the rich mine of your experience to create things that are remarkable and unique.

True to themselves

Born on Christmas Day 1908, Denis Charles Pratt was teased through his school years for his effeminacy, and in his twenties he changed his name to better reflect his outlandish camp behaviour and artistic sensibilities. As Quentin Crisp he studied journalism without graduating, took art classes, and for a time was a male prostitute in London's Soho.

After he tried and failed to enlist as a soldier in the British war effort, Crisp found work as a life model, an occupation that would provide his bread and butter for the next 30 years. The job's regularity caused him to remark that 'it was just like being a civil servant, except you were naked'. When he was 60, his autobiography, *The Naked Civil Servant*, filled with funny, sometimes outrageous stories, was published. It was well reviewed, but it took another seven years, when the book was made into a television series starring John Hurt, before he actually became famous. Crisp began doing sell-out one-man shows, and in 1981, when he was well into his seventies, he decided to emigrate to America. In New York he was invited to openings every night, famously living 'on a diet of champagne and peanuts'. He enjoyed his celebrity status for the next 18 years.

Crisp once remarked, 'It's no good running a pig farm badly for 30 years while saying, "Really, I was meant to be a ballet dancer." By then, pigs will be your style.' Through his long years as a life model, he was always trying to get noticed for his creative work and never willing to water down his personality. In his tribute to Crisp, 'An Englishman In New York', Sting sang 'It takes a man to suffer ignorance and smile/Be yourself no matter what they say.' Crisp himself once said, 'Ask yourself, if there was to be no blame, and if there was to be no praise, who would I be then?' More than most, he understood that it was never too late to become the person you truly are, and to have that truth recognised.

Staying in the theatrical realm, consider the case of Ronald Harwood. As a young man Harwood left South Africa for London to pursue a career in drama, and despite getting some acting work, his most consistent employment was as the dresser to stage legend Sir Donald Wolfit. Harwood shifted to writing and producing plays, and through the 1960s and 1970s experienced only moderate success. At one point he and his family were in danger of losing their house and he was unable to pay his children's school fees. But he kept working, and in his mid-forties had a success with *The Dresser*, a stage play and film based on his own experiences.

Major recognition, however, would have to wait another 20 years. At 68, Harwood's life changed when he won an Oscar for best adapted screenplay for *The Pianist* (2002), about a Polish Jewish musician who struggles to survive the destruction of the Warsaw ghetto in the Second World War. Today, though he could make a fortune if he moved to Hollywood, he is happier in his small flat in West London. Always attracted to stories in which people must make difficult choices to do what is right, his own career has been marked by unwillingness to compromise. Yet because of this, success when it came was all the more satisfying.

Assaying his long career, Harwood noted:

> 'The best thing about my life is that everything happened to me so late . . . No one wants to put you down when you have taken so long to get there.'

A late flowering and a comeback

We love to criticise, but hold back when it comes to the young and the old. The young are still learning, so we only want to encourage. The old . . . well, it doesn't really matter, does it? They might as well indulge themselves in the few years they have left . . .

This was exactly the attitude family and friends took of Rosalie Gascoigne as she entered her fifties and sixties.

Gascoigne grew up in the shadow of an older sister who seemed to be better than her at everything. When she was a young girl, her alcoholic father left the family home and didn't come back until she was a teenager. Along with her lack of confidence, she felt different to other children. She was never good at drawing or art, but liked making things and had a real affinity for the natural beauty of her native New Zealand.

Although not academic, her mother ensured she made it through university, and it was there she met her future husband Ben. He was a keen astronomer, and towards the end of his studies was offered a job at the Mt Stromlo Observatory just outside Canberra, the Australian capital. He took the job, the couple were soon married, and they began their life together in a new country.

Canberra was then a tiny city, a long way from Sydney or Melbourne, and Stromlo itself even more isolated. With her husband working most of the time, and two young children to care for, it was a lonely life. She took long walks in the bush, getting to know a different and less verdant landscape than the one she had grown up with, and learned how to dry and preserve wild flowers.

As the children grew up, Rosalie developed a real skill in making dried flower arrangements. Much more imaginative than the norm, they became popular for public and private events in Canberra. Rosalie took a course on Ikebana, the Japanese art of flower arranging, given by a Sydney expert. Her natural flair for the discipline was soon recognised, and a visiting master from Japan singled out her work for its artistry. The recognition was a liberating experience. 'It was the first time,' she recalls, 'I found out that I was good at anything.' She was now well into her forties.

One of her sons became a keen collector of contemporary art, and introduced her to a rising young curator, James Mollison (later the first director of the National Gallery of Australia). He took an interest in her, and she also became friends with a painter and art teacher, Michael Taylor. With their encouragement, she branched out beyond Ikebana and began making collages out of things collected on roadsides and farms.

While Gascoigne never actively looked for a 'career' in art, at the same time she knew her work was more than a pleasant pastime for a housewife. In her fifties she decided to leave flower arranging behind and concentrate full-time on her assemblages of found wood, metal and bone, so expressive of the Australian landscape. Though the word 'artist' seemed rather grand to her, she began to think of herself this way, and started having pieces in local art shows. In 1975, Taylor got her into a Sydney exhibition for 'young' emerging artists at Gallery A. She was the surprise star of the show, with critics noting her work was quite unlike anything else. The owners of the gallery offered her a solo show, her first, which was a complete success. This 'young', 'emerging' artist was now 58.

In the years following, there was tremendous demand for Gascoigne's work. She represented Australia at the Venice Biennale, the world's top contemporary art show, won various prizes, was collected by major institutions, and in 1994 was made a member of the Order of Australia.

In an interview for a national biography project, Gascoigne was asked about her route to success. In the world she had grown up in, she said, being 'artistic' for a woman meant doing a nice watercolour or decorating a Christmas tree. Anything more serious would be put away by the time their husband came home. So when Rosalie began to devote herself to her art completely, her husband was shocked at the level of her 'obsession', as he described it, forgetting that he himself was obsessed with his work.

When asked why it had taken her so long to become an artist, she replied that it could hardly have worked out another way. She had always assumed she would have children, and it was unthinkable she would not support her husband. In fact, she gave full acknowledgment to the fact that she was a 'kept woman': 'I've always been fed, and I've always been clothed. So I was free to do what I liked. And that's a great strength, because other people have to paint six more pictures that are blue, or something, because the school fees are due . . . They have to, you see, and I'm not compromised in any way. Nice clear vision.'

On the role of time in her work generally, Gascoigne reflects on the years she spent on Mt Stromlo: '. . . living

17 years in an isolated spot, without you even trying, it works on you, you know, it influences you. Everything you do influences you, but I think that really does. And it sorted it out for me.' As a New Zealander, she saw the plains and hills around Canberra with fresh eyes, and through countless walks and drives, got to know them as if they were friends. This would not have been possible if she had worked all week in a job and then allotted her Sundays to 'nature'.

On one hand then, Rosalie's housewife role was a straitjacket. But it also – particularly after the children started school – gave her large amounts of free time to develop her skills and way of seeing. She might have been 'trapped by circumstances', but they were circumstances that made her. She was asked: 'Do you regret those 50-odd years as a housewife?'

> 'Well, I have regretted them out loud to people.
> Oh, why didn't I have 30 good years under my
> belt, you see, for doing it. And they – some
> people have said to me quite comfortingly, well,
> your art probably wasn't legitimate 'til the time
> that you did it . . . And so your sort of art
> wouldn't be legitimate. And the thing that I've
> always found is that you – all your life you're
> computerising, whether you know it or not,
> you're forming yourself. You're building yourself
> up on your former selves. Everything that's
> happened to you, everybody you've met, every
> circumstance, makes you as you stand today, you

see. And so I think I did a lot of my thinking.
What I liked. I knew better what I liked than
most people who start off at 20, because they
sort through it, you see.'

Though she might have started out in art when much younger, her work would have lacked force and direction. It was only when she knew herself completely that she could become a vehicle for the expression of eternal truths. Having never been to art school, and having developed her vision in isolation, Gascoigne's work was different to anyone else's, and as she admits, the world likes the new.

When success did come, she was amazed by it, because without the usual skill base of a trained artist she had never felt confident as a capital 'A' artist. When she was asked if confidence was an essential ingredient in 'climbing the mountain' of artistic success, she replied that no, it wasn't – because she never had any. What she did have was *need*. 'You know there's something there, you don't know what it is, it's faceless. And you – well, I hate the expression "warts and all" – are going to be able to do it, you see, as long as you work hard enough.'

She reflects that 'one of the worst things' is unfulfilled potential. We have dormant seeds in us, and suddenly we can get a revelation, a ray of light hitting us in a field, Joan of Arc-style, about what it is we should be doing. 'And I think you have to sort of abandon yourself and . . . accept the fact that you can't do this and you can't do that . . . but you can do that.'

Her success provides the greatest irony: that 'the new' does not have to be the preserve of the young, who are busy imitating each other or some hero of theirs. The older person, in contrast, is usually clearer about who they are and what they can do, and their work (even if conscious of it or not, and even if not having actually embarked on their chosen field until later) may have taken a lifetime to evolve.

Gascoigne was asked what stopped her from finding out earlier 'what sort of animal she was'. She replied: 'I suppose you have silly ideas about what you are . . . You don't know yourself . . . it took me five decades to find, to sort myself out and what I really was, I think.'

Even if it takes most of your life to see it, Rosalie noted, 'There's some use in being born the way you are.'

The press writes about the 'ageing of society' as if it is some kind of calamity, when in fact it is one of the great things of our time. The extra decades we now have provide second, third, fourth or fifth chances to allow all of us a chance at greatness.

Johnny Cash made his name in the 1950s on the same label as Elvis Presley, Roy Orbison and Jerry Lee Lewis. His career dimmed in the 1960s, but was revived towards the end of that decade with his Folsom Prison recordings. He seemed irrelevant through much of the 1970s and 80s. Then, in 1993, the release of his *American Recordings* album at 61 gave Cash's career an extraordinary second wind. The three albums that followed it were also critically praised. As music journalist Mark Edwards noted, popular music is meant to be a young person's game, but 'Cash turned that idea on its head'. He observes:

> 'We accept that today's singers peak in their twenties, may perhaps sustain a reasonable level of creativity in their thirties, but then quickly fade into artistic relevance. Musicians in their sixties can churn out the old hits, like Mick Jagger, but they can't create anything new that matters. Cash blew that one out of the water . . . The work he did in his sixties was as strong as the work he did at the beginning of his career. If Cash could do it, why couldn't everyone else?'

Indeed, why can't we?

Final thoughts

Coco Chanel, who leapt onto the world fashion stage in her thirties, only to retire in her early fifties and then make a comeback in her sixties, once said:

> 'Youth is something very new: 20 years ago no one mentioned it.'

She meant that the modern world glorified youth at the same time as devaluing age and experience. Yet as the poet and humanitarian Samuel Ullman put it in his famous poem:

'Youth is not a time of life; it is a state of mind . . .

Nobody grows old merely by living a number of years. We grow old by deserting our ideals.

Years may wrinkle the skin, but to give up enthusiasm wrinkles the soul.'

If we accept that a human being is unique, then we must accept that they have a unique potential. To fulfil it is surely the one thing in life, apart from loving others, which we should ask of ourselves. It may seem like forever before this seed of potential can germinate, grow and bear fruit, but all it needs is the water of attention and some waiting.

The stories of Emily Kngwarreye, Ronald Harwood, Quentin Crisp and Rosalie Gascoigne remind us of Picasso's statement, 'I don't develop; I am.' For each, their flowering seemed such a long time in coming, but from the perspective of eternity it was, after all, just a blink.

More from the goldmine . . .

Benjamin Franklin was 70 when he helped draft the Declaration of Independence, and 78 when he invented the bifocal lens. **William Gladstone** did not become British Prime Minister until he was in his late fifties, and played a vital role in public life into his eighties. **Nelson Mandela** became President of South Africa at 76, and **Enrico Dandolo**, the great Venetian statesman, who also happened to be blind, only took up the position of Doge at 85, and was winning battles in his nineties.

William Steig was a cartoonist who provided hundreds of cartoons for *The New Yorker*. In his early sixties he wrote his first children's book, and in his eighties produced a picture book, *Shrek!* **J. R. R. Tolkien** wrote the first book in the *Lord of the Rings* trilogy when he was 62.

Laura Ingles Wilder became a columnist in her forties, but did not publish her first novel in the *Little House* series until her mid-sixties. **Elizabeth Jolley**, the celebrated English-born Australian writer, waited until she was almost 60 to publish her first.

Mary Wesley wrote her first work of adult fiction, *Jumping the Queue*, at 70.

Charles Perrault, the Frenchman who gave us the classic fairytales *Cinderella* and *Tom Thumb*, only had them published at 69. They came out not under his own name but that of his infant son, Perrault d'Armancourt. In his seventies, **Sir Henry Parkes** became the father of Australian federation. He also married his mistress and became a father.

Alexander Humbolt, the great German naturalist and traveller, did not go on his first expedition until he was 30, and only finished the last bit of *Kosmos*, his popular science work, at 90, a month before his death.

Joseph Farwell Glidden had long mulled over the question of how farmers could keep cattle within the bounds of their properties. In 1874, when he was 61, he received the patent for the first commercially available barbed wire.

Sir Christopher Wren, the architect of over 50 London churches including the great St Paul's, retired at 86. **Frank Lloyd Wright** was 91 when he finished designing the Guggenheim Museum in New York, and **IM Pei** (famous for his 'pyramide' at the Louvre Museum in Paris) enjoyed a long, almost unbroken record of architectural achievement from his early twenties until his nineties. At 91 he came out of retirement to design a new Islamic art museum in Qatar. Brazilian architect **Oscar Niemeyer**, now into his 100s, is still hard at work.

St Augustine of Hippo, founding father of the early Christian church, did not complete his magnum opus, *City of God*, until his 71st year.

Voltaire was 65 when he wrote *Candide*, and **Goethe** was 82 when he finished writing another classic of world literature, *Faust*.

Roget first published *Roget's Thesaurus* when he was 73, then kept on editing it until he was 90.

Mary Baker Eddy was not young when she wrote the classic *Science and Health*, but was 87, no less, when she launched the famous *Christian Science Monitor*.

Mary Somerville, who helped make science a popular subject in the Victorian era, was still writing influential textbooks in her late eighties.

Jared Diamond published his bestseller on how geography shapes civilisation, *Guns, Germs and Steel* at 60. At 66, **Samuel Huntington** penned his famous essay, 'The Clash of Civilizations'.

The legendary travel writer **Lesley Blanch**, who died in 2010, continued writing into her 100s. **Nirad Chaudhari** wrote his *Autobiography of an Unknown Indian* at 50, and half a century later (at 99) published the sequel, *Thy Hand, Great Anarch*.

As the climax to a successful career as a plastic surgeon, **Maxwell Maltz** wrote his self-improvement classic, *Psycho-Cybernetics*, at age 61, and became a popular lecturer.

Linus Pauling published more scientific papers between the ages of 70 and 90 than he did between 50 and 70.

The management guru **Peter Drucker** liked to say he did his best work in his thirties and forties, but he remained in high demand until his death in 2005 at the age of 94.

Falstaff, arguably **Guiseppi Verdi**'s best opera, was written when he was 80. He admitted that he had been in pursuit of perfection all of his life, and wanted to give it one more try.

Michelangelo was still doing frescoes in the Vatican at 89, and Homer wrote *The Odyssey* as a blind old man.

Louis Armstrong had to wait until he was 66 to have his defining hit, 'What A Wonderful World'.

Artist **Louise Bourgeois** had a huge installation in the Tate Modern Museum in London at 88, and enjoyed a retrospective of her work there at 96.

CHAPTER EIGHT:

THE BEAUTY
OF PEOPLE

*How background shapes us, but only to
a certain point*

Why are people joyful when a baby is born? The endless
chores and loss of free time that come with raising a child
is no cause for celebration. Studies show that, partly because
of the great sacrifices child-raising involves, parents are no
happier than single people. Perhaps, then, it is the prospect
of creating our own family, with pleasant images of kitchen-
table laughter, birthdays, holidays and a general sense of
togetherness filling our minds.

But there is something larger that invokes hope and happiness, which goes beyond what we can get *out* of the experience.
Every birth is a new beginning, bringing a new power into the
world to increase the store of love or make things better. Ask
any modern parent what they want for their child, and they
are likely to say 'For them to be happy'. But dig a bit deeper,
and you will find most want their son or daughter to have *an
effect*, to contribute something real in the public realm.

Saint Augustine famously stated, '*Initium ut esset homo*

creatus est' – 'That a beginning was made, man was created.'
Inspired by this, the philosopher Hannah Arendt wrote:

> 'It is in the nature of beginning that something
> new is started which cannot be expected from
> whatever may have happened before . . . The
> new always happens against the overwhelming
> odds of statistical laws and their probability,
> which for all practical, everyday purposes
> amounts to certainty; the new therefore always
> appears in the guise of a miracle. The fact that
> man is capable of action means that the
> unexpected can be expected from him, that he is
> able to perform what is infinitely improbable.
> And this again is possible only because each
> man is unique, so that with each birth
> something uniquely new comes into the world.'

Being born is a miracle in itself, but the real glory is in the
way we confirm our identity through our words and deeds.
While animals can only behave according to their programmed
survival instincts and impulses, human beings can *act*, going
beyond our own selfish biological needs to bring something
new into being whose value may be recognised by others
in a social and public way. Like Socrates drinking hemlock
by his choice, or someone who gives their life for another,
we can even act *against* our very survival instinct. And because
of this ability to make truly free decisions, our deeds are
never quite predictable.

Tales of the unexpected

At 50, Joanne Herring was a Texan socialite known for her pampered lifestyle, lavish parties and a stint as a talk show host. Her second husband was an oil tycoon who in the 1980s had dealings with the Pakistani government, which led her to befriend Zia-ul-Haq, head of the country's military junta. He told her about the Soviet Union's incursions into neighbouring Afghanistan and the atrocities being committed on villagers. On an undercover trip across the border, Herring witnessed these for herself, and it changed her life. At the time, the United States government was not overly concerned about the situation, but Herring returned home resolved to do something about it.

After her husband died, Herring struck up a relationship with Charles Wilson, a congressman known as 'Goodtime Charlie' for his drinking and womanising, who was also a member of a House arms appropriations committee. Herring convinced him to visit a refugee camp of displaced Afghans, which had a similarly life-changing effect on the debonair, late-forties Wilson. Over the next few years he obtained funding for arms for the Afghan rebels, who eventually drove the Soviets out in humiliating fashion. Thus, a socialite and a playboy politician became instrumental in changing the course of history. Their extraordinary story became a Hollywood film, *Charlie Wilson's War*, with Tom Hanks as Wilson.

If people such as this can, so unexpectedly, become instruments of change, why is it so unlikely that you or me can do something similar? There is nothing in the 'average' person that precludes them from doing something remarkable; as Arendt noted, the natural domain of human beings is the 'infinitely improbable'.

The idea of unexpectedness being the very essence of humanity goes against the 'smart' view that people are really just the result of their environments and the times they live in. This view says that there are no really great people, only lucky circumstances which allow a person to flourish.

In the pages ahead we will examine such an outlook by looking at the lives of two people, both successes in business. Does it turn out that they were simply the result of luck and things given? And is the idea of the self-made person a myth?

A remarkable second life

'I was convinced the best was ahead of me'

The denizens of places like Chicago often dream of moving to warmer climes. Often near the top of polls of America's most desirable cities to live, San Diego's amazing climate sees virtually year-round sunshine, yet thanks to gentle sea breezes it never gets too hot. With great beaches, pleasant suburbs, proximity to the hub of Los Angeles and great food (Mexico is just over the border), you have a recipe for high quality of life.

Such things, including the purchase of the local baseball team, the Padres, drew a wealthy couple to move there in 1974.

In the early 1950s, Joni Smith had been a young mother

earning some extra money playing organ in a St Paul, Minnesota, restaurant. Dining one night was a middle-aged businessman. There was an instant attraction and they got talking, but both were married. For a time they kept in close touch, but she was not willing to leave her husband, and there was a period of five years when they had no contact at all.

In the late 1960s, a conference reunited them. Both realised each was the love of their lives, and for the next 15 years they were together, becoming prominent members of San Diego's social and business scene. She was the daughter of a railway worker who had lost his job in the Depression, and he was a descendant of Bohemian peasants who had built a life in Chicago. Though comparatively late in life, in every sense they had found their place in the sun.

When Joni's husband died in 1984, for a few years she continued to manage the baseball team. Then, in the 1990s, she began to give money away. Passionately anti-war, she funded peace institutes at the Universities of Notre Dame and San Diego, and gave generously to nuclear disarmament causes. She built hospices, animal shelters, centres for the homeless and alcoholics, sponsored Aids research and opened her chequebook for disaster relief. Often going to some lengths to keep her donations secret, in 1997 she disbursed $15 million to thousands of Minnesota flood victims. A year later she gave over $80 million for a new 12-acre community centre in the Rolando district of San Diego run by the Salvation Army. Complete with ice rink, swimming pools, gym, meeting rooms, library, computer facilities, theatre and a performing arts school, the complex gave local people opportunities for leisure and culture they may not otherwise have had, and its success stayed in her mind.

Fifteen years later, when Joni died, the bulk of her estate went to the Salvation Army. At $1.5 billion, it was the largest donation to a single charity in American history. The money was earmarked for 30 community centres in cities across the country modelled on the one in San Diego. They are now nearly all completed. Her will also left $200 million to the non-profit National Public Radio network, by far its largest ever bequest, because she had admired its coverage of the first Iraq War.

Joni was 41 when she married her second husband, who was 26 years her senior. By this point she had already made a success of her life as a mother of three daughters, and had run a successful food franchise with her previous husband. But her true flowering came in her sixties and seventies, when she had the chance to radically improve the lives of many people through her donations. But where did that money come from?

The man that Joni met that night in the restaurant was then a milkshake machine distributor who, a few years later, would found the McDonald's company. His name was Ray Kroc.

The Kroc story is often recounted by motivational authors and business professors to show how one person can create a huge, successful company from scratch and change the face of an industry. In a foreword to Kroc's 1977 autobiography, *Grinding It Out*, one such professor described Kroc as 'a flesh-and-blood example of a Horatio Alger story' whose career was 'a dramatic refutation of all who believe risk-takers will no longer be properly rewarded'. His success '. . . reminds us that opportunity abounds, that all one needs is the knack of seizing the chances that exist, of being in the right place at the right time. A little bit of luck helps, yes, but the key element, which too many in our affluent society have forgotten, is hard work . . .'

Of course, you could debate for years (depending on your eating habits and political views) whether the McDonald's company is one of the great beacons of the modern age . . . or not. For the purposes of this chapter, however, your personal views don't really matter. Here, we look at Kroc's life merely as a generic study in achievement, and to help us answer a question that is important to all of us: is the conventional view of success, of the heroic, self-made individual who bends the world to their will, actually correct? Or was Kroc just a lucky product of his background and times?

In 2008, Malcolm Gladwell turned his attention to this question with *Outliers: The Story of Success*. Any philosophy worth its salt will cut through clichés and lazy misconceptions, and the book did just this, seemingly overturning a century or more of comfortable propaganda about the 'self-made' individual. The ethos had led us to buy hundreds of millions of motivational books and tickets to seminars, but in our keenness for personal advancement, had we ever stopped to really see whether any of it was true? After putting under the microscope the idea that success is about the triumph of the individual over circumstances, Gladwell found the opposite to be true:

> 'Successful people don't do it alone. Where they come from matters. They're products of particular places and environments.'

For Gladwell, much of the success ascribed to an individual – and that they ascribe to themselves – is in fact the result of a succession of opportunities created by others, and which they simply had the wit to seize. Not only are successful people likely to have had more resources from an early age for education or coaching, but they often enjoy the great advantages of having loving, attentive parents who teach valuable social skills and the drive to get ahead. Beyond the parental influence are cultural legacies ingrained by ancestors or national heritage, such as a predisposition to hard work (if you are Chinese, for instance, you are likely to have inherited an industrious attitude forged by thousands of years of rice farming, a form of agriculture which requires constant attention and care), or subservience to authority figures, or openness to innovation and risk.

Luck, Gladwell says, also plays a much bigger part in success or failure than we like to think. A person who comes of age just as a long economic depression descends, for instance, is never going to have the same chances as someone entering the workforce at the beginning of an era of prosperity. A child born in the midst of a baby boom will have to fight harder for places in good schools and universities than a compatriot born only a decade later or earlier. Gladwell concludes that, '. . . success arises out of a steady accumulation of advantages', the result of a lucky combination of family, culture, time and community.

Yet if he is right, his theory should apply even to exemplars of the individualistic, self-made ethos like Ray Kroc. Beyond the hype, does Kroc turn out to be simply a result of positive circumstances outside his control, more product than protagonist? We touched on this question in an earlier chapter with the example of Larry Ellison, but let's use Kroc's life to go deeper into it.

Sources of success

Kroc was not particularly distinguished as a boy; in fact he was constantly excelled by his brother Bob. Ray loved sports, and his parents Louis and Rose and the other kids tended to think he was a dreamer, always getting excited about some scheme or other. But as other boys loved play, Ray remembers actually enjoying working, including helping his mother around the house, and all through school he had various jobs. His Uncle Earl ran a soda fountain in a drugstore, and for a while he helped out, discovering, he later recalled, '. . . that you could influence people with a smile and enthusiasm and sell them a sundae when what they'd come in for was a cup of coffee.' This 'smile and sell' ethos sowed a seed in his mind that would flower decades later.

Ray showed an early interest in business, and his parents did not stand in his way when, while still in school, he started up a small sheet music shop with two friends. It did alright, but was wound up after a few months. His mother was a keen piano player and encouraged her son to learn. His skill at it would come in handy later when, as a young salesman, he played piano at nights to bring in extra money. Kroc therefore had reasonably supportive and loving parents who wanted him to do well. Confirming the Gladwell thesis, he already had something of a head start on less fortunate boys of his era.

Let's look at another possible source of Ray's later success: cultural legacy. These are the first words Kroc writes in his autobiography:

> 'I have always believed that each man makes his
> own happiness and is responsible for his own
> problems. It is a simple philosophy. I think it
> must have been passed along to me in the
> peasant bones of my Bohemian ancestors.'

Around the time of his birth in Chicago in 1902, the city had become, behind Prague and Vienna, the third-largest Czech city in the world. In the 1860s and 1870s, there had been waves of immigration there from Bohemia, then part of the Austro-Hungarian empire (now the Czech Republic), even creating a neighbourhood called 'Prague'. But unlike, say, European Jews who settled in New York with marketable skills such as garment making and jewellery, the Bohemian immigrants to Chicago were largely unskilled and uneducated, earning less than most of the other ethnic groups in the city. They had no particular fondness for risk or innovation, and their muscle was put to use in the lumber industry.

As time passed, though, prosperity saw many Czechs move out to suburbs like Cicero and Oak Park, where Ray was raised. His mother ran a well-organised, neat and clean house, and he remembers his grandmother being so worried about dirt that most of the week her kitchen floors were covered in newspaper. On Saturday, she would take the newspapers up and scrub the floor underneath with hot soapy water – a floor that had barely been touched. 'That was the old way Grandma had brought from Bohemia,' Kroc recalls, 'and she was not about to change.'

Given his later messianic attention to hygiene, this family attention to cleanliness clearly rubbed off on Kroc. A major reason for the early success of McDonald's was its shining kitchens and spotless car parks – such a contrast to the grimy reputation of burger bars and drive-ins of the 1940s and 1950s. Indeed, years after the restaurant chain had become a national success, Kroc could still be found mopping the floor of a franchise he was visiting to demonstrate just how elemental hygiene was to its success.

One of Gladwell's claims is that there are lucky and unlucky generations, with demographic factors like birth rate, wars and depressions all determining the chances an individual will get. Did Kroc belong to a lucky generation?

Because he was born in 1902, he missed the 1890s economic depression; and because he was too young to fight in the First World War (he signed up as a Red Cross ambulance driver, but the war ended before he was due to ship out), he avoided a major conflict. Finally, he came of age in the 1920s, boom years in America. In these respects then, he was lucky.

Ray Kroc's excellent life chances were in contrast to his father's and grandfather's. His grandpa had escaped poverty in Bohemia to find things almost as tough in America, but had managed to build a house and support his family. His son Louis (Kroc's father), however, never went to high school, and at 13 was working at Western Union, then a telegraph company, where he stayed a conscientious lifelong employee.

So Kroc's story seems to prove correct everything Gladwell says about people being, more than we like to admit, a product of history, culture, time and place. On several counts – cleanliness, order, hard work and personal responsibility – Kroc himself takes his hat off to characteristics of his family and culture that helped make him what he was. And by simply being born at the start of the 20th century, he was already much better off than his father and grandfather.

But recall Gladwell's idea that remarkable people were given remarkable opportunities. Were Kroc's chances really *remarkable*?

In fact, the opportunities presented to him were no greater than millions of other boys of his age growing up in early 20th-century America. Ray's parents were neither rich nor poor, and though they were encouraging, did not try to push their sons to be way ahead of their peers. Kroc's early business and retail experiences would certainly come in handy as an adult, but again they were in no way exceptional. Millions of other American boys of his time were also the progeny of cultures with an affinity for keeping things clean and orderly, and with a devotion to hard work. Could these really be held up as a decisive factor in their adult achievements? The most noticeable feature of Kroc's childhood and teenage years is their *normality*. Ray may have had plenty more opportunities than his forebears, but compared to the rest of his own generation, they were not markedly superior.

Let's continue with his story.

After leaving school at 17, Kroc was keen to earn money, so began selling ribbons door to door and making extra cash through playing the piano at summer resorts. At one of these he met Ethel, and they were keen to marry. However, his father insisted that he get a 'proper' job if he was to do so. Ray found a position as a salesman for the Lily-Tulip paper cup company. Paper cups were a relatively new thing in the 1920s, and he was keen to prove himself in the job. He was soon earning $35 a week, quite a good wage, but to help support his wife and baby daughter Marilyn he also began playing piano in nightclubs.

While the idea of selling paper cups would have put many people to sleep, Kroc was fired up. 'The ten years between 1927 and 1937,' he later noted, 'were a decade of destiny for the paper cup industry.' Such a grand phrase for a pedestrian product gives a good indication of his intensity and enthusiasm for his work, and perhaps unsurprisingly he prospered even through the Depression.

Kroc would stay with Lily-Tulip for 17 years, working his way up to becoming a sales executive. By the time he left the company he was selling five million cups a year to one account alone, the drugstore chain Walgreen's. But in the late 1930s, Ray's imagination began to move away from paper cups; he had discovered the Multimixer, a machine that made it easy for store owners to make several milkshakes at a time. Seeing unlimited potential, he wanted to branch off to become the exclusive agent for the machines, effectively becoming his own boss. But there was a problem. Believing the move would risk the family's livelihood and future, Ethel insisted that he stay with Lily-Tulip. They had a nice home in a Chicago suburb, were living the American dream. Why risk it? In one domestic contretemps, she said, disbelievingly: 'You are 35 years old, and you are going to start all over again as if you were 20?'

Ray tried to persuade her to get behind him and become involved, perhaps doing the paperwork for the fledgling operation, but still she said no. Given the importance of his work to him, her refusal felt like a betrayal.

'If you believe in something,' he noted, 'you've got to be in it to the ends of your toes. Taking reasonable risks is part of the challenge. It's the fun.' Despite the pressure at home, Kroc went ahead and struck an agreement to be the national agent for the Multimixer.

It was not easy in the early years. He had built up debt to go into the new venture and had to work day and night to pay it off. But it was a good product, and gradually, over several years, he moved into the black, selling it to large chains like Tastee-Freez and Dairy Queen. By the time he was 50, Kroc was making around $25,000 a year (or over $200,000 in today's money).

Ray could afford to coast, and began to play more golf. But he was restless. He had heard about an operation using his machines that was run by two brothers in San Bernardino, on the edge of the Mojave Desert 50 miles from Los Angeles. The Multimixers could make five shakes at a time, so most drugstores or dairy-bar operators only needed one. The San

Bernardino people were using *eight*. Curious to see what was going on, in 1954 he flew out to California to visit.

What he discovered amazed him: in contrast to the usual greasy spoon cafes or drive-in eateries with carhops that made you wait for a hamburger of varying quality, Mac and Dick McDonald were providing cheap (15 cent) but high-grade hamburgers within *30 seconds*, in a building and parking lot kept scrupulously clean. And unlike most fast food outlets of the time, it was not a teen hangout but actually attracted families. The brothers had established a perfect delivery system for the food, combining speed and freshness based on a revolutionarily small menu. Their French fries were so good that people came back for them alone. The sheer number of customers meant lots of milkshakes too, hence the need for all those Multimixers.

That night in his motel room, Kroc had visions of McDonald's restaurants dotted across America, each one of them requiring several of his machines. As the national distributor, the financial potential was mind-boggling. The next day, he drove from his motel to see the brothers again, and sitting down after the lunch-hour rush put to them the idea that they should open more restaurants around the country.

The idea was greeted with stony silence. The brothers were happy with things the way they were, they said. They had just built a nice home overlooking the city, each had new Cadillacs and were making $100,000 a year *profit*. They didn't want more worries. Anyway, said Dick, 'Who could we get to open them for us?'

At this point a light turned on in Kroc's mind. When

he leaned forward, he heard himself say: 'Well, what about me?'

All of his work experiences had readied him for this moment. The years selling paper cups had provided the selling skills and market knowledge to start his enterprise as the chief agent for Multimixers, and this in turn had led him to the McDonald brothers.

The brothers relented, and the trio made an agreement that allowed Ray to copy the brothers' system and design (complete with the golden arches making an 'M' over the building) and open outlets elsewhere.

In April 1955, Kroc opened his first McDonald's outlet close to his home turf in Des Plaines, a suburb of Chicago. It wasn't a wild success, but it was a start. As more outlets opened, the key to the company's success emerged: a franchise system which effectively made the corporation into a property developer, buying each site and leasing it to the franchisee.

By the end of 1957 there were 37 McDonald's restaurants in operation, all of them essentially serving counters in the middle of parking lots (there were no restaurants with inside seating until 1966). The detailed knowledge Kroc had built up over 30 years of the geography and demographics of towns and cities across America from selling paper cups and mixers would ensure that the choice of locations for new McDonald's stores was invariably wise, and over the next ten years the company experienced explosive growth, emerging as the behemoth we know today.

However, as the Gladwell theory gives so much emphasis to luck, we should be open to the idea that Kroc was simply lucky in starting the McDonald's corporation when he did, in the early years of a massive change in American eating habits. Many of the chains still around today began in the 1950s: Jack in the Box and Taco Bell in 1951, Denny's in 1953, Burger King in 1954, McDonald's itself in 1955, and Pizza Hut in 1958. With post-war prosperity (wages went up 30 per cent in the 1950s, with greater disposable income), the average family could afford to eat out, even if it was hardly 'dining', sitting in your car in a parking lot. Also, America was at the start of a baby boom and an accompanying move to the suburbs. The single-owner drugstores and cafes of town and city centres began to go bust as their customers moved away. In their place grew up the restaurant chains we know today on arterial roads that ran through endless suburbs.

Of course, Kroc and the other early McDonald's staffers would work extraordinarily hard in its first ten years to make sure it took advantage of every opportunity to become the dominant chain, but given the above factors it would be easy to say that luck played the biggest part, that Kroc had simply climbed onto the top of a rocket just about to take off.

An argument could also be made that Kroc received unusually good breaks in his career leading up to McDonald's. In his twenties and thirties, he certainly notched up 10,000 hours (which Gladwell says is the 'magic number of greatness') of skill development as a salesman, getting constant feedback on the success or otherwise of his abilities from customers and from his sales figures. This experience was vital for what was to come. And yet . . . there were millions of other salespeople criss-crossing America at the time, learning the same lessons, getting the same level of feedback, and having similar successes. How exactly was Kroc different?

If he began to stand out, surely it was through the seizing of opportunities that he spotted, that were of his own making. Nothing was 'given'.

How old was Kroc when he began the McDonald's we know today? As he tells it in his autobiography:

> 'People have marveled at the fact that I didn't
> start McDonald's until I was 52 years old, and
> then I became a success overnight. But I was just
> like a lot of show business personalities who
> work away quietly at their craft for years, and
> then, suddenly, they get the right break and
> make it big. I was an overnight success all right,
> but 30 years is a long, long night.'

Having only found his winning groove at 52, Kroc could hardly be classed as one of Gladwell's 'outliers'. If he eventually made himself statistically separate from the rest of the American population (by becoming, in today's money, a billionaire), it was through decades of refinement of his knowledge, skills, contacts and intuition.

Other developed traits stand out. The first is *openness to opportunity*. As he entered his sixth decade, Kroc was indeed like thousands of other successful salesman of a similar age, but there was one crucial difference: his unusual view of the second part of his life. Throughout his long career in sales he was always alert to new opportunities, and like Colonel

Sanders, another school dropout turned salesman, always believed that his life to date was simply an apprenticeship to something really great. He recalls his mindset at age 50:

> 'I was a battle-scarred veteran of the business
> wars, but I was still eager to go into action . . .
> I had diabetes and incipient arthritis. I had lost
> my gall bladder and most of my thyroid gland
> in earlier campaigns. But I was convinced the
> best was ahead of me.'

You could also argue there was nothing remarkable about Kroc's decision to fly out from Chicago to visit the first McDonald's operation. In the same year, Keith Cramer, who owned a carhop restaurant in Florida, also paid a visit, and was inspired to open Insta Burger King (later Burger King). Also, about this time the original McDonald's store made it on to the cover of *American Restaurant*, causing plenty of people in the industry to take notice. Therefore, it is not as if Kroc could be given great credit for 'discovering' it. Moreover, the McDonald brothers had in fact licensed their 'Speedee Service System' to a few other franchisees, some of which had also copied elements of the San Bernardino store, including the golden arches.

But for Kroc, these were all half-hearted steps. In his mind he could see hundreds of McDonald's stores dotting every state around the nation. It seemed obvious to him, and in the fact that the brothers were basically uninterested in the franchising side, and were doing it badly, was his golden opportunity to be the franchise operator for the whole country. In his classic management text *Innovation and Entrepreneurship*, Peter Drucker talks about the 'unexpected success' in business, and how often people fail to properly appreciate it and exploit it. Kroc had no such problem, seeing immediately the potential before him. In fact, he knew that the key to success was to copy the McDonald brothers' operation *exactly*.

It could be said that if Kroc had not seized the day and made an agreement with the McDonald brothers, chances are someone else would have. But *he* did it, and he did it *then*. A younger person might have been less sure of their judgement, or not had sufficient funds to make the commitment; someone older might not have had the stomach for the challenges ahead. But at 52, believing that 'the best was ahead of him', Kroc acted.

On the subject of opportunity, Gladwell only writes of those opportunities seized, ignoring the majority *not* taken. He is happy to admit the role of luck and then hard work to make something happen, but underplays the role of old-fashioned virtues like curiosity and courage. Yet in relation to Kroc, surely the central factor in his success is *willingness to risk*.

When he was 16 or 17, Western Union offered Kroc's father Louis a promotion that required the family to move to New York. With a settled life in Chicago, his wife Rose wasn't keen, but gave in. Perhaps predictably, she didn't like it and after only a year or so prevailed upon her husband. They moved back to Chicago.

Twenty years later, Louis' son Ray, now a husband and father himself, finds himself in a similar position. Having spent over a decade and a half with the one company, he sees an opportunity and wants to branch out on his own as the Multimixer distributor. At this point he is 35. Recall, though, that Kroc is unprepared for the views of his wife Ethel, who cannot believe that Ray is *going to start all over again as if he was 20*. Let's be clear about the 'Ethel' and the 'Ray' views of life:

Ethel	Ray
Stick with your employer.	There's more potential if I go out on my own.
Let's not blow what we've created.	Taking reasonable risks is part of life.
You're too old to start all over again.	I'm just warming up; the best is ahead of me.

Ethel thinks Ray is too old *at 35* to be starting something new, and with such divergent views on what is appropriate at a certain 'stage in life', it is no surprise they later part. If they *had* stayed together, she would have been shocked when, now in his fifties and with his array of ailments, he decided to take the biggest risk of his life – McDonald's.

Willingness to take intelligent risks is surely the crucial difference between the career of Louis Kroc and his son Ray. You could argue that Louis Kroc came of age at a time when it was enough just to have a job – you didn't want to go out on your own, particularly with a family to support. But

Ray also had a family – and took risks anyway. One man gave into pressure from his spouse, and shrunk back. The other did not, and the rest is history.

It is understandable when people choose security, even it is illusory, but let's be clear on its effects. Ray never wanted to be hemmed in, and there was certainly an element of the dreamer about him. Maybe he was lucky in some respects, but the fact is that he acted without safety netting.

Gladwell's environment-causing theory of success also takes little account of *passion*.

Kroc's big epiphany came in the form of a French fry. From the first day he visited the McDonald brothers, he noticed that they lavished attention on the making of their fries, including a long curing process in which thousands of Idaho Russetts were stored in chicken wire bins open to the outside air before they were cooked. As the fries were easily the best he had tasted, and were a big part of the restaurant's success, not to mention vital to its profitability (as they are today), Kroc went to great lengths to replicate the process in the new stores. 'The French fry would become almost sacrosanct for me,' he recalled, 'its preparation a ritual to be followed religiously.' Having found his mission late in life, Kroc would carry it out with the passion of a born-again, and thereafter often speak of McDonald's – only partly in jest – as if it was his religion. Franchisees had to demonstrate absolute loyalty, could not operate any other restaurants, and were often offered their first franchise a long way from where they lived, thus testing their 'faith' and commitment.

Thus, the humble French fry was the door that Kroc walked through to another life. You can draw a direct line back from the millions that Joan B. Kroc (to give her her full title) lavished on peace institutes, disaster victims and the Salvation Army, to her husband's obsession with the perfect fry. You may laugh, but the message is clear: follow whatever you are mesmerised by, even if to others it seems superficial or a waste of time, because when properly developed, it can bring meaning, purpose and money into your life in degrees never imagined.

The nature of productive obsessions is that they come from nowhere. Despite often being the point on which a whole life can turn, they are a gift, a mystery which we can either dismiss or use.

What are you so excited about that it sometimes stops you from sleeping? What can you spend hours thinking about or looking at that others see as a trivial waste of time? What is obvious to you, that isn't to others? What insights has your career given you that others may not have? History is full of surprising passions that lead to remarkable new products or standards. Your passion can be made universal.

The myths of luck and inevitability

History has a way of making things seem inevitable. We are more likely to marvel at the scale of someone's philanthropic giving than at the story of how it became possible. When remarkable things happen, in hindsight it always seems obvious that they would, yet life is not lived in hindsight, and real success is never inevitable. Who today, enjoying a swim in a Kroc Center pool, or being inspired by a lecture at a Kroc peace institute, will give thanks that it is the result of decisions taken in a person's life decades before – points at which they might have gone the opposite way, or done nothing?

'Whenever you see a successful business,' Peter Drucker once said, 'someone made a courageous decision.' It is too easy to forget, when looking at a corporate giant like McDonald's, that it began with a *person*. Moreover, every significant organisation or enterprise can be traced back to very specific 'inflection points' – points where something can go either way, up or down – in that person's life.

To come back to our original argument, Gladwell's theory of success could never predict the achievements of people like Kroc for a very good reason: people act unexpectedly. An interest or passion suddenly grabs them; they risk all to uncover a mystery or fulfil a potential. The odds of them taking a particular path might seem high, but they are only odds. Many people *are* mere products, never examining themselves or their reason for being. What undermines the environment-causing theory of success is that at certain points in a person's life they can move beyond this. The hole in his theory is *people* themselves.

Gladwell's success philosophy fails in another crucial respect: its preoccupation with youth. According to Gladwell, our most important opportunities come early in life, thanks to the family or school environment we find ourselves in. The danger of this is an acceptance that, because you didn't get great early opportunities, and then build on them in your twenties, you are destined to be an also-ran. While it is true that early chances can make a big difference to a person's later success, it is not as if opportunities dry up after you turn 25. Fortunately, most adults, as Kroc did, can take the longer view and settle into their own rate and pattern of achievement.

When, in his teens, Kroc was in basic training to be an ambulance driver, there was another boy in his company, also from Chicago. Though they were never actually friends, both would come to have a massive effect on America's cultural and commercial landscape. While Ray was out trying to chat up girls in local bars, his fellow Chicagoan stayed in the base doodling and drawing. The difference was that Walt Disney would become famous while still in his twenties, while Kroc would have to wait another 30 years for similar renown. Did it irk him to see a contemporary achieve so much fame and fortune while he slowly carved out a career selling paper cups and milk-shake makers? Perhaps; he doesn't say either way in his autobiography. But the important thing is that he did not give in to thoughts such as 'I will never reach the heights of Disney, so I'll settle for a good deal less'. Instead, his view was – even at 50 – 'I still have arrows in my basket; the best is yet to come.'

The older you get, the less you become a product of your upbringing or simple luck, and the more you become the result of your *own previous decisions*. While the chances we get in childhood or adolescence are largely given to us, the older we are the more likely it is that opportunities arise because of previous efforts. If the super-successful Kroc of his mid-fifties was a 'product' of anything, it was thousands of small decisions made daily over several decades to remain disciplined, focused and on the lookout for opportunities. He was specifically the 'product' of two large decisions (going out on his own with Multimixers, and taking on the franchising of McDonald's).

In saying, 'Successful people don't do it alone. Where they come from matters. They're products of particular places and environments', Gladwell is right in elevating cultural legacy to an important role in our lives. Our genes, quality of upbringing, educational opportunities and the country we are born in *are* all important. And yet, to describe a human being as a 'product', while barely mentioning free will, volition or decision, shortchanges us.

Gladwell would argue that the very things that Kroc lacked (wealth, recognition, an enterprise of his own) drove him on to be a success. Yet such deficiencies did not *create* his success, nor did it *determine* that he would be ambitious. As Kroc himself notes, his family circumstances and native abilities certainly played a substantial part in what he became, but he still willed it to happen.

Having told us at length that we are essentially products of our environments, deep in his book Gladwell comes to a surprising conclusion. He gives the example of Jewish law graduates in New York who, because they were turned away from the Establishment law firms in the 1950s had to start their own (such as Joseph Flom, who helped build the famous Skadden, Arps, Slate, Meagher & Flom). To survive, they had to take on any work that was out there and that the traditional firms found distasteful, like corporate takeovers. But in time this setback would prove a great opportunity in disguise, when the massive growth in these areas made them well placed to take advantage and prosper. 'They learned,' Gladwell writes, that '. . . if you work hard enough and assert yourself, and use your mind and imagination, you can shape the world to your desires.'

Belatedly, Gladwell arrives at the truth of success, even if it is an inconvenient one: that background and circumstances matter a lot, and yet *determine nothing*. Ultimately success is, as we noted, a mystery, because it occurs through an individual mind. Our path to success may indeed involve a reaction against our poor/wealthy/suburban/rural/white/black background, but it is still *our* reaction. Moreover, it is difficult to make clear judgements about what are 'bad' (or good) circumstances. The seeds of opportunities can be found in even the worst situations, and success requires us to see any kind of personal background as simply raw material. While personal background and circumstances may set the scene, they can never dictate the story. One person may be given all the best opportunities and yet come to little, while another may be given similar chances and yet at certain points take personal or career risks that serve to take them to another level.

This fact was illustrated by Harvard University's land-mark longitudinal study of a group of its own students, the class of 1940. In the decades passing since graduation, the study has shown that most members of the class suffered various setbacks, just as you would expect. But as George Vaillant, a key interpreter of the data and author of *Aging Well: Surprising Guideposts to a Happier Life From the Landmark Harvard Study of Adult Development* (2003), has noted, it was not the obstacles themselves that ulti-mately determined success or failure, but rather the quality of the individual subjects' *response* to them, or what he calls 'adaptation to life'. And these responses could never be predicted.

Motivational speakers tell us to persevere, but success involves perseverance combined with experimentation; if something doesn't work, try something else. Agility of mind means you will find a way forward, and it is a way likely to be perfectly suited to you. The only way you will become a 'result' is if you see yourself that way.

The truth is, we don't ever really know which way a person will go, and the longer the life, the less justified is anyone in saying that a particular event or chance 'caused' their success or failure. Every human being has some scope for action, and can be counted on to do the unexpected. We are not Pavlovian dogs that simply respond to stimuli; we choose our reactions. This is the beauty of people. The environmental view may go some way to explaining achievement, but it can never fully explain it, since it leaves out of the equation that most human thing: the ability to surprise.

Something from nothing: Howard Schultz and the creation of Starbucks

The Kroc story would be echoed, to a striking degree, 40 years later in the creation of another enterprise. Bear with me while I tell it, because it suggests that many of the lessons from Kroc's story were not unique to him, but apply equally well to others (including you and me).

In the early 1980s, Howard Schultz was a successful sales

executive for the Swedish company Perstorp. Based in New York, he was the American manager of its stylish housewares and kitchen brand Hammarplast. These were good times for Schultz. In the same city in which he had grown up in a subsidised housing block, he and his wife had bought a trendy loft apartment, they had a new company car to play with at the weekends, and come Mondays he could remind himself that he had 20 sales reps answerable to him.

In Schultz's product line was a drip coffeemaker, and he was intrigued by the large orders for it coming from a small company in Seattle. Echoing Kroc's curiosity about the McDonald brothers, Schultz flew out to investigate, finding a four-store chain that roasted and sold its own ground coffee, and whose customers were particularly choosy about the brewing equipment they used. They loved the Hammarplast product sold in the stores.

At a time when filter coffee was king, the owners, Jerry Baldwin and Gordon Bowker, had started the business to give Seattle people access to real coffee, at a time when you had to drive hundreds of miles to San Francisco to buy it. It was difficult to walk past one of their stores without being enticed by the heady aromas of coffee, tea and wood and a sense of the exotic once you stepped over the threshold. When they had started it in 1971, the literature-loving men had come up with a unique name for their business. In Herman Melville's *Moby Dick*, the first mate on the *Pequod* was Starbuck, a name which they felt captured the romance of the seafaring coffee, tea and spice traders of old. As they couldn't imagine people stopping by 'Pequods' for their coffee, Starbucks it would be.

Like most Americans at that time, Schultz had only ever drunk filter coffee, but when Baldwin served him his first cup of real, whole bean ground coffee, he remembers, 'I felt as though I had discovered a whole new continent.' Just as Kroc had discovered a world of difference between a McDonald's French fry and everyone else's, so the liquid Schultz had drunk all his adult life now seemed a travesty, and from that moment on he was on a crusade for the real thing.

If San Bernardino became the Mt Sinai of the McDonald's movement, with the commandments for a perfect system, so Seattle, to use Schultz's own imagery, became his 'Mecca'. Just as Kroc knew he somehow had to be involved with McDonald's from the moment he saw it, on his flight back to New York Schultz wondered how he could become 'part of the magic' he had seen. It was 1982, and he was only a few months from turning 30. He was restless in his job, but was he really willing to give it all up for a small outfit on the other side of the country? His mother, echoing Ethel Kroc, said, 'You're doing well, you have a future. Don't give it up for a small company nobody's ever heard of.' Schultz, however, had begun to feel he wanted to chart his own destiny, in exactly the same way that Kroc had begun to tire of simply being an employee at Lily-Tulip.

Schultz spent a year trying to convince Jerry Baldwin that he could make a real contribution to the company, and was finally invited to have dinner with the three owners (one was a silent partner). After a confident articulation of his vision for Starbucks, he believed he had the position sewn up. Then came the bad news. They didn't want to expand Starbucks. It was 'too risky, too much change'.

Most people would have just accepted the decision, but by this point Schultz felt so committed to the company he didn't feel able to just walk away. After some further convincing and pestering, he was finally, begrudgingly, taken on. As the company's new marketing director, he was taking a big cut in his salary, but much more importantly in his mind, he had a small equity stake.

In the years following, Schultz wondered what his life would have been like if he had accepted the partners' original decision:

> 'Life is a series of near misses. But a lot of what
> we ascribe to luck is not luck at all. It's seizing
> the day and accepting responsibility for your
> future. It's seeing what other people don't see,
> and pursuing that vision, no matter who tells
> you not to.'

The point about 'seeing what other people don't see' could seem like Schultz is making himself out to be a business seer with a magic touch, but it's a lot less grand than that. He was simply intent on something which seemed *obvious* to him – expanding Starbucks, just as it seemed perfectly obvious to Kroc that the original McDonald's was a brilliant system that deserved to be writ large across America.

Kroc felt that all his working life had prepared him for McDonald's; Schultz felt the same about Starbucks. *Doing what seems obvious to you* is a vitally important point in the success equation, and the vision each had for these places seemed absolutely clear to them.

Schultz's colleagues wondered why he wanted to be part of an industry that, if not dying, wasn't growing either (from a peak of three cups a day in the early Sixties, per capita coffee drinking was on the way down). Ray Kroc experienced a similar reaction when he was trying to sign up the first McDonald's franchisees. Most of his friends, successful businessmen at his country club, thought he was mad getting into a business based on 15-cent hamburgers. Apart from the low status of the field, they just couldn't see how he could make money out of it.

The dissenting voices of friends and family are one thing, but when intelligent people who have succeeded in their careers also question you, it is difficult not to take notice. Then there is one's self to contend with. When he discovered Starbucks, Schultz admits, 'I wasn't bold enough to become an entrepreneur just yet.' Yes, moving from a corporation to be the marketing person of a four-store retailer would be a big change, but at the end of the day he was still going to be an employee. Similarly, recall that Kroc did not suddenly leap from being a company salesman to starting McDonald's. He had the intervening years as the Multimixer distributor, which turned out to be the perfect bridge between employee and full-blown entrepreneur.

To finish the Schultz story . . . In his first few months in the marketing job for Starbucks, he went to a coffee trade fair in Milan. A second epiphany awaited him. Seemingly on every corner he found busy, atmospheric cafes filled with conversation and beautiful aromas, all serving a drink he had never had in America: the caffe latte, a mixture of strong espresso coffee mixed with hot, frothy milk. At the time, Starbucks was simply a roaster and seller of ground coffee, but in Milan Schultz suddenly realised that it had to get into *serving* coffee.

Back in Seattle, his idea of opening cafes in the existing stores was dismissed as a crazy idea of the marketing guy. But eventually the owners allowed him to open a coffee bar in the corner of one store. Amazingly, even though it did very well, the owners did not want to expand the idea. They were 'not in the restaurant business', he was firmly told.

At this point, Schultz's frustration was akin to the parent who knows their child is capable of so much more, but for some reason isn't willing to seize the day. He could imagine millions of people across the country having a great daily experience in a Starbucks cafe, only the owners couldn't see, or weren't interested in, the same vision.

Reluctantly, he realised he may have to go out on his own. Such a step would not be taken lightly, and would be a much bigger leap of faith even than leaving Hammerplast. For almost a year Schultz pounded the Seattle sidewalks trying to find investors for an Italian-style cafe. Of 242 people he approached, 217 gave him an outright 'No'. Many wondered why he was bothering with coffee when all the money was in technology start-ups. Eventually, he raised enough cash to open his cafe, Il Giornale in the business district of Seattle. It did quite well, and then, just as he was beginning to open other branches, he heard some interesting news: the Starbucks business was up for sale. It had been difficult enough to raise money for his cafe; how could he ever come up with the $4 million asking price for Starbucks? With his initial fundraising experience under his belt, he was able to find the investors, but only on the promise of starting up 100 more cafes across America over a five-year period. At the time, this seemed like an outlandish proposal even to him, little knowing that, only a decade later, Starbucks would have over 1,300 stores.

Schultz's success derived from more or less the same things that marked Kroc's rise: openness to opportunity, willingness to risk, and the passion of a new convert. The first two elements were things that Schultz had deliberately refined within himself, the third is a matter, as we've noted, of personal mystery. Why are we deeply and suddenly drawn to one thing and not another? Schultz found his work selling homewares interesting, but coffee made him tremble with excitement. He recognised this strong irrational element, and put it into a rule:

'If it captures your imagination, it will captivate others.'

What is startlingly and obvious to you will, given time, seem obvious to others too. But you need to *act* on what you see.

The casual observer might still put Schultz in the 'lucky' basket. You could argue that America was ripe to become a nation of proper coffee drinkers, and that Starbucks was lucky to be there as the swell of untapped demand turned into a wave, which it rode brilliantly. Yet it was not at all obvious that there was such a demand. Remember, coffee consumption was *declining*. But Schultz saw Starbucks not in terms of 'coffee' but rather 'cafe experience'. It was obvious to him that America was ripe for such an experience, but it was certainly not to just about everyone else. Schultz's auto-biography is hardly a trumpet-blowing exercise, and in fact it is full of hand-wringing concerns about whether Starbucks is getting too big or if it is treating its employees right. But his conscience doesn't prevent him from seeing the reality of his situation, and he admits the truth of Peter Drucker's statement, 'Whenever you see a successful business, someone made a courageous decision.'

Did Schultz's family background give him this courage? There was actually nothing in it that encouraged risk or entrepreneurship. His father had always worked in low-grade jobs, and the family had barely ever left the environs of New York. When Howard got accepted into college he was the first on either side of his family. Moreover, when he finished college he had little idea what he wanted to do. At 22 he had 'no mentor, no role model, no special teacher to help me sort out my options'. He worked at a ski lodge, waiting for inspiration, and after a year returned to New York and landed a position as a sales trainee at Xerox, then a highly rated company whose training programmes taught excellent communication and business skills. Schultz was put to work selling word processors, making 50-plus cold calls a day. He did well, and his commissions enabled him to pay off his college tuition loans in only three years. This confidence-raising experience in turn led to his position at Perstop.

It is easy now to think of Howard Schultz as the billion-aire founder of a huge company, but we should remember too the hard-working Xerox salesman, and later the unknown, unproven entrepreneur drumming on the doors of investors to open a cafe. Like you and me, he was trying to 'make something happen'. Schultz says he was shaped by the Xerox opportunity, but it was one he made the most of. If we are shaped by our environments, we also create new mental environments for ourselves, and at Xerox Schultz laid a psychological foundation for success on which he could build his achievements. His parents' lack of money was certainly a motivating factor in his rise, but in no way should it be said that it set up the son's success. In fact, Schultz admits that his decision to leave his position as marketing man at the original Starbucks and start his own business, just as his wife Sheri had fallen pregnant (which would mean she would have to go back to work as soon as the baby was born) went right up against the values of his parents. His father had always given him the message that a breadwinner should never quit their job, given the fearful instability it caused a family, and then there was his perplexed mother and her calls for him not to risk it all. Schultz hated the idea of possibly putting his family in jeopardy. On the other hand, he also felt that what he was doing, even if difficult in the short term, would eventually pay off and secure the family's future – but it still needed courage to actually make the jump.

Perhaps it is human nature to forget or dismiss the grind and obstacles that lead us to significant achievement, but either way we should treat with slight amusement the idea that one succeeds through being given wonderful breaks. The nature of success is that it *is* self-created. Rather than

Schultz simply being a product of his family, place and times, it is more correct to say that the institution he created *shaped* the times, just as McDonald's did. There is no demand if it is not articulated in a service or product, and Starbucks did this.

As we have seen, there was nothing at all inevitable about the rise of Schultz or Kroc. Both had their insecurities and deficiencies like the rest of us, but pushed forward regardless. They were 'products' mainly of themselves.

Final thoughts

Using words such as 'product' in relation to human beings is not only incorrect but dangerous. If people were determined by their environments, their life trajectories would be utterly predictable, but usually they are not. Yes, we underplay the role of family and heritage in success, but in correcting this, we also risk underplaying the vital spark, the burning desire, the wish to transcend, that come out of the *individual*. J.P. Stern once said of the philosopher Friedrich Nietzsche: 'He distrusts systems. He thinks there's something indecent about trying to encapsulate a human being or a human psyche within a systematic account.' Ultimately, you cannot have a universal theory of success simply because the subjects of such a theory (people) do unexpected things.

Part of our beauty is the ability to admit we are on the wrong path and change to another one. History has often been seen as a grand narrative of nations or dominant ideas leading to a certain end, but as Hannah Arendt noted, this view (subscribed to by many great thinkers, including Marx and Hegel) overlooks one crucial truth: the human capacity to surprise. History is more accurately a succession of moments in which individuals act *in defiance* of expectations. The Gladwell view is that we are driven by our pasts, but as the positive psychologist Martin Seligman rightly put it, human beings are also 'drawn by the future'.

Do you believe yourself to be the product of genes, environment or circumstances? If so, it may be limiting your life or making it more predictable than it might be. Remembering the essential human quality of surprise may help you come into your own. 'The new always happens against the overwhelming odds of statistical laws and their probability,' Arendt noted, 'which for all practical, everyday purposes amounts to certainty.' Just as financial products come with the caveat that 'indicated rates of return are based on past performance and are no guarantee of future returns', your future at this point may be based on probabilities, but these are based on past experience and determine *nothing*. Everyone 'knew' what Charlie Wilson and Joanne Herring were like, and no one expected great things of Ray Kroc as he entered his fifties, least of all his wife. Howard Schultz was just another child from the projects, and later a mediocre college football player. Yet each were just getting ready to flower into a greater role. Only a year before each decided on the courses that would make them stand out, no one (perhaps not even themselves) could have or did predict it.

You may now be at a similar point of inflection, a point where your life can go up or down on the graph of life. Moreover, having been endowed with a longer lifespan than you might have expected means that you are likely to have a *number* of points at which you are given the opportunity to truly advance. Not only can you change yourself, in some unique way you can change the world. Expect from yourself the unexpected. The future is, in fact, a blank slate.

CHAPTER NINE:

EVERYTHING BIG BEGINS SMALL

And often starts slowly

In my early twenties I took a year out from university to go backpacking around the world. My first stop was California, where I'd arranged to stay with a friend of my uncle. Charles Berolzheimer was then in his late eighties, a renaissance man who spoke seven languages and had a collection of incunabula, the earliest printed books. He was the scion of a pencil-making family that had emigrated from Germany in the 1860s, and had grown up in comfortable surroundings in New York; Charles recalled to me the family coach and horses with driver that took him around the city before the advent of cars. When he was older, his father put him through Harvard, where he studied chemistry.

When the time came for Charles to decide what to do with his life, the choice was almost made for him. In the 1910s and 1920s, the American pencil-making industry had a problem: the Eastern Seaboard's stock of cedarwood for pencils was becoming exhausted. The Berolzheimers knew about the rich forests of incense cedar growing in California and Oregon, and in his early twenties Charles moved out to California, his father putting up the money to buy a company called California Cedar Products.

Over several decades Charles built up CalCedar, and with his language skills carved out large overseas markets for the cedar slats it made for use in pencil production. A lover of Yosemite and other natural places, he was never into slash-and-burn forestry and developed sustainable sources for the company's products, innovating all the time in saw technology and wood science. Concerned with the large amount of waste sawdust that it produced, Charles tasked his research and development team to develop a slow-burning artificial firelog made out of sawdust and wax that could be used in the fireplace instead of real wood, but without a charcoaly mess being left behind. Firelogs were not new, but in the 1960s the market for them wasn't very big and involved only regional operators. But in only a few years CalCedar's premium Duraflame log created a new national market, distributed in supermarkets across the United States. It remains the bestselling firelog in America. Charles died in 1995, but had gone in to work every day well into his nineties. His son took over the running of the company, and today his grandson is in charge.

Charles and his company are an excellent example of the power of filling niches. When you pick up a pencil you never think of the slat of wood from which it was cut, and yet without the pencil slat there would be no pencils. The Berolzheimer family were wise to seek leadership in this niche, as opposed to the extremely competitive market for pencils themselves, and CalCedar is still the world's largest supplier of pencil slats. Moreover, its Duraflame firelog business would never have come into being if this first pencil slat niche had not been filled perfectly.

A company does not get big by chasing every market. It picks out a niche, or creates a niche, and aims to be the leader in it. 3M, the firm that invented the Post-it note, Scotch sellotape and an array of other useful things, started off as a struggling mining concern whose early years were littered with disaster. To survive, its staff had to experiment, finding that even a twig of research could grow into a full branch that sprouts many related products. Because it couldn't tell what would grow big, it had to try a lot of little things. It became part of the culture of the company that 'no market, no end product is too small to be scorned'.

The success law of filling small niches is true even of a behemoth like Microsoft. Its first market was just a sliver, creating a particular programming language (BASIC) for a specific operating system (CPM). Fill one particular need, and in time you notice other, bigger ones. As the power of chips and processors grew, Bill Gates knew there would be a market for desktop software that was 'easy enough for his mother to use'. The user interface that made Microsoft rich, Windows 3.0, took much longer than expected to get right (seven years), but as Gates and his partner Paul Allen found, a well-filled niche can turn into a massive business.

* * *

You may be afraid of creating too small a niche with your product, but the truth is, all large, successful companies initially grew from very specific products aimed at small markets. These segments grew, revealing other, usually unexpected products and markets.

Are you perhaps too focused on thinking big when in fact you should be thinking *small*? Do a small thing right, and growth will almost take care of itself. Never be overwhelmed by the fact that your new innovation or idea doesn't seem to have a market or an audience at the beginning; if it's good, you will create one. Everyone wants to dominate their field, marketing expert Al Ries notes, 'But the way to do this is to start small, not big.' The fact is, all great brands effectively create a market from nothing. On the day it was created, for instance, the size of the Coca-Cola market was zero. There was no electric light bulb market on the day Edison invented one, and no automobile market the week that Karl Benz saw the first car sold. CalCedar had no ready-made market for its firelogs; it had to persuade supermarkets to stock them and convey their advantages to people who were otherwise happy burning regular wood.

Raw materials are rarely the problem in finding and exploiting a new, valuable niche. After all, Charles and his family created a very big and profitable national market for a product made out of cast-off sawdust and cheap wax. What is in shorter supply is imagination and the wish to truly make life simpler and easier for people. If it seems obvious to you that there is a need that isn't being met, you are probably right – chances are, others see it too.

The time it takes

In his business classic, *Innovation and Entrepreneurship*, Peter Drucker tells the story of the chemical manufacturing company Hoffmann-La Roche of Basel, Switzerland.

Its founder, Fritz Hoffmann-La Roche, really struggled with the business in its early years; in fact, in its first three decades. It made textile dyes, cough syrups and painkillers, but never made headway against much bigger German and Swiss dye and chemical firms. Then it hit trouble during the First World War, when both Germany and France thought it was loyal to the other, and boycotted it along with Britain. To compound matters, when Russia had its revolution the company lost a million Swiss francs. It faced bankruptcy and it had to raise money publicly. Finally, there was family tragedy: Fritz died in 1919 from illness, not that long after his son, expected to take over, died in a car accident.

But in the early 1930s things finally started to look up for the company. It acquired the patents to synthetically produce vitamins from a team working at ETH (the Swiss government-funded equivalent of MIT), and Roche lured these scientists with big salaries. It bet everything it had on these new substances, and in 1934 began selling the first commercially available vitamin C capsules. As we know, vitamins became a massive business, and until the 1980s, the company still had about *half* the worldwide market for them.

Though it sold its vitamin business in 2002, Roche's big vitamin bet was the foundation of its success. One well-filled niche opens up others, and the company later poured money into another untried area of pharmaceuticals, muscle-relaxing tranquillisers that could make you calm but not tired. In the 1950s it introduced Librium and Valium (now Diazepam), which turned the firm into an industry giant (Roche is now the third-largest pharmaceutical company in the world, with revenues of $50 billion). And though Fritz himself died just as the 1920s dawned, his descendants still own a sizeable chunk of the company.

You may think this is just another 'big company' story, but as Drucker notes, 'Hoffmann-LaRoche was not a big company when it started.' It was a family affair battling against the big firms, trying to come up with products that would give it an edge.

Could this be where your company or your organisation stands today?

One of Drucker's disciples was Jim Collins, the author of *Good to Great*, about the often unlikely journeys and successes of some of America's best-known companies. After 20 years studying these firms, Collins observed:

> 'No matter how dramatic the end result, the good-to-great transformations never happened in one fell swoop. There was no single defining action, no grand program, no one killer innovation, no solitary lucky break, no miracle moment. Rather, the process resembled relentlessly pushing a giant heavy flywheel in one direction, turn upon turn, building momentum until a point of breakthrough, and beyond.'

This shouldn't be a great insight, but it feels that way because we are so used to looking for a big effect in a hurry. So blinded are we by the glamour of the grown-up, we forget about the love and attention that needs to be lavished on the baby.

The first one per cent

Futurist Ray Kurzweil is known for the accuracy of his predictions on technology and society. In the 1980s, for instance, before anyone really knew about it, he presaged the massive growth of the internet in the 1990s, and he has now made bold predictions about the rise of 'intelligent machines' that will also transform the way we live.

Kurzweil notes that the trajectory of everything from the spread of telephones, to money spent on education, to computing power, does not follow a neat diagonal upwards line over time, but is more like a ramp that starts off on a slight angle but doubles the rate of its upward climb before long.

Many people, he says, dismiss his predictions because they do not appreciate the fact of exponential growth. That is, most things do not seem remarkable in their early phases because their rate of growth is slow:

> 'Scientists imagine they'll keep working at the present pace . . . They make linear extrapolations from the past. When it took years to sequence the first one per cent of the human genome, they worried they'd never finish, but they were

right on schedule for an exponential curve. If
you reach one per cent and keep doubling your
growth every year, you'll hit 100 per cent in just
seven years.'

Why is this so important for personal or business achievement? Because when you embark on something new, your
rate of progress in the early years can seem *so* slow. When
you look at them on a graph, the remarkable thing about
exponential upward curves is how unremarkable they are at
their beginning, because they are so gradual. Without much
positive feedback, this is the point at which most people
give up.

But the longer you stick at something, the more likely that
that law of accelerating returns will kick in, and the day will
come when you will barely be able to keep up with your rate
of progress. But the key is to not bite on the reins in the early
years, and be comfortable with the natural rate of growth.

A perfect example of exponential growth is Lonely
Planet.

In 1972, twentysomethings Tony and Maureen Wheeler
arrived in Australia at the end of a long overland trip from
England across Asia. The final part of their trip included a
few weeks on a leaky boat from Bali that eventually disem-
barked them on a West Australian beach.

After hitchhiking across the Nullarbor, they reached
Sydney with 27 cents to their name and rented a furnished
single room in a house overlooking Sydney Harbour. It was
$16 a week, and from it they could see a strange, beautiful
structure being built: the Sydney Opera House.

The couple had met on a park bench in London. Tony was a business school student and Maureen was temping as a secretary, having moved from Belfast only the week before. Originally their plan was just to save enough to get back to Britain, but they decided to spend a year in Sydney and do another year's travelling. People kept asking them about the overland trip they had done to Australia, and many of the questions were the same. The thought struck them: why not put out a little guidebook on their experience and sell it?

In October 1973 they had the pages printed for 1,500 copies of *Across Asia on the Cheap*, and stapled it together themselves. Tony went off to cities around Australia going directly to bookshops and taking orders, then delivering the books from a couple of suitcases he was keeping in left luggage. They soon had to do a reprint of 3,500. It was 'a totally unplanned success,' Tony remembers. The thought occurred to them that they could make a living doing this, or at least pay for their next trip.

In 1974 they scraped enough money together (mostly from jobs, rather than cash from the first guide) and travelled around South-East Asia, at a time when most people did not think of it as a place that tourists go. Bali was still a backwater island paradise. Tapping out *South-East Asia on a Shoestring* in a steamy Singapore room, they put their second production together. In their first proper year in business, sales were £15,000, but given the books were retailing for £1 each, they had to sell a lot to stay afloat. At the end of 1975, Maureen recalls, 'The business was still so small that we could load all the paperwork into the boot of our humble Ford.'

Thanks to a government grant, the following year Tony attended his first Frankfurt Book Fair to promote the fledgling company (which they named Lonely Planet), and he could only afford to stay in a flea-bitten room in the red light district. It would be like this for several years. On their travels, the Wheelers would often be forced to rely on the hospitality of friends when they had literally ran out of money (this was before the time of credit cards for emergencies). Tony even moonlighted, writing parts of other company's guidebooks to bring in extra cash.

In 1976 they had published four titles, and the following year it was eight. 'Looking back at those books,' Tony notes, 'they were often fairly shoddy productions, but simply getting them on the shelves helped make the business viable. Furthermore, they were often filling empty niches, so even if they weren't very good, by our later standards, they were still better than anything else around.'

For Tony and Maureen, 'Doing what we wanted was still much more important than doing what made the most sense financially.' In the late 1970s they published books on Sri Lanka and Burma, which didn't promise great sales but were simply places they wanted to go. Yet in the longer term, they knew that doing this kind of book was important in building their credibility. As it happens, the Sri Lanka book did very well and came at the right time, just before the country descended into civil war. Even so, six years after starting the business, there were only three people involved full-time.

The make or break moment for Lonely Planet was its

guide to India. At the time there were only more upscale Fodor's and Frommer's guides to the country, plus the famous Murray's *Handbook for Travellers in India*, first published in the 1850s. India was perhaps the number one destination for budget-conscious travellers at the time, and they felt there had to be a market for a backpacking guide. The couple set off for the subcontinent in 1980, just as Maureen fell pregnant, and at the hottest time of year. Towards the end of 1980 it still looked like Lonely Planet might go broke. Their business partner Jim was in hospital with a cerebral aneurysm, Maureen was sidelined following the difficult birth of their daughter Tashi, and Tony had developed high blood pressure trying to keep everything afloat. Finishing India was 'a long slog' and came to 700 pages, three times the size of their regular titles.

However, when the book finally came out at the end of 1981 it was a runaway success and won the Thomas Cook 'Guidebook of the Year' award. Ten years after Lonely Planet had begun, the little company was firmly in the black. By 1984/85 it had a list of 33 titles, and the following year made a profit of £250,000. By the mid-1990s, it had sales of almost £10 million.

Yet its rise tested the couple's marriage because in the early years Maureen didn't believe Lonely Planet would ever become big enough to support both of them. She had enrolled at university, first studying psychology and then social work. But her doubt had a positive effect, in that it put pressure on Tony to work furiously to make the company a profitable concern. Tony summed up their experience in an interview:

'For the first ten years we were sitting around
with no money and all our friends were onto
their second company BMWs, or buying houses
and having kids. Meanwhile, we're struggling
because we had an idea.'

With hindsight it is easy to see that *of course* there was a
massive market to be tapped for backpacker travel guides,
but at the time they started, this market was tiny compared
to conventional travel. Now, there are guides to every con-
ceivable place on earth, but in the 1970s much of the world
was roped off by the larger publishers as being where nice
people didn't go. The Wheelers had discovered, though, that
there were lots of people like them, passionate about travel
but also culturally sensitive, wishing to immerse themselves
in a place instead of being just a tourist.

'The story of Lonely Planet,' Maureen notes, 'seems to
resonate with anyone who has ever dreamed of turning their
passion into their work.' They ended up employing hundreds
of freelance writers to produce guides to every corner of the
world, and to Maureen's surprise the company grew into
something big. In 2007, the Wheelers decided to sell Lonely
Planet to the BBC. Though the terms of the deal were kept
under wraps, the figure floated was $250 million – quite a
lot of money for an enterprise begun in the boot of a car
35 years before.

'Nothing is revolutionary, it's evolutionary'

It seems obvious to say it, but every big enterprise that changes the way things are done always begins as a single, often simple idea. The mistake is in looking at the monolithic company or organisation and imagining it *always* existed.

When business guru Al Ries advises new companies, he tells them *not* to try to emulate big companies in their quest for success. Instead, noting that all large companies have a humble beginning, the start-ups should find out what these big companies were doing *before* they became successful, when they were also small.

> 'Brand building is slow, patient, methodical work. It takes several decades, goes the old saying, to become an overnight success. Sure, there are some exceptions, which we call shooting stars . . . but these exceptions usually take place in industries that are exploding in growth, carrying the leading brands along with them. In the vast majority of cases a brand takes many years (or many decades) to successfully establish itself.'

Volkswagen, for instance, took almost twenty years to peak as a brand, and many of today's famous names have been with us for a long time. General Electric goes back to 1892, Mercedes-Benz to 1885, and Wedgwood pottery, Moet & Chandon champagne and Remy Martin cognac all began in the 1700s.

True, the online era can condense the time in which it takes to build a powerful brand, with word spreading quickly about the utility of a particular service or application. Yet even online it takes time to build a brand. Facemash, the precursor to Facebook, was launched by Mark Zuckerberg at Harvard in 2003, but it still took another three years before the firm became a household name, when it had spread well beyond its college roots. Google's search engine went live in January 1998, but despite the lightning-fast speed at which word spreads online, it still took another three years to be recognised as the best around.

Mike Moritz was one who saw Google's early potential, pushing the venture capital firm where he worked, Sequoia, to invest $12.5 million in 1999. Five years later, the stake was worth $2 billion. Yet Moritz has had plenty of failures as well as successes, and notes the extraordinary effort and lead time that goes into making a dot com star:

> 'People don't understand. Most of our
> companies are not overnight successes even
> when they become well known. It's the same
> with Silicon Valley.'

People beat a path to his door to get advice on how to set up a 'Silicon Valley' where they are. But this can't be done overnight, Moritz notes. The Valley as it is today was 50 years in the making. As he puts it, 'You're not going to be able to put it in a bottle and go and sprinkle it on parched earth that hasn't been properly fertilised.'

Sequoia Capital's founder, Don Valentine, who came to Silicon Valley in 1959, gives his view:

> 'The duration of the venture industry is probably only from something like 1960 through the present, so you talk about not even half a century. It's still a new and sort of closet-like form of financial engineering. We don't think of it as investing at all. We think of it as building companies, often times building industries. And it's an entirely different mentality and attitude than in the traditional idea of buying and selling things. And this is not a place where you buy things; this is a place where you build things. And you participate in the founding team that creates an entirely new company and sometimes a new industry.'

In Silicon Valley, Valentine remarks, 'Nothing is revolutionary; it's evolutionary.'

Perhaps a surprising remark from a major figure in the dot com and technology field, and yet the name of Valentine's company says it all. The Sequoia tree can live for 1,500 years and tower over 100 metres high, dominating the forest around it, yet like every other tree it begins as a sapling.

Go slow to get big

You have probably heard of the 'microloans' that are helping to lift millions out of poverty around the world. Yet the story of how the microcredit movement came into being is worth retelling.

Muhammad Yunus was an economics professor at Chittagong University in Bangladesh who didn't need to bother too much about what was happening outside the walls of his faculty. But when a famine started to grip his native Bangladesh, with emaciated people appearing on the streets, he began to wonder about the value of his economic theories. What was their worth when babies could die for the simple lack of food?

Yunus decided to go into a nearby town and learn about poverty first-hand. He discovered that otherwise capable people were trapped into a cycle of poverty caused by lack of capital, and that if he lent small amounts of money to them at low interest, they could buy materials to make products for sale, and no longer be at the mercy of money lenders and their exorbitantly priced loans. Yunus's first loans, to 44 families in Jobra, amounted to $27. These were people no bank would ever consider lending to, since they had no collateral and were mostly illiterate, not even able to fill in a form. Yunus did not consider himself a banker, yet here was a clear need that could be satisfied with tiny resources. His experiment was the beginning of an institution, the Grameen (or 'village') Bank, which by 2008 had lent over $7 billion to the world's poorest families, lifting most of them out of poverty for good.

What was the secret of its success, particularly the impressive rate of its growth over 30 years? Yunus's surprising answer: 'Whenever Grameen starts functioning in a new location, it is never in a hurry to do anything.'

Setting up in a new village, it doesn't try to find more than *100* borrowers in its first year. But from these seeds of trust, word spreads to surrounding areas. Yunus gave this advice to his field officers: 'Go as slow as you can! The slower the better. One can pick up speed only when everything is in order.'

As slow as you can. This is radical advice for anyone in the early stages of an enterprise, but as Yunus notes, with the basic structure set you can always move faster when you're ready. Not letting the concrete cure and dry only sets you up for problems later.

Spiritual movements and religions also turn out better when their growth is not forced. Sects and cults tend to rise up fast on the back of a charismatic leader, but a lack of timeless principles or teachings to sustain them sees them wither just as quickly. A stock of principles or spiritual laws has to be tested over a long period, with each generation being able to experience their truth, before something called a religion can really take shape. After Jesus of Nazareth's death, it still took centuries for the Christian church to establish itself. Likewise for Siddartha Gautama (the Buddha). Despite his undoubted personal power during his lifetime, it was still a long time before his teachings really began to shape the world.

However, an offshoot or reformed version of an existing spiritual tradition can move ahead quite quickly, particularly if it is transplanted to a different part of the world from its origins. Karma Kagyu or Diamond Way Buddhism, for instance, a separate lineage within Tibetan Buddhism to the Dalai Lama's, developed over many centuries in one of the most remote parts of the world. Until well into the twentieth century, hardly any Westerners (only a few intrepid anthropologists, missionaries and travellers) had had any contact with this exotic, self-contained culture. But in the late 1960s two newly married young Danes, Ole and Hannah Nydahl, made their way to the Himalayas and became the first Western students of the 16th Karmapa, the lineage's spiritual leader. He transmitted to them many of the powerful meditations and mantras, which transformed the couple from drug-addled hippies into strong people who now sought to work for the benefit of others. The Karmapa now gave them a life's mission: to go back to Europe and teach what they had learned, applying the philosophy and techniques in a fresh way suited to Western lifestyles.

In 1972, the couple returned to Copenhagen to establish the first Diamond Way centres outside Tibet and India, at a time when Tibetan Buddhism seemed, if not a threat, certainly something strange and exotic in the West. Today, 40 years after this modest beginning, there are hundreds of such centres and groups around the world, making Diamond Way one of the largest Buddhist organisation outside Asia. Yet true to the Buddhist ethos, it all happened not by preaching or missionary work, but through the attraction of like minds. The message: 40 years may seem like a long time, but it's not even a person's whole life – indeed, Ole Nydahl did not even discover Buddhism until his late twenties.

In most people's minds, organic growth means slow growth, but this misses the point. As with the Grameen example, the most important thing with any organisational 'tree' is the thickness and depth of the roots. These may take a while to take hold, but once they do, growth is virtually assured, and in time he or she who planted the tree is amazed at its height, strength and productive output. By taking it slow at first, we can make sure that everything is in order. If it is, things will naturally speed up when the time is right. And let's be reminded: more than any other time in history, we have the time to take this approach.

Final thoughts

When you embark on something new, the rate of progress in the early years can seem painfully slow. Not only does everything big or great begin small, it can seem to *stay* small for an uncomfortably long time. Yet the longer you stick at something, the more likely it is that that law of accelerating returns (or exponential growth) will kick in. But the first one per cent of any project is special, so don't try to hurry it.

Tiny things, if nurtured and given time to grow their own way, can flower into something substantial. This seems obvious, but in our quest to do big things, we too easily forget the basic laws of growth.

What worthwhile project are you now working on that seems like a sapling in the wind? What big effort are you making that seems like scrabbling around at the foot of a mountain?

Comparisons with the people waving from the summit will only discourage. Instead, be reminded that they were once where you are. It is easy to be blinded by the light reflecting off a great person, product or enterprise. But get closer and you will discover tiny, inauspicious origins.

An interviewer once asked Warren Buffett whether he expected to be so successful. 'No,' he replied. What, then, she asked, was his secret? The man who had created, and was now in the process of giving away his $50 billion fortune, replied in seven words:

'One foot in front of the other.'

By starting small, you are obeying the immutable laws of growth and time. These laws can raise up a beautiful garden or a towering forest within your lifetime, and after you have gone, enrich the lives of those who come after you. 'The best use of a life,' William James said, 'is to create something that outlasts it.' It is not too late for *your* life to have such an effect.

EPILOGUE

In *The Structure of Scientific Revolutions*, Thomas Kuhn showed that knowledge proceeds on the basis of inconvenient facts overturning existing paradigms of understanding, which then form the basis of new, more accurate ones.

In this book, I have sought to draw attention to two such facts:

1. Things often take longer than we expect to achieve.
2. We are living longer, healthier lives.

The first fact overturns the notion of overnight success, that 'something can happen' and we will be transported out of our mundane world to fame, riches, glory or permanent happiness. Manifestations of this belief are many in contemporary life: television shows that hoist people from obscurity to eminence for a short time, massive lottery prizes with huge subscriptions, and a self-development culture of changing your life in seven days, or even '59 Seconds' as one book had it. While it's true that a change in state of *mind* can happen in an instant, changing your actual *life* is another matter. For 99.9 per cent of us, there is no sudden lifting up to a higher world, and the success we achieve is dreamed, designed, worked for and maintained over many years.

The second fact overturns the conventional wisdom that life is short. Real achievement may be a longer, tougher road than we ever like to admit, and yet we have more time to travel that road than any time in history. You don't have to 'change your life in seven days', because you have decades to do it.

An understanding of how long it generally takes to master something, and the span of time we may have at our disposal to put in that effort, is fundamental to our understanding of what it takes to succeed. Most people's mental images of time are drawn from fear, but in seeing time as a help, not a hindrance, in a speed-obsessed world we give ourselves an unusual advantage. The motivational field does not like to talk about how long real achievement takes because it thinks people will be turned off. Yet by looking unflinchingly at the timescales of success, surely it has a greater chance of actually happening when our decisions and actions are grounded in truth, not mere wishes.

Let's remind ourselves of what's been observed in this book:

- Factor in enough lead time, and virtually any big project, skill or enterprise is achievable. Take the long view of your life and work, and you will move to a place beyond your peers.
- If you are frustrated by the pace of your achievements so far, recall the Bristlecone Pine or

the Raramuri runners. Most probably, even if you consider yourself a success now, you have just been warming up for the real event or contribution of your life.

- Don't be overawed by fame or great achievements. Everyone has to start somewhere, and the valuable thing is to study what a particular person or organisation was doing before they made their mark.

- Be open to opportunity, remain curious, have a willingness to take intelligent risks, and follow whatever you are passionate about. Most people lose these qualities in adulthood, but those who keep them often experience great flowerings when others of their generation are winding down.

- Do what seems obvious to you. If you see a need for something, chances are others do too. If the times are not right for your offering right now, wait; stay true to yourself and things will swing back your way.

- Human beings, by nature, are never quite predictable, and every person represents a new beginning through which the world can be changed in some way. Never discount your ability to have an effect. The first 30, 40 or 50 years of your life may simply have created a platform that provides the skills, experience and wisdom on which to build something important.

- Motivational speakers talk about persistence, but it is hard work combined with experimentation that leads to the breaks characterising the lives of remarkable people.

- Start modestly, give your idea or enterprise enough time to put down roots, and it will have enough time to build into something that lasts.
- Thinking big can get you somewhere, but combine it with thinking long and you have a recipe for greatness.

Finally, remember that we are never simply products of our past. If this were so, people would never do anything unexpected, and yet they do. We are also drawn by the future, and what we strongly imagine tends to be made real.

If you did not do the Schwartz exercise earlier in the book, do it now. It will show you that you have more time than you think to embark on what you've always wanted, and that 'too old' is hardly ever a sound excuse.

Never let anyone suggest to you that you are simply an animal with various urges for survival, or that you are a 'consumer' who is little more than a collection of tastes or preferences. Rather, your birth represented a truly new beginning, and you have a natural readiness to act according to what seems obvious to *you*. The way you see the world is never quite the same as anyone else, and this is why your actions are so potentially valuable.

Final thought

We are beings that live in time and space. The extent to which we love, prosper, fulfil our potential and serve humanity ('success', in a word) will depend to a large extent on our appreciation and awareness of time's role in our flourishing. Edward Banfield was right: by changing how you see time, you change your life, for the longer we are around on the planet, the less our original conditions matter, and the more our success is the result of our own decisions and use of the hours and days that we have.

The remarkable and somewhat shocking truth is that we can build uniquely powerful lives, but only if we take a long-term view which can accommodate the inevitable reversals, obstacles or changes of direction that come along. In the 1930s, in the middle of a Depression, Napoleon Hill told audiences that the 'supreme secret' of life was *whatever the mind of man can conceive and believe, he can achieve*. To many people of that era, conditioned by reduced prosperity and shorter lifespans, this idea must have seemed outlandish. Yet in *our* time and *with* our time, this land of possibility is ours to take. Yes, things often take longer than we might like – big life projects, by their nature, unfold over decades – but today we really do have the time for them.

If that is the case, why not aim to do something that will benefit a lot of people over a long period, instead of just yourself? Life is wasted if all we are concerned about is building big edifices for ourselves. Greatness, in contrast, is constantly working for the benefit of others. This naturally brings you closer to people, and the smaller ego it entails will make you a lot happier.

The radical scientist Buckminster Fuller often had to run against the wind to gain credence for his work and ideas, but in the process discovered a secret:

'You can rest assured that if you devote your
time and attention to the highest advantage of
others, the Universe will support you, always and
in the nick of time.'

In your journey of greatness, I hope that you will discover
this liberating, happy truth.

ACKNOWLEDGEMENTS

This book is a tribute to the authors of the great self-development books of the last 150 years, from Samuel Smiles and Orison Swett Marden to major 20th century names including Dale Carnegie, Napoleon Hill and David Schwartz, and contemporary figures such as Stephen Covey, Anthony Robbins, Wayne Dyer, and Catherine Ponder. Though this book is in part a critique of the motivational field, there is a large amount of value in the personal development literature itself.

I live in Britain, am a native of Australia and my work has focused on the personal development and business literature, much of which is American. My place, time and personal interests have naturally influenced who and what I've written about, and I fully acknowledge that there are thousands of stories of thinking long and slow-cooked success from around the world that I'm ignorant of, and from domains I know little about. I therefore don't make any claims for the representativeness of the examples. However, I'm grateful to everyone who has suggested examples.

Sally Holloway of Felicity Bryan Associates agreed to represent me on the strength of the book, helped finesse the concepts and showed me how to write a proper proposal to find the right publisher. Thank you Sally. I'm grateful to Ed Faulkner and his colleagues at Virgin Books for their enthusiasm from the outset, and for implementing a strategy to see it read by as many people as possible. Thanks to Clare Wallis for editing.

Sarah Ravenscroft loved the idea of the book from the start and felt it was a message that needed to be heard. My mother, Marion Butler-Bowdon, was also excited by the concept and believed this would be my best work. Thanks so much to you both.

A number of readers of my previous books, plus friends and family, offered to read and comment on an outline and a couple of chapters in their early form. Thanks to Rob Cover, Ian Hunter, Irfan Alvi, Vanessa Vinos, Jennifer Baker, Stuart Moses, Andrea Molloy, Rick Richardson, Dean Beal, Daniel Midson-Short, John Avon, Sean Cook, George Ravenscroft, Sacha Ravenscroft, Eddie Butler-Bowdon and Richard Koch. Your enthusiasm was a nice surprise and encouraged me to think that the book could be helpful to people. Thanks also to Warwick Mayne-Wilson for allowing me to tell your story.

Tamara Lucas was there at the book's conception and rightly sceptical of its worth when the working title was 'Slow-Cooked Success'. Your comments on a revised outline were valued. And Cherry, you've naturally made me think in longer timeframes while helping me to have a greater appreciation of the present. *Vos duae nescitis quantopere amemini.*

ENDNOTES

Introduction

'People overestimate . . .' quote is from Anthony Robbins, *Awaken the Giant Within* (1991). Robbins does not claim it as his own, but gives no attribution either.

Chapter One

Buffett:

Quote from Berkshire Hathaway 1985 Annual Report, reprinted in *The Essays of Warren Buffett: Lessons for Investors and Managers* (The Cunningham Group), Selected, Arranged and Introduced by Lawrence A. Cunningham, 1997.

Epictetus:

Quotes from Epictetus, *A Selection from the Discourses of Epictetus with The Encheiridion*, translated by George Long, (1909), Project Gutenberg, www.gutenberg.org.

Erickson:
Sidney Rosen quote from Rosen, S., *My Voice Will Go With You*, Norton, New York, 1982, p. 182.

Schopenhauer, Arthur, *The World as Will and Representation*, Falcon's Wing Press, Colorado, 1958. Preface to Third Edition (1859).

Richard Koch:
Koch, Richard, *The 80/20 Revolution: why the creative individual is king: how you can create and capture wealth and well-being*, Nicholas Brealey, London, 2002. p. 87.
This title was later republished as *The 80/20 Individual*, Currency Doubleday, New York, 2003.

Chapter Two

Danish researchers:
Christensen, Kaare; Doblhammer, Gabriele; Rolan Rau; Vaupel, James W., 'Ageing Populations: The Challenges Ahead', *The Lancet*, October 2009.

Lynne Cox, Tom Kirkwood: quoted in 'Our growing lifespans show no sign of slowing this century', Robin McKie, *The Observer*, 6 March 2011.

'. . . worldwide market of 5 trillion': Canton, James, *The Extreme Future: The Top Trends That Will Shape the World in the Next 50 Years*, Plume, New York, 2007. See Chapter 5, 'Outliving the Future: Longevity Medicine'.

Julian Savulescu:

Quoted in 'Woe, Superman: Science is opening up the possibilities of significant human enhancement and provoking a debate on the ethics involved.' Peter Snow, *Oxford Today* (University of Oxford), Vol. 22, No. 1, Michaelmas, 2009.

Schwartz exercise:

Schwartz, David J., *The Magic of Thinking Big*, Simon & Schuster, New York, 1959, 1965. See Chapter 2, 'Cure Yourself of Excusitis, the Failure Disease'.

Warwick Mayne-Wilson:

Biographical sketch drawn from notes provided by subject, 2011.

Chapter Three

Banfield:

Banfield, E. C., *The Unheavenly City*, Little, Brown, New York, 1970.

Elliot Jacques:

Key works include *Requisite Organization: Total System for Effective Managerial Organization and Managerial Leadership for the 21st Century* (1997); *Executive Leadership: A Practical Guide to Managing Complexity,* and *Human Capability: A Study of Human Potential and its Application*, the last two both 1994 and written with Kathryn Cason.

Jeff Bezos:
Quote from interview for Academy of Achievement (www.achievement.org). Interview can also be seen by searching for 'Jeff Bezos' on YouTube.com.

Bee Gees:
BBC 4 documentary, *In Our Own Time*. Broadcast 15 May, 2011.

Franzen:
One of the best articles on the author is 'Jonathan Franzen: Great American Novelist' by Lev Grossman, *Time*, 12 August 2010.

Estée Lauder:
My principal source on the early years of Estée Lauder is Israel, Lee, *Beyond the Magic*, Macmillan, London, 1985.

Morita and Sony:
Morita, A., Reingold, E. & Momomura, M., *Made in Japan: Akio Morita and Sony*, Signet, New York, 1988.
John Nathan, *Sony: A Private Life*, HarperCollins Business, 2001.

Toyota:
Hino, Satoshi, *Inside the Mind of Toyota*, Productivity Press, New York, 2005.
Liker, Jeffrey, *The Toyota Way: 14 Management Principles from the World's Greatest Manufacturer*, McGraw Hill, New York, 2004.
'The Birth of the Prius', Alex Taylor III, *Fortune*, 6 March 2006.

Jack Welch:

His autobiography is *Jack: Straight From the Gut*, Warner Books, New York, 2003.

Jeffrey Immelt:

Source for the quotation is Geoff Colvin's *Talent is Overrated*, Nicholas Brealey, London, 2008. The original Harvard Business Review article is 'Growth As A Process: The HBR Interview', Harvard Business Review, June 2006.

Antony Gormley:

Nicholas Wroe, 'Leader of the Pack', *Guardian*, 25 June 2005.
John-Paul Flintoff, 'Antony Gormley, the man who broke the mould', *The Sunday Times*, 2 March 2008.
Charlotte Higgins, 'Antony Gormley', *Guardian*, 8 September 2007.

Fritjof Capra:

Capra, F., *The Tao of Physics: An Exploration of the Parallels Between Modern Physics and Eastern Mysticism*, Shambhala, Boston, 1975, 1983. p. 105.

Chapter Four

Erika Sunnegardh:

Daniel J. Wakin, 'Stepping Onstage as a Waitress, She May Exit the Met as a Star', *New York Times*, 1 April 2006.
James Bone, 'Fame at last for the diva in waiting', *The Times*, 3 April 2006.

David Usborne, 'An unforgettable night at the opera for the waitress who dreamed of a starring role', *Independent*, 3 April 2006.

Samuel Smiles:
Quote from Samuel Smiles, *Self-Help: With Illustrations of Conduct and Perseverance*, 1859. The Ruskin, Voltaire and Buffon quotes are also from Smiles.
Orison Swett Marden: quote from *Pushing to the Front*, Biblio Bazaar, 2009, p. 303. Both works available at Gutenberg.org.

Chess study:
Chase, W, and Simon, H, 'Perception in chess', *Cognitive Psychology*, 1973.

John Hayes:
Hayes, J.R., 'Cognitive Process in Creativity', Occasional Paper No. 18, January 1990, Center for the Study of Writing, Berkeley, CA.; Center for the Study of Writing, Pittsburgh, PA.

Schonberg:
Schonberg, Harold C., *The Lives of the Great Composers*, W. W. Norton & Company, New York, 1970, p. 103.

John Hunter:
Samuel Smiles quote from *Self-Help*, ibid., p. 80.

Erik Erikson:
Erikson's *Young Man Luther: A Study in Psychoanalysis and*

History (Norton, New York, 1958, 1962) is a fascinating read on the subject of wilderness periods, or 'moratoriums' as he calls them, and of course on Luther himself. Direct quote, p. 176.

Brin, Page, Gates, Dell: information from a range of sources, but Dell's autobiography *Direct From Dell: Strategies That Revolutionized an Industry* (HarperBusiness, London, 1999) and James Wallace and Jim Erickson's *Hard Drive: Bill Gates and the Making of the Microsoft Empire* (HarperBusiness, New York, 1992) are excellent.

Twitter:
Dorsey, Jack, *Twitter for Dummies*, Wiley, Indianapolis, 2010 (foreword).

Malcolm Gladwell:
Gladwell, Malcolm, *Outliers: The Story of Success*, Penguin, London, 2009.

Larry Ellison:
The best source on his life and rise is Mike Wilson's *The Difference Between God and Larry Ellison*, William Morrow, New York, 1997.

Joel Morgenstern:
'The studio is not enough: When filmmakers only know about other films, expect turkeys', *Wall Street Journal* (Weekend), 19-21 May 2006.

Michael Stipe:
Quoted in Louise Gannon, 'We did it our way . . . REM's rules of rock', *Daily Mail*, 19 August 2008.

Csikszentmihalyi:
His findings are expressed at length in Csikszentmihalyi, M., *Creativity: Flow and the Psychology of Discovery*, HarperPerennial: New York, 1997.

Robin Warren:
My first introduction to his story was Frances Andrijich's piece 'Gut Instinct' in *The Weekend Australian*, 10-11 December 2005.

Ogilvy:
Quote from Colvin, ibid, *Talent is Overrated*, p. 33.

Chapter Five

Gail Sheehy:
Sheehy, G., *Passages: Predictable Crises of Adult Life*, Ballantine, New York, 1974.

Carl Jung:
His idea of the quaternity is mentioned in *The Portable Jung* (edited by Joseph Campbell) and the autobiographical *Memories, Dreams, Reflections*, but for more depth see his *Collected Works*.

Mother Teresa, Mohandas Gandhi, Eleanor Roosevelt:

The facts of these subjects' lives can be found anywhere, but I particularly enjoyed *Mother Teresa: A Simple Path*, compiled by Lucinda Vardey, Rider, London, 1995; Gandhi's classic *An Autobiography: The Story of my Experiments With Truth* (any edition), and Robin Gerber's *Leadership the Eleanor Roosevelt Way*, Prentice-Hall, New Jersey, 2002.

Nidetch:

Information drawn principally from an article by Louise France, 'The woman who taught the world to slim', *The Observer*, January 2008, and a profile by the Horatio Alger Association of Distinguished Americans (horatioalger.org). See also Jean Nidetch's *The Story of Weight Watchers* (Signet, 1972), and *The Jean Nidetch Story: An Autobiography* (Weight Watchers Publishing Group, 2010).

Bill Wilson:

Primary source is Susan Cheever's *My Name is Bill: Bill Wilson – His Life and the Creation of Alcoholics Anonymous*, Washington Square Press, New York, 2004.

Benenson:

Quote from an obituary in *The Human Rights Defender*, Amnesty Australia, April/May 2005.

Joan Birman:

Sources include an interview in *Notices*, American Mathematical Association, May 2006, conducted by Allyn Jackson and Lisa Traynor (http://www.ams.org/notices/200701/fea-birman.pdf); and a piece on the American

Mathematical School website, 'In Her Own Words', (http://www.awm-math.org/articles/notices/199107/six/node1.html) written by Birman herself.

Tony Mendoza:
Tony Mendoza, 'Speaking Personally; Succeeding as a Photographer', *The New York Times*, 26 June 1988.

Colonel Sanders:
Pearce, John Ed, *The Colonel*, Doubleday, New York, 1982.

Stephen Fry:
Quote from Stephen Fry, Episode 3 of *Stephen Fry in America*, BBC Television. Aired 26 October 2008.

Hugh Grant:
BBC's *The One Show*, 28 January 2009. Interviewer Adrian Chiles.

Al Ries:
Ries, Al, *Focus: The Future of Your Company Depends On It*, HarperBusiness, New York, 1996, p. 274.

Lichtenstein:
Quote '. . . was too shy to introduce himself' from chronology of Lichtenstein's life, LichtensteinFoundation.org.
Quotes '. . . remained an art world outsider' and 'At 37 . . .' from 'Wham! Suddenly Roy was the darling of the art world', M. Gayford, *Daily Telegraph*, 25 February 2004.

Lee Child:

David Smith, 'Sacked at 40 and on the scrapheap. Now Brummie tops US book charts', *The Observer*, 22 June 2008. 'I think it's vital' quote from 'The Persuasive Lee Child', Ali Karim, *January* (januarymagazine.com/profiles/leechild.html).

Pitkin:

Pitkin, Walter B., *Life Begins at Forty*, McGraw-Hill, New York, 1932.

Chapter Six

Daniel Libeskind:

Libeskind, Daniel, *Breaking Ground: Adventures in Life and Architecture*, John Murray, 2004.

Gaby Wood, 'The Belly of an Architect', *The Observer*, 23 September 2007.

Momofuko Ando:

Dennis Hevesi, 'Momofuko Ando, 96, Dies; Invented Instant Ramen', *The New York Times*, 9 January 2007.

Obituary, 'Momofuko Ando', *The Times*, 10 January 2007.

Chester Carlson:

Owen, David, *Copies in Seconds: How a Lone Inventor and an Unknown Company Created the Biggest Communication Breakthrough Since Gutenberg – Chester Carlson and the Birth of Xerox*, Simon & Schuster, New York, 2004.

Julia Margaret Cameron:

Hill, Brian, *Julia Margaret Cameron: A Family Portrait*, Peter Owen, London, 1973.

Victoria & Albert Museum, 'Julia Margaret Cameron' (http://www.vam.ac.uk/content/articles/j/julia-margaret-cameron-biography/).

Bryce Courtenay:

Quote from Courtenay interview on *Talking Heads with Peter Thompson*, ABC (Australia), screened 8 May 2005.

Lionel Shriver:

Quotes from Lynn Barber, 'We need to talk', *The Observer*, 22 April 2007; and Ian Youngs, 'Honest is key for Orange winner', BBC News (http://news.bbc.co.uk/1/hi/entertainment/4071564.stm).

Chapter Seven

Sami El-Raghy/Sukari mine:

Article in *Egypt Today*, September 2006.

John Synnott, 'Aussie miners take on the world', *The Australian*, 2 April 2008.

N.B. In 2009 Sami El-Raghy stepped down as chairman of Centamin, but remains a large shareholder.

Emily Kngwarreye:

Rebecca Hossack, 'Emily Kngwarreye: Obituary', *Independent*, 6 September 1996.

'Emily Kame Kngwarreye', National Gallery of Australia, http://nga.gov.au/exhibitions/Kngwarreye/teachers.htm.

Ronald Harwood:
Quote from Alice Thompson and Rachel Sylvester, 'Interview with Ronald Harwood: I am deliriously happy because they are putting on both my new plays in the West End', Jewish-Theatre.com, 2009.
John Nathan, 'Ronald Harwood: Interview', *The Jewish Chronicle*, 14 May 2009.

Rosalie Gascoigne:
All quotes from National Library of Australia audio biography, 'Rosalie Gascoigne', interviewer Robin Hughes, recorded 11 November 1998.
(http://www.australianbiography.gov.au/subjects/gascoigne/)

Johnny Cash:
Mark Edwards, 'The Man Comes Around', *The Sunday Times*, 2 November 2002.

Chapter Eight

Happiness of parents:
See Kahneman, D., Kruger, A., Schkade, D., Schwartz, N., & Stone, A. (2004). 'A survey method for characterizing daily life experience: The Day Reconstruction Method (DRM)'. *Science*, 306, 1776-1780.

Hannah Arendt:
Quote from *The Human Condition*, University of Chicago Press, 1958, 1998, p. 178.

Joan B Kroc:
'Joan B. Kroc, 75; Widow of McDonald's Chief "Radiated Joy" as Philanthropist', *Los Angeles Times*, 13 October 2003.
Obituary, 'Joan B. Kroc, 75, Owner of Padres and Philanthropist, Dies', *The New York Times*, 14 October 2003.

Kroc centers:
See http://en.wikipedia.org/wiki/Kroc_Center.

Ray Kroc:
Kroc, Ray, *Grinding It Out: The Making of McDonald's*, St Martin's Press, New York, 1977.
Quote, 'People have marveled . . .', p. 100
Quote, 'I was a battle-scarred veteran . . .' p. 13
Quote, '. . . its preparation a ritual to be followed religiously.' p. 10.

Love, John F., *McDonald's: Behind the Arches*, Bantam, New York, 1986, 1995.

Gladwell:
Quote, 'Successful people don't do it alone', p. 119, *Outliers*, ibid.

Chicago:
Alicia Cozine, 'Czechs and Bohemians', Encyclopedia of Chicago (http://encyclopedia.chicagohistory.org/pages/153.html).

Fast food industry:
Smith, Andrew F., *Encyclopedia of Junk Food and Fast Food*, Greenwood, Westport, Connecticut, 2006.

Unexpected success:
Drucker, Peter F., *Innovation and Entrepreneurship*, Harper-Business, New York, 1993, see Part 1, Chapter 3, which covers sources of innovation.

Vaillant, George, *Aging Well: Surprising Guideposts to a Happier Life From the Landmark Harvard Study of Adult Development*, Little, Brown & Co, New York, 2003.

Howard Schultz and Starbucks:
Schultz, Howard, with Dori Jones Yang, *Pour Your Heart Into It: How Starbucks Created a Company, One Cup at a Time*, Hyperion, New York, 1999.
'Life is a series of misses' quote, p. 44.

J. P. Stern:
Stern, J. P., Dialogue 11: Nietzsche, Bryan Magee, *The Great Philosophers*, Oxford University Press, 1987.

Martin Seligman:
Full quote: 'Human beings are often, perhaps more often, drawn by the future than they are driven by the past, and so a science that measures and builds expectations, planning and conscious choice will be more potent than a science of habits, drives, and circumstances' – from M. Seligman, *Flourish: A New Understanding of Happiness and Well-Being*

– and How to Achieve Them, Nicholas Brealey, London, 2011, p. 106.

Chapter Nine

California Cedar Products:
Information based on personal knowledge, also see:
http://companies.jrank.org/pages/741/California-Cedar-Products-Company.html.

Hoffman-La Roche:
See Drucker, Innovation & Entrepreneurship, p. 210-218.

Ray Kurzweil:
John Tierney, 'The Future, Radically Different and Coming Soon', excerpt from The New York Times in the Observer, 15 June 2008.

Lonely Planet:
The best source for the Wheelers' story is their auto-biography:
Wheeler, Tony and Maureen, The Lonely Planet Story: Once While Travelling, Crimson, London, 2008.
Quote 'For the first ten years . . .' from interview with Tony Wheeler, Boss magazine, Australian Financial Review, April 2005.

Al Ries quote, 'Brand building . . .', Ries, Al and Laura, The Fall of Advertising and Rise of PR, HarperCollins, New York, 2002, p. 223.

On Ries' advice to small companies not to emulate big companies, but to find out what they did before they became successful, see 'Tips for India Inc: Narrow Down On Focus', *The Financial Express* (India).

Silicon Valley:
Mike Moritz's quote, 'People don't understand . . .' is from David Williamson, 'Dotcom success in internet warning', 13 November 2006, WalesOnline.co.uk. See also James Ashton, 'Sage of Silicon Valley start-ups', *The Sunday Times*, 10 April 2011 and Paul Durman, 'The Brit with the Midas internet touch', *The Sunday Times*, 12 November 2006.
Don Valentine's quote is from a Stanford University interview conducted 21 April 2004. For transcript: http://silicongenesis.stanford.edu/transcripts/valentine.htm.
Alorie Gilbert, 'Legendary venture capitalist looks ahead', CNET News, 27 November 2004.

Ole and Hannah Nydahl:
Nydahl, Lama Ole, *Entering the Diamond Way: Tibetan Buddhism Meets the West*, Blue Dolphin Publishing, Nevada City, CA, 1999.

Epilogue

Thomas Kuhn:
Kuhn, Thomas S., *The Structure of Scientific Revolutions*, University of Chicago Press, Chicago & London, 1969.

INDEX

ABC 79, 80
achievement, genuine:
   lead time and 81, 82, 84
   rich time and 7
   shortcuts and 6
   'slow-cooked' success and xiv
Adams, Richard 162
'age excusitis' 14–15
ageing of society 9–23, 167, 175,
    220–1, 243
   in Britain 9–10
   disease and 8–9
   exercise and 11–12
   obesity and 10–11
   medicines and 9–10, 12–13
   new life at 49 18–22
   Schwartz exercise and 14–18
   slowing of 10–11
   technology and 12
   the new (time) rich 10–14
   in United States 9
   see also life expectancy
*Ageing Well: Surprising Guideposts to
    a Happier Life From the
    Landmark Harvard Study of
    Adult Development* (Valiant)
    209–10
agility of mind 210
Albeniz, Isaac 58

Alcoholics Anonymous 5, 104–8
Alexandria, Egypt 165–6
Allen, Paul 69, 72, 225
Almodovar, Pedro 76
Altman, Robert 76
American Graffiti 87
Amnesty International 109
Ampex 68–9
Ando, Momofuko 149–50, 160
appearance of genius 60
Apple 68, 69, 74–5
Aquinas, Thomas 134
Arden, Elizabeth 38
Arendt, Hannah 184, 186, 219–20
Aristotle 8
Armstrong, Louis 181
Autobiography of an Unknown Indian
    (Chaudhari) 180

babysitter, the Harvard-educated
    113–15
Bacon, Francis 88
Baldwin, James 78
Baldwin, Jerry 211, 212
Banfield, Edward 25–7, 39–40, 247
Beast and Man (Midgley) 163
beauty of people, the 183–221
   Howard Schultz and 210–19
   Joni Smith and 186–8

Malcolm Gladwell and 189–91,
    206–10, 220
myths of luck and inevitability
    and 205–10
Ray Kroc/McDonald's and
    188–9, 191–208
second life, a remarkable 186–7
something from nothing 210–19
sources of success and 191–205
Starbucks and 210–19
unexpectedness of humanity and
    185–6
Beckham, David 61
Bee Gees 33, 60
before they were successful,
    comparing yourself to people/
    companies xvi, xix, 245
Al Ries and 119–20
companies 235, 245
Hugh Grant and 118–19
Hugh Laurie and 118
humdrum nature of early years
    86
lead time and 67, 85
Stephen Fry and 117–18
'trying to be a remarkable
    person' 120
behind the curve, feeling xiii–ix
Bell Labs 151
Benenson, Peter 108–9
Benz, Karl 226
Berolzheimer, Charles 223–4
best for last, saving 165–77
comebacks and 175–6
late flowering 170–5
true to themselves 167–9
Bezos, Jeff 28–9, 40
big begins small, everything 223–42
CalCedar 223–5, 226
Diamond Way Buddhism 239–41
first one per cent, the 229–34
go slow to get big 237–9
Grameen Bank 237–9
Lonely Planet 230–5
microloans 237–9
Microsoft 225
niche markets and 223–42

nothing is revolutionary, it's
    evolutionary 235–7
Roche 227–9
the time it takes 227–9
Big Sleep, The (Chandler) 136
Birman, Joan S. 109–13
birth/children 183–4
Blair, Tony 30
'blame the victim' 25
Blanch, Lesley 180
Bomis 70
books that waited for their writer
    153–60
Adam Smith 162
Bryce Courtenay 154–5
Charles Bukowski 161–2
Dan Brown 155–6
Geoffrey Chaucer 161
Immanuel Kant 162–3
John Stuart Mill 162
Lionel Shriver 157–60
Mary Midgley 163
Wallace Stevens 162
Boorman, John 76
Borlaug, Norman 161
Bourgeois, Louise 181
Bowker, Gordon 211
Bradman, Donald 61
braid and knot theory 109–13
Braids, Links and Mapping Class
    Groups (Birman) 111
brainstorming 82
Brin, Sergey 66, 67, 69
BritArt 50
British Museum 141–2
Brokaw, Tom 80
'Brokeback Mountain' (Proulx) 144
Brown, Blythe 121, 123
Brown, Dan 121–4, 127–8, 133,
    155
Buck, Peter 80–1
Buddha 239
Buffett, Warren 1, 137, 242
Buffon, George-Louis 57
Bukowski, Charles 161–2
Bulova company 41–2
Burchard, Brendon 29

Burger King 199, 201
Burgess, Anthony 135–6
Bush, George W. 137
business:
    comebacks and 75
    courage and 206, 217
    emulating big companies 235
    long-view of 35–47, 52
    niche 227–9, 231–4
    time and 7, 35–47, 52
    'unexpected success' in 202
    see also under individual business
        and businessperson name

CalCedar 224–5, 226
Cameron, Charles Hay 140
Cameron, David 31
Cameron, Julia Margaret 140–2,
    160
Campbell, Joseph 136
'can do anything' xvi
Canterbury Tales, The (Chaucer) 161
career change 18–22
    caution and 20
    Dan Brown 121–4
    family and 20, 29
    finances and 20, 129
    importance of experience and
        130–1
    Jeff Bezos 28–30
    Jim Grant/Lee Child 128–31
    period of transition and 21
    productive life and 22
    Roy Lichtenstein 124–8
    Warwick Mayne-Wilson 18–22
careers going nowhere...and then
    121–31
Carlson, Chester 151, 152, 160
Carson, Rachel 91–2
Cash, Johnny 175–6
catch-up, playing xii
CBC 79
Cedar Bar 125
Chain, Ernest 137
chance *see* luck
Chandler, Raymond 136
Chanel, Coco 176–7

charity 187–8
Charlie Wilson's War 185
Chase, William 57, 66
Chaucer, Geoffrey 161
Chaudhari, Nirad 180
chess players 57
Chicago 117–18
    Joni Smith and 186, 187
    Larry Ellison and 67
    Ray Kroc and 192–3, 196, 198,
        201, 202, 207
Child, Julia 133
Child, Lee 128–31
Christian Science Monitor 180
Churchill, Winston 32–3, 35,
    159–60
CIA 68
class and perception of time 25–6,
    39–40
Clockwork Orange, A (Burgess) 135
Clooney, George 118
Coca-Cola 226
Codd, Ted 68
Collins, Jim 228
Columbia Pictures 87
comebacks:
    Johnny Cash 175–6
    Steve Jobs 74–5
composers 57–60, 75
Corrections, The (Franzen) 34–5
courage:
    artistic advances and 126
    Chinese, long view and 52
    Howard Schultz and 217, 218
    Joan Birman and 111
    long view takes 34, 52
    Malcolm Gladwell overlooks
        202, 206, 217, 218
    moral 33
    Mother Teresa and 96, 97
    Peter Drucker and 206, 217
    Ray Kroc and 202, 206
    Roy Lichtenstein and 126
Courtenay, Bryce 154–7, 160
Courtenay, Damon 154–5, 156
Cox, Dr Lynne 10–11
Craigslist.org 71

creative discoveries 82
    books that waited for their writer 153–60
    chance and 83–5
    comebacks and 176
    early success and 77–81
    financial necessity and 128, 129
    long preparation period and 56
    long view and 30
    luck and 82–5
    'sunset years' as dawn of 167, 176
    we get creative when we master a domain 81–5, 90, 128
Crisp, Quentin 167–9, 177
Critique of Pure Reason (Kant) 163
Cruise, Tom 79
Csikszentmihalyi, Mihaly 81–2
Csuri, Lee 125
cultural legacy/family background 190
    Annie Proulx and 142
    Anthony Gormley and 50
    Bill Wilson and 104–8
    birth year and 72–4
    Charles Berolzheimer and 223, 224–5, 226
    family companies and 38, 39, 40–4, 46, 76
    Fritz Hoffman-La Roche and 227–8
    Howard Schultz and 214, 217, 218, 219
    Julia Margaret Cameron and 140–2
    long view and 25–7
    Malcolm Gladwell and 203–4, 207–9, 217, 219, 220, 246
    Ray Kroc and 192–4, 196, 202, 203–4, 206–7
    Ronald Harwood and 169
    Rosalie Gascoigne and 170
    Roy Lichtenstein and 124
Curie, Marie 84–5
Curie, Pierre 84–5

d'Armancourt, Perrault 179

Da Vinci Code, The (Brown) 123–4, 127–8, 155
da Vinci, Leonardo 162
Dandolo, Enrico 178
Darwin, Charles 162
decade:
    give me a decade and see what I can do 56–61
    ten years of silence/ten-year rule 56–61, 62, 64, 66, 76, 81–2, 114, 144
    thinking in terms of 39, 45, 48, 49–50, 56–61, 62, 64, 66, 76, 81–2, 114, 144
    underestimation of what you can achieve in a xiv, xix
dedication 82, 91
'deep domain expertise' 46
defiance of expectations 220
deliberate practice 61
Dell Computing 66
Dell, Michael 66, 67, 69, 73–4
Denny's 199
Depression 99, 151, 187, 195, 247
desire xviii, 22, 82, 209, 219
Diamond Way/Karma Kagyu Buddhism 239–40
Diamond, Jared 180
Dion, Celine 60
Dior, Christian 134–5
discipline 43, 56, 91, 127–8, 145, 171, 207
discoveries, creative 82
    books that waited for their writer 153–60
    chance and 83–5
    comebacks and 176
    early success and 77–81
    financial necessity and 128, 129
    long preparation period and 56
    long view and 30
    luck and 82–5
    'sunset years' as dawn of 167, 176
    we get creative when we master a domain 81–5, 90, 128
discovery of a mission 101
Disney 65

doing what seems obvious to you
213–14, 245
done other things xv, 75–7
Dorsey, Jack 71–2
down the mineshaft, working in the
mud 61–5
Drucker, Peter 181, 202, 217, 227,
228
duos, great 69–70
Duraflame firelog 224–5, 226

early success 30–3, 77–81
Keith Urban 78–9
Peter Jennings 79–80
REM 80–1
William Hague 30–1
William Styron 78
Winston Churchill 32–3
East India Company 140
Eddy, Mark Baker 180
Edison, Thomas 45, 60, 226
education 50
class and 26, 40
John Stuart Mill ix, 162
longevity and 11
social mobility and 25
success and 190, 208
Edwards, Mark 175–6
Egypt 165–6
Einstein, Albert 7
Eliot, T. S. 137
Ellison, Adda 68, 69
Ellison, Larry 67–70, 191
El-Raghy, Sami 165–6
Entrepreneurship & Innovation
(Drucker) 227
environment, success and 12
creating a new mental
environment for ourselves 218
education and ix, 11, 25, 26, 40,
50, 162, 190, 208
family and *see* family
background/cultural legacy
human being as a 'product' and
208, 210
Malcolm Gladwell and 190, 204,
206, 208–9

passion and 204
unexpectedness and 186, 206,
208–9, 210, 219, 220
Epictetus 1–2
Erickson, Milton 4
Ericsson, Anders 61, 66–7
Erikson, Erik 63–4, 100
Evans, Nicholas 138
everything big begins small 223–42
CalCedar 223–5, 226
Diamond Way Buddhism 239–41
first one per cent, the 229–34
go slow to get big 237–9
Grameen Bank 237–9
Lonely Planet 230–5
microloans 237–9
Microsoft 225
niche markets and 223–42
nothing is revolutionary, it's
evolutionary 235–7
Roche 227–9
the time it takes 227–9
evolutionary, nothing is
revolutionary, it's 235–7
experimentation:
Chester Carlson and 151
Momofuko Ando and 150
painters 88, 125, 127
perseverance combined with
123, 127, 132, 210, 245–6
3M 225
explosion of purpose 94–5, 101
exponential growth 229–31, 241
expression of a successful idea can
happen quickly 85
extra projects 149

Facebook 236
family:
companies 38, 39, 40–4, 46,
227–8
resistance from/time pressure
and xviii, 12, 15, 20, 110, 112,
124–5, 128, 130, 196, 202–4,
214
family background/cultural legacy
190

Annie Proulx and 142
Anthony Gormley and 50
Bill Wilson and 104–8
birth year and 72–4
Charles Berolzheimer and 223,
    224–5, 226
family companies and 38, 39,
    40–4, 46, 76
Fritz Hoffman-La Roche and
    227–8
Howard Schultz and 214, 217,
    218, 219
Julia Margaret Cameron and
    140–2
long view and 25–7
Malcolm Gladwell and 203–4,
    207–9, 217, 219, 220, 246
Ray Kroc and 192–4, 196, 202,
    203–4, 206–7
Ronald Harwood and 169
Rosalie Gascoigne and 170
Roy Lichtenstein and 124
Falstaff (Verdi) 181
50s 139–64
    Annie Proulx and 142–5
    examples of successes in 162–4
    Julia Margaret Cameron and 160
    no greatness without
        foundations 145–7
    spare time and 149–51
    the books that waited for their
        writer 153–9
    transferring expertise 147–9
    we never know when a calling
        may be revealed 140–2
financial crash, 1929 105
first one per cent 229–34
first, do the old things well 81–2
Fisher, Bobby 57
fitness boom, personal 11–12
Fleming, Alexander 137
Fleming, Ian 137–8
Florey, Howard 136–7
flow, state of 82
focus xii, xiii
    choosing the one big thing and
        50–1

on your own domain of
    experience 86
finding success through 126
lack of 68
lead time and 85
long view and 35
narrowing in our 40s 93, 94,
    101, 112
sense of calm and 33
targets and 27
on thinking small 226
Focus (Ries) 119–20, 226, 235
Fontenot, Alice 161
Ford, Harrison 87
Ford, Henry 33
40 factor 93–138
    Agnes, Mohandas and Eleanor
        95–101
    before they were famous 117–21
    careers going nowhere...and then
        121–31
    chance reading that changes a
        life 108–10
    gas station owner who loved
        chicken 115–17
    keeping your oar in the water
        109–11
    life begins at 40 131–3
    second life metamorphoses
        101–8
    the Harvard-educated babysitter
        113–15
Fosdick, Harry Emerson 91
Franklin, Benjamin 178
Franzen, Jonathan 34–5, 92
free decision-making 184
Freud, Sigmund 61–4
Friedan, Betty 133–4
Friend, Jonathan 77
Fry, Stephen 117–18
Fuller, Buckminster 247–8
future-orientation 25–6

Gandhi, Mohandas 97–8, 100, 101,
    133
Gary, Romain 78
Gascoigne, Rosalie 170–5, 177

Gates, Bill 66, 67, 68, 69, 72, 89, 158, 225
Gaugin, Paul 87
General Electric (GE) 45–7, 235
genius:
    is patience 57
    work and 56, 57, 59–60, 91
genuine achievement:
    lead time and 81, 82, 84
    rich time and 7
    shortcuts and 6
    'slow-cooked' success and xiv
Gervais, Ricky 137
getting back your breath 4
Giardini, Felice 60
Gladstone, William 178
Gladwell, Malcolm 72–3, 158, 189–91, 192, 193, 194, 198–9, 200
    born at the right time theory 72–3
    cultural legacy/family background theories 203–4, 206–9, 217, 219, 220, 246
    luck and 72, 190–1, 193, 198–9, 202, 206–9
    people acting unexpectedly and 206
    preoccupation with youth 206–7
    'product' of our environment, see people as 203–4, 207–9, 219, 220, 246
    shows that background and circumstances determine nothing 209
    10,000 hours theory 199
    underplays curiosity and courage/risks 202, 206, 217, 218
    see also Outliers: the Story of Success (Gladwell)
Glidden, Joseph Farwell 179
Goethe 180
gold mining 165–6
'good life' 8
Good to Great (Collins) 228
Google 66, 68, 72, 236
Gormley, Antony 49–51

Graham, Benjamin 137
Graham, Katherine 133
Grameen Bank 238–9, 240
Grant, Hugh 118–19
Grant, Jim 128–31
Gray's Sporting Journal 143
Great Basin Bristlecone Pine (Pinus longaeva) 2–3, 4, 244
'great moments' motivation xviii
Great Sequoia 3
Grove, Andy 89
Guns, Germs and Steel (Diamond) 180

Hague, William 30–1, 35
Haloid company 151
Hammarplast 211, 215
Handel 58
Handler, Ruth 138
Harry Potter 65
Harvard Business Review 46
Harvard University 13, 25, 113–15, 209, 223, 236
Harwood, Ronald 169–70, 177
Hayes, John 57–8, 59–60, 66–7
health:
    50s and 139, 145
    life expectancy and 11–14, 243
Hero With a Thousand Faces, The (Campbell) 136
Herring, Joanne 185–6, 220
Hill, Napoleon 247
Hobbes, Thomas 10
Hoffer, Eric 152–3
Hoffman, Hans 88
Hoffman-La Roche 227, 228
Hoffman-La Roche, Fritz 227, 228
Hogan, Ben 61
Holden, William 87
Homer 181
Hugo, Victor 142
Humbolt, Alexander 179
humiliations:
    Hugh Grant 119
    Lionel Shriver 159
Hunter, John 61
Huntington, Samuel 180

Huston, John 76
hygiene 193

IBM 68, 69, 70, 72, 73, 151
   Chester Carlson and 151
   Craig Newmark at 70
   Oracle and 68, 69
   relational databases 73
   technology talent pool and 72
IBM Journal of Research and
   Development 68
Ibuka, Masuru 40, 41
Ikebana 171
Immelt, Jeffrey 46–7
Immelt, Joseph 46
implementing ideas:
   Larry Ellison 73
   lead time and 56
   Mother Teresa 97
   Roy Lichtenstein 128
'inflection points' 206
Innovation and Entrepreneurship
   (Drucker) 202, 228
Institute for Ageing and Health, UK
   11
International Congress of Working
   Women 99
Interpretation of Dreams, The (Freud)
   62–3, 64
Israel, Lee 36
it's not too late xvi, 242

Jack in the Box 199
Jackson, Michael 60
Jackson, Samuel L. 135
Jacques, Elliott 27–8
James, William 242
Japan 149–50
Jennings, Peter 79–80
Jesus of Nazareth 239
Jobs, Steve 68, 69, 72, 74
Jolly, Elizabeth 178
Joy, Bill 72
Joyce, James 77
Jumping the Queue (Wesley) 178
Jung, Carl 93–4

Kandinsky, Vasilly 88
Kant, Immanuel 162–3
keeping your oar in the water
   109–13
Kentucky Fried Chicken 114, 115–17
Khorkova, Svetlana 60
Kidman, Nicole 79
King, Stephen 91
Kinsey Reports 147–8
Kinsey, Alfred 147–8
Kirkwood, Professor Tom 11
Kline, Franz 125
'knack' 7
Kngwarreye, Emily Kame 166–7,
   177
knowing how long it takes to
   succeed 56
Koch, Richard 6–7
Kooning, Willem de 125, 127
Kroc, Ethel 195, 196, 203, 212
Kroc, Joan B 186–8, 204–5
Kroc, Louis 202, 203
Kroc, Ray:
   family background 191–5,
      202–4, 206–7
   french fry and 204–5
   Grinding It Out 188–9
   Howard Schultz and 210, 211,
      213, 214, 216, 219
   meets Joni Smith 187, 188
   Lily Tulip and 195
   Malcolm Gladwell and 191, 194,
      198–200, 202, 204, 206–8
   McDonald's and 197–205,
      206–8, 210, 211, 213, 214,
      216, 219, 220
   Multimixer, sells 195–7, 203,
      208
   openness to opportunity 200–1
   persistence 199–201
   productive obsessions and 204–5
   risks, willingness to take
      intelligent 203–4
   story of success 191–205, 206–8,
      210, 211, 213, 214, 216, 219,
      220
Kroc, Rose 202

Kuhn , Thomas 134, 243
Kurzweil, Ray 229–30

Lady Gaga 60
Laffoon, Ruby 116
large projects broken up into
    smaller pieces xv
late-starters/bloomers/ late flowering
    139, 170–5
Lauder, Estée 35–9
Laurie, Hugh 118
Lauter, Joseph 36, 37, 39
Lauter, Leonard 36
Lauter, Ronald 37
lead time 21, 33, 55–92, 244
    early success and 77–81
    'I don't know of any time when
        there are not great
        opportunities' 67–75
    give me a decade and see what I
        can do 56–61
    life experience and 75–7
    mastering a domain and 81–4
    wilderness periods/'ten years of
        silence' and 61–5
    wunderkinds and 65–7
League of women Voters, U.S. 99
Lean, David 76
Leo Castelli gallery, New York 126
Libeskind, Daniel 145–7
Lichtenstein, Dorothy 127
Lichtenstein, Isobel 124, 125
Lichtenstein, Roy 88, 124–8
Life Begins at 40 (Pitkin) 131–2
life expectancy 9–23, 167, 220–1,
    243
    in Britain 9–10
    disease and 8–9
    exercise and 11–12
    obesity and 10–11
    medicines and 9–10, 12–13
    new life at 49 18–22
    Schwartz exercise and 14–18
    slowing of 10–11
    technology and 12
    the new (time) rich 10–14
    in United States 9

life experience xv, 75–7, 131
'life is short' 4, 22, 244
life isn't short 9–23
    new life at 49 18–22
    productive lifespan chart and 17
    the new (time) rich 10–14
    the Schwartz exercise and its
        surprising results 14–18
Liker, Jeffrey 44, 45
Lily-Tulip Paper Cup company 195
Little House series (Wilder) 178
Lonely Planet 230–4
long time perspective 6, 25–53
    in business 35–51
    of your career 27–35
    philosophy 45–6
long-distance running 3–4
longevity, how increased is giving
        us multiple chances to
        succeed 9–23
    new life at 49 18–22
    Schwartz exercise and 14–18
    the new (time) rich 10–14
Lord of the Rings (Tolkien) 178
Loreto sisters 95
lower class people, view of time of
        25–6
luck:
    a lot of what we ascribe to luck
        is not luck at all 213, 216–17
    as 'cause' of success 210
    breaks and 6, 120, 228
    discovery and 82–5
    life expectancy and 131
    lucky years 67–8
    myth of 82, 205–7
    reading that changes a life 108–9
    success and 190–1, 193, 198–9
    youth and 206, 207
Luther, Martin 62, 63–4

Magic of Thinking Big, The
    (Schwartz) 14
Maistre, Xavier De 87
Major, John 30
Malmo Opera 55
Maltz, Maxwell 180

Mandela, Nelson 178
Marden, Orison Swett 57, 91
Marriott, J. W. 89–90
Marquis, Samuel 33
Mary Poppins 64–5
master a domain 81–5, 86, 144
mathematics 109–13
Mayne-Wilson, Warwick 18–22
McCain, John 17
McDonald, Dick 197, 211
McDonald, Mac 197, 211
McDonald's, Ray Kroc and birth of
        188–205, 206, 208, 211, 212,
        213, 219
medical technology/disease
        prevention 12–13
Mendoza, Tony 113–15, 117
Mercedes-Benz 235
Michelangelo 181
microloans 237–8
Microsoft 66, 89, 225
mid-century magic 139–64
    Annie Proulx and 142–5
    examples of successes in 162–4
    Julia Margaret Cameron 160
    no greatness without
        foundations 145–7
    spare time and 149–51
    the books that waited for their
        writer 153–9
    transferring expertise 147–9
    we never know when a calling
        may be revealed 140–2
Midgley, Mary 163
Mill, John Stuart 162
Miller, George 76
Miller, Henry 135–6
Miner, Bob 68–70, 73, 74
missed opportunities xiii, xvii–xviii,
        67–8, 73–4
Missionaries of Charity 96–7
Moet & Chandon 235
Mollison, James 171
Mona Lisa (da Vinci) 162
Mondrian, Paul 88
Monet, Claude 88
money:

decreasing value of compared to
        health 14
giving away 152, 187–8
microloans 237–8
parents lack of as motivation 218
persistence and lack of 50, 51,
        68, 71, 114, 115, 121, 124,
        125, 154, 157, 192, 231, 232,
        234
raising 215–16
Moore, Gordon 89
'Moore's Law' 89
Morgenstern, Joe 75–5
Mori, Taikichiro 164
Morita, Akio 40–3, 44
Morita, Kyuzaemon 40–1, 43
Moritz, Mike 236
Moses, Ann Mary Robertson 88–9
Moses, Grandma 89, 114
motivational speakers/books xiii,
        xiv–xv, xvi, xviii, 14, 123, 159,
        188, 189, 210, 244, 245–6
Mozart 59–60, 60, 75
Mt Stromlo Observatory 170
Multimixer 195–7, 198, 208, 214
Myers, Dr John 36

National Public Radio 188
natural unfolding, power of our 2
NBC 79
never giving in 159–60
new does not have to be preserve of
        the young 175
new life at 49 18–22
New Yorker, The 178
Newmark, Craig 70–1, 74
Newton, Isaac 91
niches, filling 224–9
Nidetch, Jean 5, 102–8
Nidetch, Marty 102
Niemeyer, Oscar 179
Nietzsche, Friedrich 219
Nightingale, Earl 90
no greatness without foundations
        145–7
nothing is revolutionary, it's
        evolutionary' 235–7

Nupedia 70
Nydahl, Hannah 240
Nydahl, Ole 240

Oates, Ed 69
Observer, The 108
obsessions, productive:
  Michael Dell/Bill Gates 66
  Ray Kroc 205
  Rosalie Gascoigne 172
  Roy Lichtenstein 127
  Vera Rubin 83, 84
Odyssey (Homer) 181
Ogilvy, David 90
Ohio State University 115, 124
Olympics, Amsterdam, 1928 3–4
On Liberty (Mill) 162
openness to the new/opportunity
    245
  Malcolm Gladwell and 190
  Ray Kroc and 200–1, 216
  Roy Lichtenstein and 127
Oracle 68–9, 70
Orange Prize 157, 158
Origin of the Species, The (162)
other things, doing xv, 75–7
Outliers: the Story of success
    (Gladwell) 72–3, 158,
    189–91, 192, 193, 194,
    198–9, 200
  born at the right time theory
    72–3
  cultural legacy/family
    background theories 203–4,
    208, 217
  luck and 72, 190–1, 193, 198–9,
    202, 206–9
  people acting unexpectedly and
    206
  preoccupation with youth 206–7
  'product' of our environment,
    shows people as a 203–4,
    206–9, 219, 220, 246
  shows that background and
    circumstances determine
    nothing 209
  10,000 hours theory 199

underplays curiosity and
    courage/risks 202, 206, 217,
    218
outsiders:
  Lionel Shriver 158–9
  Martin Luther 63
  Peter Jennings 79
  Roy Lichtenstein 125
overnight success:
  Jack Dorsey 71–2
  Lady Gaga 60
  Lionel Shriver 158
  myth of xiv, xix, 85, 86, 235, 243
  Ray Kroc 200
  Silicon Valley 236
  William Styron 78
Oxford Group 106, 107

Page, Larry 66, 67, 69–70, 71, 73
Pale King, The (Wallace) 91
Paris Review 78
Parkes, Sir Henry 179
*Passages: Predictable Crises of Adult
    Life* (Sheehy) 93
passion xv, 245
  discovering 99, 141
  Howard Shultz and 216
  Malcolm Gladwell takes little
    account of 204, 205, 206
  Ray Kroc and 204, 205, 206, 216
  Wheelers/Lonely Planet and 234
Pasteur, Louis 85
Patek Philippe 39
Pauling, Linus 180
pay by the hour/monthly salaries
    27–8
Peck, M. Scott 135
Pei, IM 179
people, the beauty of 183–221
  Howard Schultz 210–19
  Joni Smith 186–8
  Malcolm Gladwell and 189–91,
    206–10, 220
  myths of luck and inevitability
    205–10
  Ray Kroc/McDonald's 188–9,
    191–208

second life, a remarkable 186–7
something from nothing 210–19
sources of success 191–205
Starbucks and 210–19
unexpectedness of humanity
185–6
Perls, Fritz 161
Perrault, Charles 178–9
persistence, value of 58–9, 121, 123,
127, 132, 159, 245–6
personal mystery 216
personnel changes 45–7
perspective, long time 6, 25–53
in business 35–51
of your career 27–35
philosophy 45–6
Perstop 211
philanthropy 187–8
Photographic Society of London
141
photography xii, 113–15, 141–2,
151
Pianist, The 169
Picasso, Pablo xix, 177
Pitkin, Walter B. 131–2
Pixar 75
Pizza Hut 199
Pollock, Jackson 88, 125, 127
Pop Art 126, 127
possibilities, 'I don't know of any
time when there are not great
possibilities' 67–8
potential:
fulfilling xvii, 6, 50, 60, 77, 174,
206, 246–7
seeing early 68, 117, 167, 195–6,
197, 202, 203, 206, 236
unique 177
Power of One, The (Courtenay)
155–6
practice 7, 57, 60–1, 85
'present-orientation' 25–6
Princeton University 111
Prius 44
problem or need, perceiving 150–1
productive lifespan 13–18, 22, 23,
132, 167

Protestant Work Ethic and the Spirit of
Capitalism, The (Weber) 134
Proulx, Annie 142–5, 160
Psycho-Cybernetics (Maltz) 180

quality of decisions, advantage of
long view 30
quaternity 94

radium, discovery of 84–5
Raramuri Indians 3–4, 245
Rather, Dan 80
redundancy, seeing opportunity in
130
'regret minimisation framework' 29
REM 80–1
remarkable person:
40s and 93, 104, 109, 111,
119–21, 133–8
given remarkable opportunities
194, 201, 205, 246
a remarkable second life 186–91
trying to be a 22, 61, 120
Remy Martin 235
retirement 16, 17, 18, 19–20, 132,
163, 179
Revlon 38
'rich time' 7
risk:
career change and 20–1, 27, 130,
196, 202, 203–4, 206
openness to 190, 209–10, 245
Ray Kroc and 196, 202, 203–4,
206
Starbucks and 213, 216, 217, 218
Road Less Travelled, The (Peck) 135
Robbins, Anthony xix
Roche 227–8
Roget's Thesaurus 180
Roosevelt, Eleanor 98–100, 101
Roosevelt, Franklin Delano 98–9
Roosevelt, Teddy 98
Rosen, Sidney 4
Rothko, Mark 88
Rousseau, Theodore 87, 135
Rowling, J. K. 65
Royal Perth Hospital 82–3

Rubin, Vera 82, 83, 84
Rubinstein, Helena 38
Ruskin, John 57
Russell, George 64
Rutgers University 125

Sanders, Colonel 114, 115–17, 133, 200–1
Satyagraha 98
Savulescu, Julian 13
Schmidt, Eric 72
Schonberg, Harold 59
Schopenhauer, Arthur 6
Schubert, Franz 58
Schultz, Howard 210–19, 220
Schwab, Charles 71
Schwartz exercise 14–18, 22, 23, 246
    do the exercise yourself 15–18
    productive lifespan chart 17
Science and Health (Eddy) 180
second life:
    metamorphoses 101–8
    remarkable 186–7
Second World War 9–10, 76, 87, 124, 145–7, 149–50, 153, 155, 169
Security analysis (Graham) 137
seeing early potential/what other people don't see:
    Colonel Sanders 117
    Larry Ellison 68–9
    Mike Moritz and Google 236
    Ray Kroc 195–6, 197, 202, 203, 206
self-created, success 218–19
self-development xi–xiv, xvi, 6–7, 243–4
self-destruction 78, 81
Self-Help (Smiles) 43, 56, 61
self-knowledge, deep 101
self-made individual 186, 189, 191
self-reflection 77
Seligman, Martin 220
Sequoia Capital 236–7
Seth, Vikram 47–9
Shakespeare, William 78

shame over time it takes to do worthwhile things xix
shortcuts:
    'break through' and 159
    natural to seek 86
    starting young as a 61
    time may be condensed but never shortcutted 61, 85
    universe rarely offers 6, 61
Shrek! (Steig) 178
Shriver, Lionel 157–60
signs of success, too subtle 5
Silent Spring (Carson) 92
Silicon Valley 75, 236–7
Silkworth, Dr 105, 107
Simon, Herbert 57, 66
Singer, Bryan 118
Sir George Williams University 143
slow development of character 75–7
slow to get big, go 237–8
'slow-cooked' success 145, 156
    dullness of success and 89–90
    early success and 81
    hard work, experimentation and 127
    as the norm xix
    as the only path to genuine achievement xiv, 6
    Prius and 44
    self-reflection and 77
Smiles, Samuel 43, 56, 61
Smith, Adam 162
Socrates 184
Somerville, Mary 180
Sony 41–3, 44
Sorbonne 124
Soros, George 137
sources of success 191–205
    Malcolm Gladwell and 192–4, 198–199, 200, 202, 204
    Ray Kroc/McDonald's and 191–205
South Africa 98, 101, 154, 155, 169, 178
spare time 149–53
Spirit of the Laws, The (Montesquieu) 55–6

St Augustine 179, 183–4
St Therese of Lisieux 95, 96–7
Star Wars 87
Starbucks 210–19
Steig, William 178
Steinway, Henry 161
Stern, J.P. 219
Sternbach, Leo 161
Stevens Institute of Technology 110–11
Stevens, Wallace 162
Stigwood, Robert 33
Stipe, Michael 81
Structure of Scientific Revolutions, The (Kuhn) 133, 243
Stuart Mill, John xi, 162
Sturges, Preston 76
Styron, William 78, 90
success:
    early xiii, 30–3, 74–5, 77–81
    environment and 12, 186, 190, 204, 206, 208–9, 210, 218, 219, 220
    examples of in their 50s 162–4
    genuine xiv, 6, 7, 81, 82, 84
    luck and 190–1, 193, 198–9
    overnight xiv, xix, 60, 71–2, 78, 85, 86, 158, 200, 235, 236, 243
    signs of success, too subtle 5
    'slow-cooked' xiv, xix, 6, 44, 77, 81, 89–90, 127, 145, 156
    sources of 191–205
    unexpected 5, 103, 202
successful, comparing yourself to people/companies before they were xvi, xix, 245
    Al Ries and 119–20
    companies 235, 245
    Hugh Grant 118–19
    Hugh Laurie 118
    humdrum nature of early years 86
    lead time and 67, 85
    Stephen Fry 117–18
    'trying to be a remarkable person' 120

Suitable Boy, A (Seth) 48–9
Sukari Project site 166
Summa Theologiae (Aquinas) 134
Sun Microsystems 72
Sunnegardh, Erika 55, 77
sunset years 167
Sunset Boulevard 87

Taco Bell 199
take the time to dream, muse, meditate or just play around 149
talent:
    birth year and 72
    finding an outlet for 78, 142
    making the most of your 100, 123
    overrated/hard work and 43, 56, 57, 58, 60, 61, 75, 77, 91, 144, 145
    time and 1, 2
Talent is Overrated (Colvin) 144
Talleyrand 51–2
Tao of Physics, The (Capra) 52
Taylor, Michael 171
ten years of silence 56–61, 62, 64, 114, 144
ten-year rule 56–61, 62, 64, 114, 144
    Annie Proulx and 144
    composers and 57–60
    Martin Luther 63–4
    Pamela Travers 64–5
    Sigmund Freud 62–4
    Tony Mendoza and 113–15
10,000 hours 199
Tennyson, Alfred Lord 140, 141, 142
Teresa, Mother 95–7, 100, 101, 120, 123–4, 133
30-year goldmine 165–77
thinking long, the power of ix, xix, 7–8, 23, 246
thirties 'deadline' 93
3M 225
Thy Hand, Great Anarch (Chaudhari) 180

Tibetan Buddhism 239–40
time 1–2, 7
  adjusting the timescales xv
  class and perception of 25–6,
    39–40
  40s and 93–138
  50s and 139–64
  in between 55–92
  lead 21, 33, 55–92, 244
  limits breed efficiency 112
  long view and 6, 25–53
  longevity and 9–23
  rich 10–14
  spare 149–53
  take the time to dream, muse,
    meditate or just play around
    149
  talent and 1, 2
  10,000 hours 199
  ten years of silence 56–61, 62,
    64, 114, 144
  ten-year rule 56–61, 62, 64, 114,
    144
  thinking about as a separate
    dimension of our lives 7
  thinking long, the power of ix,
    xix, 7–8, 23, 246
  30-year goldmine 165–77
Tokyo Telecommunications
    Engineering Corporation 40–1
Tolkien, J.R.R. 178
Toyoda, Eiji 44
Toyoda, Kiichiro 43–4
Toyoda, Sakichi 43
Toyota 43–5
transferring expertise 147–9
'transforming your life' xiii, 158,
    228, 240
trapped by circumstances 25, 173,
    238
Travers, Pamela 64–5
Trejo, Danny 135
Tropic of Cancer (Miller) 135–6
True Believer, The (Hoffer) 152–3
true to themselves 167–9
Turandot 55
Turner Prize 50

twenties 'anything is possible' 93
Twitter 71–2

Ullman, Samuel 176–7
unexpected:
  people act unexpectedly 184,
    185–6, 206, 210, 219, 221,
    246
  success 5, 103, 202
unfulfilled potential xvii, 6, 50, 60,
    77, 174, 206, 246–7
Unheavenly City, The (Banfield) 25
United Nations 109
  Universal Declaration of Human
    Rights 100, 109
University of Chicago 67
University of Georgia 14
University of Illinois 67
'university of life' 153
University of Michigan 44
University of New York 125
University of Vermont 143
University of Vienna 62
Unix 70
Urban, Keith 78–9, 80

Valentine, Don 75, 237
Valliant, George 209–10
van Ameringen, Arnold Lewis 36
venture industry 237
Verdi, Guiseppi 58, 181
Volkswagen 235
Voltaire 57, 180

Wales, Jimmy 70, 74
Walesa, Lech 136
Walker, Murray 163
Wallace, Alfred Russell 162
Wallace, David Foster 91
Walt Disney 207
Walton, Sam 135
Warhol, Andy 126
warming up 1–8
  Annie Proulx 144
  Epictetus 1–2
  Great Basin Bristlecone Pine 2–3
  Raramuri Indians 3–4, 245

rich time and 7
Warren Buffett 1
Warner Bros 80
Warren, Robin 82–4
Washington Post, The 133
Watership down (Adams) 162
We Need to Talk About Kevin
    (Shriver) 157–9
we never know when a calling may
    be revealed 140–2
Wealth of Nations (Smith) 162
Weber, Max 134
Wedgwood 235
Weight Watchers 5, 102–8
Welsh, Jack 45–6
Wesley, Mary 178
Western Union 202
'what works', finding 132
Wheeler, Maureen 230–4
Wheeler, Tony 230–4
White Cube Gallery 50
Whitechapel Gallery 49–50
Whitehouse, Mary 163–4
Wilder, Billy 76, 87
Wilder, Laura Ingles 178
wilderness periods 52–3
    Jesus in the desert 94, 97
    Martin Luther 64–5
    Pamela Travers 64–5
    Sigmund Freud 61–4
    Steve Jobs 74–5
    Theodore Rousseau 87
    Winston Churchill 32
willpower 105
Wilson, Bill 5, 104–8
Wilson, Charles 185–6, 220
Wilson, Lois 105
Wilson, Mike 73
Windows software 89, 225
Wolfit, Sir Donald 169
Women's Trade Union League, U.S.
    99
Woods, Tiger 60, 158
Woolf, Virginia 140
workers:
    indefatigable 56
    pay 27

working in the mud 61–5
    Martin Luther and 62–4
    Pamela Travers and 64–5
    Samuel Smiles and 61
    Sigmund Freud and 61–4
working life, productive 13–18, 22,
    23, 27–35, 132, 167
    chart 17
    new life at 49 18–22
    Schwartz exercise 14–18
World as Will and Representation, The
    (Schopenhauer) 6
worldliness 75–7
Wozniak, Steve 69, 74
Wren, Sir Christopher 179
Wright, Frank Lloyd 179
writer, books that waited for their
    153–60
    Adam Smith 162
    Bryce Courtenay 154–5
    Charles Bukowski 161–2
    Dan Brown 155–6
    Geoffrey Chaucer 161
    Immanuel Kant 162–3
    John Stuart Mill 162
    Lionel Shriver 157–60
    Mary Midgley 163
    Wallace Stevens 162
wunderkinds 65–7, 85
Wynfield, David Wilkie 140, 141

Xerox 151, 152, 217–18

Yale University 113
youth:
    early success and xiii, 30–3,
        74–5, 77–81
    longevity and 13, 17
    Malcolm Gladwell's
        preoccupation with 206–7
    modern world glorifies 176–7
Yunus, Muhammad 238–9

zeitgeist 126
Zia-ul-Haq 185
Zuckerberg, Mark 236

ABOUT THE AUTHOR

A graduate of the London School of Economics and the University of Sydney, Tom Butler-Bowdon was working as a political advisor in Australia when, at 25, he read his first personal development book. Captivated by the genre, at 30 he left his first career to write the bestselling *50 Self-Help Classics*, the first guide to the personal development literature.

The subsequent books in this series, *50 Success Classics*, *50 Spiritual Classics*, *50 Psychology Classics*, *50 Prosperity Classics* and *50 Philosophy Classics*, have been published in 22 languages. USA Today described him as "a true scholar of this type of literature".

Tom has also written critical introductions to Napoleon Hill's *Think and Grow Rich*, Sun Tzu's *Art of War*, Machiavelli's *The Prince*, Adam Smith's *Wealth of Nations* and Plato's *The Republic*.

Visit his website at www.Butler-Bowdon.com.